ERROR OF JUDGEMENT

Error of Judgement

THE BIRMINGHAM BOMBINGS

by Chris Mullin

Chatto & Windus

LONDON

Published in 1986 by
Chatto & Windus Ltd
40 William IV Street
London WC2N 4DF

Second Impression 1986

British Library Cataloguing in Publication Data
Mullin, Chris
Error of judgement.
1 . Provisional IRA—History
2. Bombings—England—Birmingham (West Midlands)—History—20th century
3. Criminal investigation—England—Birmingham (West Midlands)—History—20th century
I. Title
364.1'31   HV6433
ISBN 0–7011–2978–6

Photoset and printed by
Redwood Burn Limited
Trowbridge, Wiltshire

'The new evidence I have seen would be sufficient to create in my mind what's sometimes called a lurking doubt as to whether the convictions in these cases were safe.'

ROY JENKINS Home Secretary at the time of the bombings, speaking on Granada Television, 28 October, 1985

To

Hugh Callaghan
Patrick Hill
Gerry Hunter
Richard McIlkenny
Billy Power
Johnny Walker
and their families

and to

all the other victims
of the Birmingham
pub bombings

Contents

List of illustrations

between pages 114 and 125

Acknowledgements

This story could not have been told without the help of many people, some of whom would be seriously embarrassed were I to name them. I would like to place on record my thanks to all those who have assisted in the nine months' investigation which preceded the writing of this book.

In particular I thank Charles Tremayne, Ian McBride and Ray Fitzwalter of the Granada Television programme, *World in Action* – one of the last refuges for inquiring journalists. But for the willingness of *World in Action* to invest substantial resources in the investigation on which most of this book is based, the truth might never have been told.

I must also pay special tribute to those wives and relatives who have stuck by the six men throughout the eleven years of their ordeal, and who provided me with much valuable assistance. In particular I thank Eileen Callaghan, Sandra Hunter, Brian and Lily Kelly, Kate and Theresa McIlkenny, Paddy McIlkenny, Nora, Patsy and Betsy Power, and Bernadette Walker.

Although lawyers do not emerge from this story with credit, there are notable exceptions. Among them Gareth Pierce and Brian Rose-Smith.

Most journalists don't emerge with credit either, but two deserve special mention. Peter Chippindale, formerly of the *Guardian*, who first suggested to me eleven years ago that the six men were wrongly convicted, and David Brazil formerly of the *Irish Press*. Among the many reporters who covered the trial, Chippindale and Brazil were alone in recognising that there was more to this story than met the eye.

I must also thank a number of retired police officers who consented to be interviewed. Among them were Inspector Ken Brown, Chief Superintendent Alf Collins, Detective Superintendent Andrew Crawford, Detective Superintendent Bernard Ibison, Sergeant Dennis Holt, Superintendent Roy Lenton, Superintendent Joe Matthews, Detective Sergeant Brian Morton, Chief Inspector Ronald Rawsthorne, Detective Superintendent George Reade and Inspector Ken Teale.

Others who have given valuable help include Kenneth Austen (formerly Littlejohn), Steve Bundred, Anthony Curtis, Sister Sarah Clarke, Bob Clay MP, Adrian Dart, Father Denis Faul, Jan Mayman, Joan Maynard MP, Father Raymond Murray, Kieran Morgan, Sue Milne, Pat

Murtagh, Jo Moloney, Marion Neville, Dr David Paul, Clare Riley, John Shirley, Bob Satchwell, Thomas and Rose Watt, Bob Westerdale and Ruth Winstone.

We are grateful to the following for permission to reproduce the photographs: *Coventry Evening Telegraph*, page 115 (top); Pacemaker Press International, page 115 (bottom left); Express Newspapers, page 118 (bottom); Press Association, pages 118 (top), 123 (bottom); Granada Television, pages 119 (Hill, Callaghan and Walker), 120, 124 (top and bottom right); Syndication International, page 119 (McIlkenny, Hunter and Power); *Express and Star*, pages 122, 123 (top); and the *Cork Examiner*, page 124 (bottom left).

Finally, I pay tribute to the convicted men, each of whom I have interviewed and each of whom displays an extraordinary degree of dignity and good humour in the face of the nightmare that has overtaken their lives.

CHRIS MULLIN

Preface

This is the story of how six innocent Irishmen were convicted of the biggest mass murder in British history.

On August 16, 1975, after a trial lasting forty-five days, six Irishmen were sentenced to life imprisonment for planting bombs in two Birmingham public houses, killing twenty-one people and injuring one hundred and sixty-two. The evidence against them consisted mainly of confessions signed by four of the defendants during their three days in police custody, and forensic evidence which proved positive against two of them.

The men said at their trial that they were innocent and that the confessions were beaten out of them by West Midlands police officers. Today they still tell the same story.

Although most of them have not had access to trial papers since their appeal was rejected nine years ago and although they are presently held in four separate jails, they tell stories replete with circumstantial detail which corroborate each other to an extent that would be almost impossible if the men were fabricating.

At their trial, they were said to be members of the IRA. The men denied then and they deny now that they have ever been members of either the IRA or its political wing, Sinn Fein. Like many Irishmen, however, they regard themselves as Republicans. For their part, the IRA and Sinn Fein have always maintained that none of the men were members of either organisation. Unlike other IRA prisoners, their names have never appeared on any Sinn Fein list of 'prisoners of war' held in British jails.

This account of the Birmingham pub bombings is based on a wide variety of sources, official and unofficial. I have interviewed each of the six convicted men, their wives and other members of their families. Together with Charles Tremayne of the Granada Television programe *World in Action*, I have traced and interviewed many of the police officers involved. The allegations against the police were made at the trial and it is on these that my account of the six men's time in police custody is based. It is important to bear in mind that these allegations were denied by the police and that these denials were accepted by the jury. That remains the situation to this day.

World in Action also commissioned two distinguished forensic scientists to test the forensic evidence which was one of the two main planks of the convictions. The result of their experiments effectively destroys the evidence given at the trial by the Home Office forensic scientist.

Finally I have traced three of the four men responsible for the bombings – including one of the two who planted the bombs in the Tavern in the Town and the Mulberry Bush, who has given me a detailed account of what happened.

Chapters 1 to 25 consist of a detailed reconstruction of the events leading up to the arrest of these men, their three days in police custody and their ordeal in Winson Green prison. Chapters 25 to 34 deal with the trial and subsequent attempts to have the case retried. Chapters 35 to 37 examine new evidence that has come to light since the convictions. The final three chapters are based upon interviews with twelve former members of the Birmingham IRA.

I am aware that by resurrecting this subject so long after the event, I am reviving painful memories for the victims and their families. For that I apologise. Nothing can bring back the lives of the twenty-one people who died on that terrible night, November 21, 1974. We can, however, restore to six men, who have served eleven years in prison for a crime they did not commit, what remains of their lives.

CHRIS MULLIN
April, 1986

No one in Birmingham will ever forget the evening of Thursday, November 21, 1974. Ian Cropper certainly won't. He was the telephonist on duty at the *Birmingham Post and Mail*. At 8.11 he took a call from a man in a call box. First came the pips and then a voice with an Irish accent said, 'The code word is Double X.' The man's voice was calm and clear. He went on, 'There is a bomb planted in the Rotunda and there is a bomb in New Street...' There was a slight hesitation and he added quickly '... at the tax office.' Then the line went dead.

Cropper scribbled a note, and then rang the Information Room at Lloyd House, headquarters of the West Midlands police. The news hardly came as a surprise. IRA Bombs had been going off for months in and around Birmingham. An alert was immediately flashed to all policemen in the area.

Police Constable Brian Yates was one of the first on the scene. He was on foot patrol in New Street at about 8.15 when a message came over his radio that there was a bomb in the Rotunda, the huge cylindrical monstrosity of glass and concrete which dominates the junction between New Street and St Martin's Circus, and which had been bombed twice already that year. PC Yates raced down New Street to the Rotunda. As he got there he met two colleagues, PC Derek Bradbury and WPC Margaret Adams. Inside, at the reception, they found two police sergeants already organising a search of the building. It would not be easy. The Rotunda was twenty storeys high and the bomber's message offered no clues.

PC Yates, PC Bradbury and WPC Adams were told to search the even numbered floors. As they got into the lift they felt the building tremble. From somewhere below there came the sound of a huge explosion. They were too late.

The bomb had exploded at 8.17, just six minutes after the warning. It had devastated the Mulberry Bush, a public house on two storeys built into the base of the Rotunda. At that moment, PC Rodney Hazelwood was racing toward the scene in his Panda car. 'We were about three hundred yards away, just cresting the hill, when there was the loudest thunderclap and rumbling and ground shock. Debris was coming down all over the road. It was like a volcano had erupted, people running and screaming ... the Mulberry Bush had sort of exploded out onto the pavement – rubble, half a staircase, glass, carpets, bar-tops and furniture blown to bits, and injured people staggering out.'

Bus driver Anthony Gaynor was driving his number 90 bus around St Martin's Circus at the moment the pub exploded. 'I had just passed the Mulberry Bush when I felt a loud bang. I thought at first someone had hit the bus in the back, but when I looked round I saw that a lot of windows on the bus had been blown in.' Mr Gaynor pulled his bus round the corner into New Street and went to help his passengers. The bus was a write-off.

Maureen Carlin was in the Mulberry Bush with her fiancé, Ian MacDonald Lord, when the bomb went off. 'I didn't actually hear the explosion. The lights just sort of flickered and then went out and I was being carried through the air.'

Ian said afterwards: 'I knew immediately what it was and even before I landed, I was shouting "bastards".' He was referring to the IRA.

PC Hazelwood reached the scene to find PC Bradbury and WPC Adams already there. They began moving the injured out of the devastated pub and into St Martin's Circus. The bomb seemed to have exploded in the centre of the pub, near the stairway. The stairs had been blown away.

The dead included John Rowlands, a forty-six year old electrician at the Rover car works, fifty-six year old Stan Bodman, a former RAF fighter pilot, and Trevor Thrupp, a British Rail guard at nearby New Street railway station.

The bodies of two youths were recovered from under a pile of rubble and timber outside. They had apparently been passing the pub at the moment of the explosion.

Forensic scientist Douglas Higgs later said that the explosion had been caused by between twenty-five and thirty pounds of explosive, placed against the wall of a liquor storeroom not far from the rear entrance of the pub. The force of the blast had blown a hole forty inches in diameter through the ten inch thick concrete floor. Mr Higgs said he had recovered fragments of two Smith's Industries alarm clocks, a D-shackle, and a keyhole plate from a briefcase or suitcase which, in his view, had contained the explosives. The explosion had been caused by two separate devices, probably in the same container.

The explosion at the Mulberry Bush could be clearly heard in the Tavern in the Town, three hundred yards up New Street. Unlike the Mulberry Bush, the Tavern was situated below street level with only a door opening out onto New Street. The clientele consisted almost entirely of young people. That night there was over a hundred youngsters crowded into the dimly lit bar.

Barmen John Boyle and Patrick Daly were on duty in the Tavern. They heard the explosion but they had no idea where it came from. Daly went down into the cellar, opened the door at the back of the pub, looked in the direction of the railway station from where the explosion seemed to have come. Seeing nothing unusual, he returned to the bar. Boyle, meanwhile, had gone to the front doorway to check for suspicious packages. Finding nothing, he also returned to the bar. Minutes later everything went black, the building shook and the air was thick with dust. Boyle described it: 'There was an almighty blast and there were screams and shouts from everywhere. The ceiling fell in and the bar blew back at me ... It was just a screaming mass of people. I saw one man with the side of his head blown off.'

Daly said afterwards, 'There was a big flash and I was surrounded by darkness. I was knocked to the floor and the next thing I remember is removing debris from about my body and getting up.' He escaped through a hole in the back wall.

A young woman customer described what happened to her. 'I had come into the Tavern a few minutes before. I went over to the bar with my girlfriend and was just about to buy a drink when there was a bang and everything started falling upon us. The lights went out and there was screaming and moaning everywhere. I flicked on my lighter and saw my friend next to me had lost her foot. I thought I was dead and that my spirit was just carrying on.'

Once again, P C Brian Yates was among the first on the scene. After the explosion at the Mulberry Bush he had rushed out of the Rotunda and run up the left-hand side of the New Street yelling at people to cross to the other side. As he reached the entrance to the Tavern the bomb exploded, throwing him backwards into a bus shelter. Shaken but uninjured he picked himself up and went back to the Tavern. There was smoke coming from the entrance and the steps leading down into the pub were blocked with debris. P C Yates scrambled over the debris and down into the pub. It was pitch dark and the air was thick with dust. He switched on his torch and could see people staggering about, their clothes blasted from their bodies. There was screaming and people were calling to each other in the blackness.

By the time Yates had made his way to the doorway, a number of passers-by had gathered. He asked them to help clear the rubble from the stairs so that those who were still able to walk could get out. Then he climbed back into the darkness to search for the injured. He was followed into the ruin by Police Inspector Baden Skitt. It was so dark that they could only locate survivors by feeling under the rubble.

P C Yates found two girls trapped by falling masonry beneath the stairs. He dragged them clear and continued searching. In one corner he found three bodies stacked one on top of the other. He pulled a man out of the debris who had lost the back of his skull and the lower part of both legs. 'The people who were obviously dead were left and the living were dragged clear. I tried to keep count of the dead but gave up after the fifth.'

P C Yates stayed in the ruined pub until the last of the retrievable bodies had been recovered, while Inspector Skitt climbed back into New Street to take charge of the rescue operation. Although in a state of shock, some of those who had survived the blast stayed to help P C Yates search the ruin. As they worked, masonry showered down on them.

Outside in the street, ambulances were ferrying the injured to hospital. Taxi drivers from the cab rank at nearby New Street rushed to offer their services. At Birmingham's General Hospital fifty doctors and one hundred and eighty nurses worked flat out to cope with the injured. One surgeon said, 'Go to the casualty ward and you could be forgiven for thinking that roast beef was cooking. The smell of burns was still there long after these people had been removed. You want to put drips on an arm and it isn't there. You look for a leg and there isn't one'.

Forensic scientist Donald Lidstone later testified that the explosion at the Tavern in the Town had been caused by about thirty pounds of blasting explosive wired to two clocks. The bomb had been placed in a corner at the furthest point from the bar, on the right hand side of the staircase as you entered the pub from New Street. As with the Mulberry Bush, the explosion had blown a hole in the ten inch concrete floor about three feet by three feet six in diameter. Among the parts of the bomb recovered from the debris were fragments of two General Time of Scotland alarm clocks, a 4.5 volt Ever Ready battery, a Phillips-head screw and two sets of D-shackles from the handles of a hold-all or briefcase that had apparently contained the bomb.

There was a third bomb that night. It was found at the rear of a Barclay's Bank office in Hagley Road, Ladywood, two miles from New Street station. It was discovered at around 9.15 – an hour after the other bombs had exploded – by Alfred Meeks, a caretaker with General Accident Insurance Company. Mr Meeks had been for a drink in the Ivy Bush pub in Hagley Road and was returning to his flat on the top floor of the insurance offices. Access to the flat was through a door at the back of the building. As he went to open the door he noticed two parcels in plain white plastic bags about a foot away. They had not been there when he left for the pub at around 7.30. He bent down and touched the top bag and felt something hard and flat inside. Then he rang the police.

The Hagley Road bomb was the subject of a controlled explosion. It was later said to have consisted of thirteen and a half pounds of an explosive known as Eversoft Frangex made by Irish Industrial Explosives Limited of Enfield, in the Irish Republic. It cannot be legally imported into Britain.

The explosives were said to be divided into two packages to each of which was taped a detonator mechanism consisting of a Smith's alarm clock, an Ever Ready 126 battery, a light bulb and a Phillips-head screw with the point broken off. The Phillips-head screw was to prove to be the bombers' trademark. It was inserted into the face of the clock and protruded about an inch – a dangerous practice since it risked causing a short circuit and could have resulted in a premature explosion.

Forensic evidence later showed that the Hagley Road bomb contained similar ingredients and was of similar construction to both the bombs that went off in Birmingham that evening. It also bore a marked similarity to seven other bombs and incendiary devices placed at premises in Birmingham, Wolverhampton and Coventry in the sixteen days before the pub bombings. Donald Lidstone later told a court that in his view all the bombs were the work of the same team.

There were many reported sightings of the bombers that night.

Roy Findon and his brother, Michael, were walking up New Street minutes before the bombs exploded. They had just passed the Rotunda when they saw two men in their twenties standing outside Lloyds Bank. According to Michael, one of the men was carrying a parcel. As the brothers approached, they saw two policemen coming towards them, checking shop doorways. The policemen disappeared briefly into a deep shop entrance and the two men ran off in the direction of New Street station. The brothers then boarded a number 33 bus and, as they took their seats on the top deck, there was a huge explosion. That was the Mulberry Bush going up.

George and Edna Pugh also saw a man acting suspiciously. They were in the Odeon cinema further up New Street watching *The Planet of the Apes*, sitting three rows from the back in the 'No Smoking' area. Just before eight, after the film had been showing for some time, a man pushed past them and sat down on the right of Mrs Pugh. As soon as he had sat down he took a hand-rolled cigarette, not from a packet but from the breast pocket of his jacket, and started smoking. Mrs Pugh said, 'It was the fact that he was smoking in a "No Smoking" area which drew my attention to him.' She went on, 'During the twenty minutes he sat next to me he smoked three or four cigarettes more or less continually. I kept looking at him and noticed that he frequently looked at his wrist watch for the time. I thought this extremely strange, having apparently just come into the cinema. During the last five minutes prior to the first explosion, he sat looking at his watch all the time and I felt uneasy about him.'

At the sound of the first explosion the man's demeanour changed. He got up and walked casually to the end of the row, passing two other people on the way. Mrs Pugh last saw him walking towards the exit. She later described the man to police as aged about forty to forty-five years and five feet eight inches tall, with dark hair. He was wearing a dark jacket and carrying what appeared to be a dark raincoat. Although Mrs Pugh thought she would recognise the man if she saw him again, no trace of him was ever found.

There was one other suspicious incident that night. A Mercedes sports car was seen speeding away down Stephenson Street which runs off New Street between the Midland Hotel and the ramp leading into the station. A youth in his shirt sleeves was spreadeagled across the roof and the car was chased by police officers, one of whom shouted to the driver of a passing bus, 'Ram the bastard, he's a bomber.' After about twenty-five yards, the youth fell off the roof and the car sped away. The incident was filmed by a camera crew and shown on television that night. For years, it has given rise to speculation that the men in the car were the real bombers. In fact the occupants of the car were just people who had panicked trying to flee the bomb zone. They were swiftly eliminated from police enquiries.

The most promising lead came from Clifford Godwin, a clerk in the booking office at New Street Station. He reported that, shortly before the bombs exploded, three Irishmen had purchased return tickets to Belfast via the Lancashire port of Heysham. The train for Heysham had left at 7.55. Police at Heysham were put on the alert.

It was some days before the full extent of the carnage was known. Twenty-one people had died, and one hundred and sixty-two were injured – the biggest murder in British history. The Birmingham pub bombings came seven weeks after pub bombings at Guildford and just two weeks after a pub in Woolwich had been blown up. The pub bombings seemed to indicate that the indiscriminate murder of civilians was now a permanent feature of IRA strategy. But the Guildford and Woolwich pubs had been blown up because many of their customers were British soldiers based at nearby barracks. This was not the case in Birmingham. Many of the Birmingham victims were Irish.

One Irishman, John Reilly, was called to identify the body of his twenty-three year old son Eugene, and was shown instead the body of another man ... his other son Desmond, whom he had believed to be working two hundred miles away. Unknown to Mr Reilly, Desmond had returned unexpectedly to Birmingham to meet his brother for a drink at the Tavern in the Town. They both died.

The bombings triggered off a wave of anti-Irish sentiment. Revenge attacks on Irish property began almost at once. Within hours, the Irish Community Centre at Digbeth was petrol bombed. A petrol bomb was thrown through the window of the College Arms at Kingstanding, a public house with many Irish customers. Lighted petrol-soaked rags were thrown into lorries at an Irish owned haulage firm at Small Heath. A fire was started at St Gerard's Catholic School in Castle Vale.

Revenge attacks were not confined to Birmingham. Irish owned premises in London were also petrol bombed – a pub and a tobacconist's shop in the London Borough of Ealing were hit. So was a tobacconist's shop in Streatham, South London.

At the British Leyland plant at Longbridge there was a mass walk-out by workers who took to the streets carrying makeshift placards saying 'Hang IRA Bombers'. The National Federation of Licensed Victuallers telegrammed the Home Secretary, Roy Jenkins, calling for the immediate re-introduction of the death penalty. At Liverpool and Manchester airports, workers refused to handle flights bound for Belfast or Dublin.

In the House of Commons, Roy Jenkins promised tough measures

7

against the IRA and its sympathisers. 'Under the present circumstances,' he said, 'one could be justified in enabling the police and others to take exceptional measures in order to protect our people from indiscriminate killing.'

A week later, the Prevention of Terrorism Act was rushed through the House of Commons in a seventeen-hour emergency sitting. It passed through the House of Lords in only two minutes. The Act made membership of the IRA illegal and gave the police power to hold IRA suspects for up to one week without charge. It also gave police and immigration authorities power to expel or refuse entry to suspected terrorists and anyone suspected of harbouring them. A clause saying that the possession of documents relating to the IRA or any proscribed organisation was evidence of membership was dropped at the last moment.

An editorial in the *Guardian* caught the mood of the hour. 'A liberal society,' it said, 'cannot let its freedom, and its concern for the rights of the individual be abused in order that it shall be torn to pieces. From now on anybody who complains that he is being harassed by the police bomb squad will find a less than sympathetic audience.'

2

The trail that led to the disaster in Birmingham began seven days earlier outside the Central Telephone Exchange in Greyfriars Lane, Coventry. It was there, on the evening of November 14, 1974, that a young Irishman named James McDade blew himself to smithereens while planting a bomb. Another young Irishman, Ray McLaughlin, was arrested running away from the scene.

McDade's thumb-print (the only clue to his identity) was said to match that on an incendiary device found the previous week at the premises of Guidex Limited, an office equipment manufacturer in Constitution Hill, Birmingham. Forensic evidence showed that the ingredients of McDade's bomb included a General Time of Scotland alarm clock, an Ever Ready battery and a socket for the warning bulb. Similar items were found in nine other explosive or incendiary devices planted in and around Birmingham that month, including the bombs which seven days later devastated the Tavern in the Town and the Mulberry Bush.

Two days after McDade's death, tributes began appearing in Republican newspapers in Ireland. One read: 'James McDade, Lieutenant, Birmingham Battalion, Killed in Action'.

James McDade was born in the Ardoyne district of Belfast, a tiny Catholic enclave surrounded by the Protestant strongholds of Cliftonville, Heathfield, Lower Park Road and the Crumlin Road.

Ardoyne was a village until the 1870s. It grew up around the textile mills that were almost the sole source of employment. The mill-owners built the houses and if a worker lost his job, he also lost his house. With the decline of the textile industry, the mills began to close. Today they are all derelict and more than half the population is out of work. It has been that way for two generations. For many, the only hope of work was to emigrate to England and almost every family in Ardoyne has relatives in England.

There was no way a young man brought up in Ardoyne could remain neutral. Whenever Cliftonville football team played at home, gangs of Protestant youths would descend on Ardoyne smashing windows and shouting abuse. Catholic women and children would barricade themselves indoors while their men stood guard outside with sticks.

Every July 12, on the anniversary of the Battle of the Boyne, a Protestant band would march to the Catholic chapel of the Sacred Heart, on the corner of Glen View and Park View Roads, and stand outside playing loud Loyalist tunes. When Catholic children threw stones, the Royal Ulster Constabulary would give chase shouting, 'Get indoors you Fenian scum.'

It was to get him away from this that James McDade's mother encouraged him to go to England in search of work. McDade arrived in Birmingham in 1968 and lodged with Gerry Hunter and his wife in their back-to-back house in Aston. Hunter was also a refugee from Ardoyne and had known McDade since they were at St Gabriel's Secondary School together. He was a short, quick-tempered youth who had come to Birmingham in 1963, at the age of seventeen, and collected a couple of minor convictions: one for being a passenger in a stolen car and the other for being involved in a brawl with some Asians. Soon, however, he settled down, married a Birmingham girl, Sandra, and found work as an industrial painter. It was through the Hunters that McDade met his future wife, Jackie.

McDade stayed with the Hunters for about nine months. It was an unhappy arrangement since he was given to drinking and argument. Eventually, after a fight with Gerry, he left. Although they were never again close friends, the Hunters continued to see McDade and his wife. Sandra last saw McDade at his brother's wedding party in August 1974. It was memorable because there was another row and McDade stormed off leaving Jackie to make her own way home.

Gerry Hunter last saw McDade in late September when the two men worked on a contract for Carness and Pearson, a firm of industrial painters in Handsworth. Six weeks later McDade blew himself up.

McDade found other friends in Birmingham from his school days in Ardoyne. Billy Power was one of these. Power had emigrated to England in 1963 to escape unemployment in Belfast. His father had been a sergeant major in the British army and five of his six brothers and sisters had come to live in England. He had known McDade since they were together at the Holy Cross Primary School in Ardoyne.

Billy Power was a gentle, soft-spoken young man. He was never much of a worker. As a boy he had been sent to an approved school for truancy. For years he had drifted in and out of work, first as a labourer on building sites in London, and later as an industrial painter in Birmingham, sometimes working with McDade and Gerry Hunter. When he wasn't working he would get up late and spend the afternoon watching the racing on television. He was an obsessive gambler, always nipping in and out of betting shops to lay money on horses.

Two years after coming to Birmingham, he met Nora, a girl from Cork. They rented a room in Handsworth and lived together. Nora became pregnant and they talked about getting married. Three times they arranged to marry and three times Nora backed down. When at last they did marry, at a church in Aston, they already had one child and there was another on the way. On the day of the wedding they didn't have the price of a drink between them. Billy went to a betting shop and Nora went home and changed the baby's nappy.

Even after the second child arrived they were still living in the single room in Handsworth. Then, in 1968, they were allocated an old council house in Aston. It had no bathroom and the toilet was outside, but it was a step up in the world. Five years later, in 1973 they moved to a modern council house in Cranwell Grove, Erdington. By this time they had four children. Billy was still drifting in and out of work but he had his good points. He loved his children and if he had a win on the horses he always handed most of the money to Nora.

Paddy Hill was another of McDade's friends from Ardoyne. Hill was born in the hospital next to the jail on the Crumlin Road. His father had worked for a Belfast engineering firm. According to Hill, he was sacked when he was discovered to be a Roman Catholic. Like McDade and Power, Hill was also a graduate of the Holy Cross Primary School. He was a couple of years older than McDade and remembers walking young Jamsie home from school. In February, 1960, Hill's father went to Birmingham in search of work. Hill, his mother, three brothers and a sister followed six months later.

Paddy Hill is short, stocky and tough. He has a deep scar leading down from the left-hand side of his mouth, a memento of his turbulent early years in Birmingham. By 1970 he had collected seventeen convictions, mainly for brawling, but also for breaking and entering. In 1962 he served three months' detention for safe-breaking and in 1970 he served thirteen months in prison for stabbing three night-club bouncers in a fight. His appearance might have been considered menacing but for a ready smile and a devilish sense of humour.

Hill, too, drifted in and out of work. Like McDade, Power and Hunter, he had worked as an industrial painter. He also did a bit of painting for nuns at the local convent. Hill says he never became a close friend of McDade's in Birmingham. He estimates that they met only half a dozen times in the seven years before McDade blew himself up.

By the time of his death, McDade was a popular figure in Birmingham's Irish clubs and pubs. By all accounts he had a fine singing voice. His drinking habits, however, led to trouble at home. For some time, McDade, his wife and young child lived with his mother-in-law but she eventually evicted them and, about a year before McDade's death, they went to stay with Billy and Nora Power in their new council house at Erdington. Jackie, McDade's wife, was expecting their second child. 'I felt sorry for Jackie,' says Nora Power, 'I think Jamsie knocked her about a bit.'

The McDades stayed several weeks with Billy Power and his family. Nora Power remembers clearly what brought about their departure. 'One day Jamsie asked if Billy had a gun. Billy was shocked. I told Billy they had to go and they left soon after.'

Nora Power never saw James McDade again but, a few days before he blew himself up, she saw a photofit picture of a man police wanted in connection with the latest outbreak of bombings in Birmingham. 'I said to Billy, "That's Jamsie." Billy said, "Don't be so bloody stupid."'

Those who knew McDade say that he was not obvious IRA material. When he first came to Birmingham he had such a baby face that he had to carry his birth certificate with him in order to get served in pubs. In the early years, at least, he showed no interest in Republican politics.

The turning point seems to have come in December, 1971, when his brother Gerry, who had stayed in Ireland and joined the Belfast Brigade of the IRA, was shot dead by British paratroopers during a raid on a Republican club. Even so, most of those who knew McDade claim not to have connected him with the bombs that were going off all over Birmingham throughout 1973 and 1974. Sandra and Gerry Hunter both say they were shocked by his death. 'My reaction was "If that's what the IRA are recruiting, they are wasting their time,"' says Sandra. Someone else who knew McDade said, 'He was a very nervous fellow. I couldn't believe it when I heard he was in the IRA. I thought to myself, "Bloody hell, they must be hard up for recruits."'

12

Only Billy Power conceded there were any grounds for suspicion. 'We'd be having a pint and Jamsie would say he had to go somewhere. We used to laugh and say, "As soon as Jamsie gets a bit of money he prefers to drink on his own." It didn't stick out a mile. Only when you look back.'

3

A few days after McDade's death, funeral notices began to circulate in Irish pubs and clubs in Birmingham. They were headed, LIEUTENANT JAMES MCDADE and read:

'On November 21 at 3.30 the remains of our comrade, James McDade, will be escorted from Coventry to Birmingham and on to Belfast. We consider it the duty of all Irish people to be present at Coventry mortuary. The coffin will be draped in the tricolour that covered the coffin of Michael Gaughan who died on hunger strike. Transport will be available for mourners.'

The Birmingham branch of Sinn Fein was determined that McDade should have a hero's funeral. The government and the West Midlands police were equally determined that he should not.

Home Secretary, Roy Jenkins, assured the House of Commons that Sinn Fein supporters would not be allowed to escort the coffin to Birmingham's Elmdon airport. Such a demonstration, said Mr Jenkins, 'affronts the tolerance of long-suffering people'.

The Public Order Act was invoked to ban the procession. Since the road between Coventry and the airport passed through the territory of three different local authorities – Coventry, Solihull and Birmingham – each had to call an emergency council meeting to bring the act into operation. All police leave was cancelled and 1,300 policemen were drafted to line the route to the airport and many more were on duty in Coventry and Birmingham in case of reprisal bombings. In death, James McDade was far more trouble to the British authorities than he had ever been in life.

It was Gerry Hunter's idea to go to Belfast for the funeral. He suggested it to his friends Johnny Walker and Richard McIlkenny over a lunchtime drink at the Crossways pub in Erdington after McDade's death.

Walker and McIlkenny were a good deal older than Hunter. Both had large families – Walker had six daughters and a son, McIlkenny five daughters and a son. Both had steady jobs at Garrington's Forging and Presswork factory at Witton. Walker was a crane driver in the maintenance section, McIlkenny a millwright.

14

Everyone who knew Johnny Walker agrees that he was one of the nicest men you could hope to meet. He was a tall, balding man whose white hair made him look much older than his thirty-nine years. He was popular with the neighbours. Sociable, but not a big drinker. He worked hard to keep his family, sometimes seven days a week. Thomas Watt, one of his workmates, who would eventually give evidence against him, says today, 'Johnny Walker was one of the kindest men I knew. He was very popular at work and always the first to help anyone in trouble. If a worker was off sick for a few weeks, Walker would arrange a collection for him – and it made no difference whether the man was Irish, English or any other nationality.'

Walker was born and bred in Londonderry. He had lived in England since he was seventeen. Despite being born a Catholic in Londonderry, he did not come from a particularly Republican background. His brother, Eddie, was a sergeant major in the British Army and Walker had served two years National Service. He went back to Ireland only two or three times in twenty years. What seemed to have opened his eyes to the troubles in Ireland was the death of his father in 1972. Walker went to Derry for the funeral. His family lived in the Bogside where, six months before, British soldiers had shot dead thirteen unarmed civilians in what became known as Bloody Sunday. The visit to Derry was an eye opener.

The Catholic estates were under siege. On one occasion when Walker went out with his brother-in-law they had to take cover from a shoot-out between the British army and the IRA. Walker's father had had a bad chest and, shortly before his death, had been tear-gassed by British soldiers. Walker believed the tear-gas had helped to kill his father. One of his daughters recalled that he sometimes said, 'The British killed my father.' When he returned to Birmingham, he took with him, as a souvenir, a plastic bullet fired by British soldiers at Catholic civilians. From that time on, Walker was an ardent Republican. He started organising raffles and totes for the families of internees in Northern Ireland. He and Richard McIlkenny would sell the tickets at work, in the Crossways pub and at the Kingstanding Ex-Servicemen's Club. Gerry Hunter and Paddy Hill also helped to sell tickets. At first, Gerry Hunter was treasurer, but Walker took over in the summer of 1973. The raffles made about £8 a week profit. Walker kept scrupulous records and handed the proceeds over to a workmate, Mick Murray, who sent it to the Prisoners' Dependents' Relief Fund at Sinn Fein headquarters at Kevin Street in Dublin. Murray also helped to provide the prizes which his wife purchased at a discount warehouse. These included table lamps, teddy bears, cutlery, ornamental clocks, alarm clocks and watches – from which in due course sinister inferences would be drawn.

Walker was not a member of the IRA (which was legal at that time) or of Sinn Fein, but many of his friends and acquaintances were. This began to be the subject of rows with his wife, Theresa. Once they went to a Sinn Fein social at the White Horse pub in Nechells. Jamsie McDade was singing and many of those present were IRA members. Theresa said she would never go there again and that he ought not to either.

Walker had known McDade for two years. McDade had sometimes helped out with the raffles, but Walker didn't know him well. Had his friends not been going, Walker would not have gone to the funeral. When he got home that evening in November and said that he was going to McDade's funeral, Theresa was angry. Why waste money on a trip to Ireland, especially so near to Christmas? And for what? As far as she was concerned, Jamsie McDade had got what was coming to him.

Richard McIlkenny and his wife, Kate, were both natives of Ardoyne. Although at forty-one he was much older than McDade, he had known the McDade family all his life. After McDade's death, Kate looked after his youngest child for a few days before the funeral.

Like all natives of Ardoyne, Richard McIlkenny and his wife were staunch Republicans. Two of Richard's brothers, Anthony and Ambrose, were interned in Ireland, and so was one of Kate's cousins. Richard worked hard organising raffles, totes and dances among the Irish community in Birmingham to raise money for the families of internees. He was also in the habit of buying half a dozen copies of the Sinn Fein paper, *Republican News*, and distributing them to friends. He was not, however, a member of Sinn Fein.

When Gerry Hunter suggested going to Belfast for the funeral, both Walker and McIlkenny expressed interest, but no definite arrangement was made. As yet, it was unclear when the funeral would be held, since McDade's remains were still in police custody at the mortuary in Coventry.

The next day, Sunday, November 17, Gerry Hunter and Johnny Walker met Billy Power at a bus stop in Kingstanding. Power was with his brother, Tony, and the four men repaired to the nearby Fisher and Ludlow social club for a drink.

Hunter asked Power if he was going to the funeral, and said it would look good if all McDade's friends went. Power replied that he would go if he could find a few days' casual work to pay the fare.

Next day, his plans for casual work having fallen through, Billy Power told his wife Nora that he would not be going to the funeral. Nora offered to help out. She was owed social security money and, if she could get it in time, she told Billy he was welcome to borrow it. Nora says it was she who encouraged him to go. 'He had got stuck to the house. Not working. Just a few casuals here and there. I blame myself. If I had said "Don't go," he would never have gone that night.'

On Tuesday, November 19, Billy Power went to the social security office and asked for the money owed to his wife. He was told that it would be forwarded to her. Still more or less penniless, he went in search of Gerry Hunter. He called at Hunter's house in Wyrley Way, Erdington, but Hunter was not there. He looked in at the Crossways but there was still no sign of Hunter. Leaving the Crossways, he ran into Richard McIlkenny, who said that he understood that a mass was being arranged for McDade instead of a collection.

Hunter, meanwhile, had gone with Walker to St Chad's Roman Catholic cathedral to buy mass cards to take to Belfast in memory of the dead man. They bought a dozen and had them signed by McDade's friends at the Crossways. Next day they went back and bought more, about twenty in all.

On Wednesday, November 20, Power called at Hunter's house just after midday and they went to the Crossways for a drink. There they met Walker and some other friends and discussed arrangements for going to the funeral. The main topic of conversation was how Power and Hunter could raise money for the fare. Hunter had been out of work for seven weeks, and, like Power, he was broke. After about fifteen minutes, Walker left for work – he was on afternoon shift. Hunter and Power stayed on until closing time. That evening they heard that McDade's remains would be released from the Coventry mortuary the following day and flown to Ireland. It therefore seemed likely that the funeral would be on Friday. When he got home, Billy Power's wife, Nora, told him that her brother Eddie would lend him the fare to Belfast. He would be going to the funeral after all. At the time it seemed a stroke of luck. Looking back, it was the greatest disaster of his life.

At around eleven o'clock on Thursday, November 21, 1974, Billy Power again went round to Gerry Hunter's house, to tell him the good news – that he was going to the funeral. Hunter had still not raised the fare, but thought he might be able to borrow it from Johnny Walker. They called round at Walker's house and found him sorting out the mass cards before taking them up to the church to be countersigned by the priest. On their way to the church, they called back at Hunter's house to pick up two more mass cards – one for Power and one for Hunter. Then they went to the church of St Margaret's and St Mary's on Perry Common Road. The parish priest, Father Ryan, was out, so they left the cards with the house-keeper and said they would call back at five o'clock.

Outside the church, Walker took leave of them, saying he had to collect the wages he was owed from work. He needed the money to pay his fare to Belfast. As he left, Walker promised that he and the others would try and make up Gerry Hunter's fare between them.

Having nothing to do, Hunter and Power decided to call on Hunter's cousin, Seamus McLoughlin, at Holland Road, Aston, where McDade's widow, Jackie, was staying. They arrived at Holland Road to find the house crowded with people come to offer condolences to Jackie McDade. Sandra Hunter and Nora Power were there, and so was Richard McIl-kenny's wife, Kate, and McLoughlin's wife, Mary. Hunter and Power were shown into a room at the back of the house with the wives. They may have been hoping for a lift to Coventry, but since there was no room in the car leaving from Holland Road they decided to go down to the Irish Com-munity Centre at Digbeth where Sinn Fein was supposed to be laying on coaches. Sandra Hunter and Kate McIlkenny walked with them to the end of the road. Gerry Hunter and Billy Power caught a bus into town, Kate McIlkenny went home and Sandra Hunter went to collect her chil-dren from the Hastings Road Infants School.

Hunter and Power arrived at the Irish Centre in Digbeth only to find that the free transport to Coventry had been cancelled. The police, however, were much in evidence, standing in pairs on every corner. Since they didn't have the money for a bus fare to Coventry – let alone to Ireland – they decided to go to a pub where they had just enough money for a light and bitter each. Later, they were to reflect that, had they had the price of the bus fare to Coventry, they could not have got back to Birmingham in time to catch the train for Ireland.

In the pub they got talking to a couple of Irishmen who bought them each another drink. Then, at Power's suggestion, they called in at a nearby betting shop where he put his last thirty pence on a pair of greyhounds called Paul's Pride and Blue Bass. Power was lucky. He won £5.50. he placed one more bet and lost. Then they called in at another bookmaker's further up Digbeth where Power place a couple more unsuccessful bets. This left him with about £4 which he offered to split with Hunter, but Hunter refused his share. By now it was about three o'clock and they both went their separate ways home. Before parting they agreed to meet at New Street Station in time to catch the 6.55 train for Heysham and the ferry to Belfast.

After leaving Hunter and Power outside the church, Walker called in at the Crossways where he ran into Richard McIlkenny. Walker told McIlkenny that the funeral was to be the next day in Belfast and that he was definitely going. McIlkenny said that he would come too. First, however, they had to collect the wages owed them. Walker, who had been due to start an afternoon shift at one thirty, was about to phone the office but McIlkenny pointed out that it would be shut. Instead, they decided to call in. When they arrived, McIlkenny stayed talking to the gateman while Walker went in and saw the foreman, Martin Murrihy. He was told to come back for his money at about two thirty. Walker also ran into a workmate, Dennis Turner, who had a side-line mending watches. Turner had several times mended watches and clocks for Walker and McIlkenny. He later estimated that over the previous eighteen months Walker had given him three or four clocks or watches to repair, and that Dick McIlkenny had brought him two alarm clocks and several watches. On this occasion he had just repaired a wristwatch for Walker and he told him it was ready for collection. Walker reached in his bag and produced an alarm clock with a broken spring which he asked Turner to repair. Much significance would later be attached to Walker's association with clocks.

Walker and McIlkenny then walked down to the nearby Yew Tree pub and had a couple of pints of Guinness before going back for their money. When they got back, they saw the shift foreman, Martin Murrihy, again, and the shop foreman, Bob O'Dwyer. They told them they were going to the funeral of a friend in Belfast, collected their money and departed. Both Walker and McIlkenny insist that, apart from the two foremen, the watchmender and the gatekeeper, they spoke to no one else during their short visits to their workplace. However, another workmate – Tom Watt – later testified that he met Walker in the locker room. Watt said that he already knew Walker was going to McDade's funeral because Walker had told him the previous day. In the locker room, according to Watt, Walker said he was going to Belfast and had given him the key to the tea cupboard. The conversation would be of no significance except that Watt added that Walker warned him not to go out that night, 'I said, "Why?" and he said, "That's enough."' Watt claimed that this was only the latest of several such warnings given him by Walker and that these had usually been followed by explosions. Walker denies that he ever said anything of the sort. As for the conversation on the day of the bombing, he denies he even met Watt. Much was made of Watt's evidence in court and it is a subject to which we shall return.

Having got their money, Walker and McIlkenny then went to call on Eddie Lewsley, another regular at the Crossways and a workmate at Garringtons. Walker borrowed a black tie from Lewsley, then he and McIlkenny separated and went back to their respective homes. Before parting, they agreed that McIlkenny should call at Walker's house at about six o'clock. They would then call for Gerry Hunter and make their way to New Street station in time to catch the 6.55 to Heysham.

4

Until the last minute, Paddy Hill did not know whether he would make it. Like Gerry Hunter and Billy Power, he was flat broke. He had not worked for the best part of a year and he supported his wife and six children on £60 a week social security money.

Hill had seen Hunter two days after McDade's death and said he was hoping to go to Belfast for the funeral. Although he had been at primary school with McDade, Hill had not been a close friend. Nevertheless he was tempted by the prospect of a trip to Belfast. An eighty year old aunt had just had a stroke and was not expected to live. Hill had promised to visit her before Christmas. McDade's funeral provided an opportunity and also offered the prospect of some congenial company.

On Tuesday, November 19, Hill learned that his aunt had taken a turn for the worse and he made up his mind to go. Money remained a problem, however. Thursday, November 21, dawned and he was still no nearer raising the money. He spent most of the day at home with his wife and three of his children and by 3.30 he was getting desperate. Taking his two year old son, Sean, with him, Hill went to visit Johnny Walker at Perry Common. The journey from Hill's home at Kingstanding involved two buses and took about half an hour. Hill planned to ask Walker if he could borrow the raffle money to pay his fare to Belfast. Walker, however, said he had nothing to lend. He had sent the proceeds from the raffle to the Prisoners' Dependents' Fund the previous week.

On leaving Walker's house, Hill telephoned his wife, Pat, from a call box at the end of the street. She said she would lend him £2 from her money box, the key to which was in the custody of a family friend, Rose Murphy. The reason for Mrs Murphy's custody of the key to the money box remains obscure. Hill says that this was the first he knew of it. Pat Hill also suggested that he might try to raise a loan from Sister Bridget, a nun at the Little Sisters of the Assumption Convent at Old Oscott Hill, a five minute walk from home. Sister Bridget had known the Hill family for about two years and helped them out on several occasions. She was not in when Hill phoned. He was told to call at the Convent at six o'clock.

Hill then called at Rose Murphy's house, collected the key to his wife's money box and went home. He arrived home around five o'clock, shaved, bathed and put a few clothes in a small blue suitcase. He went to the convent where Sister Bridget lent him £15 which, added to the £2 from his wife's money box, gave him more than enough for the £15 return ticket to Belfast.

At five o'clock, Johnny Walker went to collect the mass cards from Father Ryan. When he got back, one of his daughters made him scrambled eggs. He sent his son, Sean, round to Gerry Hunter's to collect a hold-all which Hunter had borrowed for his father's funeral seven weeks earlier. The zip had broken and Sandra Hunter mended it. When Sean returned with the hold-all, two of Walker's daughters, Bernadette and Veronica, packed him a few clothes, ham sandwiches and Granny Smith's apples for the journey.

Dick McIlkenny called for Walker, as arranged, at about six o'clock. He brought with him Hughie Callaghan, another regular from the Crossways.

Hughie Callaghan, an unemployed labourer, lived with his wife and sixteen year old daughter in a council house in Erdington. He was forty-four years old and had lived in Birmingham since 1947. Like McIlkenny, Hunter, Power and Hill he was born in Ardoyne. As a boy he had known the McDade family, and over the last two years he had become acquainted with Jamsie, but did not know him well. Callaghan's wife, Eileen, describes Hughie as a timid, inoffensive man with no political beliefs. He suffered from ulcers and had not been in regular work for three years.

The day of the disaster was also Eileen's birthday. Hughie Callaghan went to collect his £17.20 social security money from the post office at Stockland Green. He had arranged to meet Eileen near the post office later that morning to hand over the money which she needed for the family's housekeeping. Hughie, however, needed the money to repay a debt, so when he met Eileen he told her that the post office would not pay out the money until the afternoon. He was owed £12 for casual work he had picked up from a man he had met in Yates' Wine Lodge in Corporation Street. He would go to Yates' that evening, collect the money he was owed and take it home to his wife who would be none the wiser. That, at least, was the plan.

After leaving his wife at Stockland Green, Callaghan had gone for a drink at the Crossways. On the way he met Gerry Hunter and Billy Power going to Seamus McLoughlin's house. They stood chatting for a few minutes, during which Hunter and Power mentioned that they were trying to raise the money to go to Belfast for McDade's funeral, then they parted company. Walker and McIlkenny were in the Crossways, but Callaghan did not speak to them beyond passing the time of day. He stayed at the Crossways until closing time and consumed three or four pints of Guinness. After closing time, he strolled up to the Kingstanding Ex-Servicemen's Club, where he had a couple more Guinnesses. Then, reluctant to go home until he could pay his wife's housekeeping, he called at Richard McIlkenny's house in Epsom Grove to repay £1 he owed.

Callaghan arrived at McIlkenny's house shortly after four and found McIlkenny getting ready for his trip to Belfast. He sat playing with McIlkenny's children while Richard packed. Callaghan had no intention of going to Ireland, but, having nothing better to do, said he would come to New Street station to see them off.

Unlike Theresa Walker, Kate McIlkenny was keen that her husband should go to Belfast. She was a cousin of James McDade and had been brought up in the same street as his family, but it wasn't only sympathy for the McDades that prompted her to encourage her husband to go. 'Richard usually went back every year and took one or two of the children with him. This was one year he hadn't been back to see his family and I said, "Why don't you go?"'

Richard McIlkenny says the funeral was not his main interest. 'I thought I'd like to see my mother for a couple of days and be back on Sunday.'

Kate McIlkenny arrived home from work at around five o'clock and set about helping her husband prepare for his journey. She drew up a shopping list of Irish food which she wanted him to bring back – soda bread, potato bread, Irish sausages, vegetable rolls. She then called on a neighbour and asked to borrow a suitcase. It was a blue case with a zip fastener. She had borrowed it before, when they went to Belfast for her father's funeral. Into the suitcase Richard packed a new shirt, a tie and the jacket of his new suit, still in its plastic wrapping. The trousers were with Sandra Hunter who was turning up the legs for him.

Shortly before six, McIlkenny and Callaghan left to call for Johnny Walker, a walk of about ten minutes. 'See you on Sunday,' McIlkenny said to his wife as they left. He was never to return.

Walker was waiting when McIlkenny and Callaghan arrived. One of

23

Walker's daughters handed him the maroon hold-all, and the three men set off down Enderby Road to the bus stop on Witton Lodge Road. On the way they passed Paul Wickett, son of Walker's next-door neighbour. Wickett later testified that the hold-all Walker was carrying appeared to be so heavy that he stopped to change hands. He said he had called to Walker, but Walker had ignored him. At Witton Lodge Road the three men caught a number 5 bus to Ridgeway. At Ridgeway they got off and walked to Gerry Hunter's house in Wyrley Way.

Hunter had with him a large overcoat left behind by a friend from Belfast who had once lodged with him, and which Hunter planned to return. He asked Walker to put it in his bag. Walker unzipped the bag and tried to squeeze it in. At which point Sandra Hunter intervened. 'Don't do that,' she said, 'you'll crease your shirts.' She emptied the contents of Walker's bag onto the dining-room table. There were sandwiches, the Granny Smith's apples, two shirts, socks, a jacket, trousers and a shaving kit. She then put the overcoat into the bag and tried to put the clothes and other things back on top, but they wouldn't fit so the coat had to come out again. Since Hunter had no bag, he also gave Walker two pairs of socks and a shirt and asked him to put them in his case. In the confusion over the coat, however, the shirt was left behind.

Richard McIlkenny then asked Sandra if she had his trousers. She went to get them, then opened McIlkenny's case. There was a Chelsea Girl carrier bag inside with his shaving gear in it. She moved it over so that she could lay the trousers flat.

Johnny Walker then produced the mass cards for McDade. Sandra was neither Irish nor was she a Catholic, but she had known Jamsie on and off for six years. She signed and the men went off. There were now four of them – Walker, McIlkenny, Callaghan and Hunter.

They set off from Gerry Hunter's house at about 6.30 to catch a bus into the centre of town. As they reached the Ridgeway, Hunter's two small sons caught them up and gave Hunter a pound note from his wife. At Ridgeway they caught a bus into the city centre. As they were getting off, at Colmore Row near the cathedral, three girls tried to push their way onto the bus and the driver ordered them to get to the back of the queue.

From Colmore Row they went across the churchyard, across Temple Row and down Needless Alley, the narrow passage which runs past the Windsor pub. They came into New Street up the ramp into the shopping precinct above the station. As they hurried along, Hunter said, 'I told Billy we'd meet him at 6.30. He'll think I'm not coming.'

24

Billy Power was first to arrive. He had been waiting at New Street since about 6.40. His only luggage was a brown paper bag containing a clean shirt and a pair of socks. He had scraped together the train fare by borrowing £10 from his brother-in-law and £4 from his wife Nora. This added to the £4 left over from his win on the dogs that afternoon gave him enough for the return fare.

After glancing around the station and seeing no familiar faces, he went to a cigarette kiosk and bought a packet of twenty Embassy tipped. As he walked away from the kiosk, he noticed a man staring at him.

The Heysham train was due out at 6.55 and it occurred to Power that his friends might already be on board. He went back to the cigarette kiosk and bought a box of matches to get change for a platform ticket machine. He then bought a platform ticket and went to platform nine to search the train. The man whom he had noticed watching him seemed now to be following.

Seeing no one he recognised, Power surrendered his platform ticket and went back to the station concourse. At 6.57 he was just about to give up and go home when he saw Walker, McIlkenny, Hunter and Callaghan coming down the escalator. By now they were too late to catch the 6.55. Or so they thought – later they learned that the train had been delayed and did not in fact depart until 7.08.

At the ticket office, Walker, McIlkenny and Power purchased return tickets to Belfast. Walker and McIlkenny each stumped up half the cost of a single ticket for Hunter. They then had the best part of an hour to kill until the next train at 7.55 so they decided to have a drink. By an eerie coincidence, Callaghan suggested the Mulberry Bush in the Rotunda, about two minutes' walk away. The beer was cheaper there, he said. Eventually, however, they opted for British Rail's Taurus Bar at the end of the station concourse.

All the seats in the Taurus were taken and so they stood by a pillar near the doorway. There were several railway workers sitting at a table nearby and a young couple near the bar. Two Jamaican girls were serving behind the bar. Callaghan bought the first round. Gerry Hunter went out to a phone box to ring his mother in Belfast. Hunter's mother was not on the phone so he rang a neighbour, Felix Doherty, and said he would ring back in ten minutes if Doherty would arrange for his mother to be available by the phone. As he came back into the bar to rejoin the others, he noticed a man outside who appeared to be watching them through the plate glass window at the front. 'There's a man outside staring at us,' he said. The man was in his forties and Hunter speculated that he might be a policeman, to which Walker replied, 'So what? We're not doing nothing.' The police later said there were no officers on New Street station at that time.

The men later said they were in the bar from about 7.10 to 7.45. The timing is crucial since it was later alleged that they went from here to plant the bombs in the Tavern in the Town and the Mulberry Bush. At first, according to the men, they were standing by the pillar. Later, when a table became vacant, they moved to a table on the left-hand side of the bar and sat down. The young couple near the bar seemed to be having a tiff. At one stage the man walked off leaving the girl in tears. After a few minutes he came back and they kissed and made up. The five Irishmen kept themselves amused watching this little cameo.

After about twenty minutes Johnny Walker bought another round and Hunter went out to telephone Felix Doherty again. Doherty said that Hunter's mother was out and so Hunter asked if he could arrange for them to be met at the boat. Doherty said he would ask a mutual friend, Diddler Dunlop, to meet them and suggested Hunter ring back to confirm the arrangement.

Hunter estimates it was about 7.40 by the time he got back from the second phone call. The train was due out in fifteen minutes. They were just getting ready to leave the bar when Paddy Hill walked in.

After collecting his money from Sister Bridget, Hill had taken two short bus rides to the Crossways pub at Kingstanding. Landlord Noel Walsh later recalled that Hill, who was one of his regulars, arrived between 6.30 and 6.45. He was dressed smartly and was carrying his small blue suitcase. Hill told Walsh he was going to Ireland and jokingly asked for a couple of pounds. Hill had ordered a drink and then went next door to the library where there was a public telephone. From there he called his wife, Pat, and told her that the nuns had come up with the money for his fare and so he would be going to Belfast. He then went back to the Crossways and finished his drink. His suitcase was the subject of some amusement and as he left he told the landlord, Mr Walsh, 'You'll be sorry if I leave that here.' Walsh later testified that he clearly understood this to be Hill's idea of a joke. 'He was always cracking jokes.' And in any case jokes about parcels left in pubs were all the rage at the time, though after that night they would never again seem funny. Walsh said he heard

26

at least one such crack a day and had heard Hill make similar remarks several times before.

Hill left the Crossways at about 7.10. There were many witnesses to his departure. He tried unsuccessfully to cadge a loan from Ray Cook. Then he tried to cadge a lift into town from Tommy Jolly. Jolly excused himself on the grounds that he was driving his firm's lorry. Out in the carpark, Hill met Brian Craven and Arthur Southall. He said he was going to catch the train to Ireland and was afraid he would miss it. They too refused to take him. Hill then crossed the road and caught a bus, number 42K, into town. He got off the bus at Dale End, a few minutes' walk from New Street station. By the time he reached the Taurus Bar it was after 7.45.

The others were surprised to see Hill. No one had mentioned he was coming. 'And where do you think you're going?' asked Johnny Walker.

'I'm going with you'se.'

'Where did you get the money?'

'I tapped it off the nuns.'

'You what, Paddy?'

'I'll make it up to them with a bit of decorating.'

Hill then went to the bar and was about to buy himself a drink when Richard McIlkenny told him there was no time. Instead, he bought a packet of twenty Park Drive plain cigarettes and had a sip out of Billy Power's glass. Then they left the bar, and Hill went to buy a ticket. He walked away from the ticket office leaving the ticket on the counter. The booking clerk called him back.

The others didn't wait for Hill. Callaghan bought himself another platform ticket and they went through the barrier. At the Menzies shop, just inside the barrier, Walker and McIlkenny bought cigarettes and they then made their way to platform nine. On the platform Hunter gave Power, who had no overcoat, the coat he was carrying for his friend in Belfast. Hill caught up with them on the platform and everyone except Callaghan boarded the train. It pulled out within a minute and Callaghan stood on the platform waving them off.

It was 7.55 on the evening of November 21, 1974. The pubs in the city centre were filling up, mostly with young people. By now the bombs must already have been ticking away. All the victims were in their place.

5

Jamsie McDade's remains left Coventry mortuary at about four o'clock on a twilight November afternoon. He departed with a minimum of ceremony. In the mortuary chapel two priests conducted a short funeral in defiance of a ban by the Archbishop of Birmingham. Mourners included McDade's twenty year old widow, Jackie, and his two year old son, Gerard. As the IRA notice had promised, the coffin was covered with the flag that had once adorned the coffin of the dead hunger striker, Michael Gaughan. Gaughan's brother, John, was among the mourners. So was Brendan McGill, national organiser of Sinn Fein in Britain, and George Lynch, Birmingham organiser.

Outside, a crowd of about three hundred Sinn Fein supporters faced a three-deep police cordon. Nearby, a group of National Front supporters chanted anti-IRA slogans. The demonstrators were kept well back from the entrance to the mortuary. The badges on the police helmets twinkled in the television lights.

Before the coffin emerged, police ordered the flag to be removed and Brendan McGill addressed the crowd through a loud hailer. 'In a few moments the remains of Lieutenant James McDade will leave the mortuary. Please stay as orderly as possible. I want no trouble.'

As the coffin appeared, a lone bagpiper, dressed in a kilt, played a lament. (The piper was later suspended by his employers, the car components firm Joseph Lucas, after threats from his workmates.)

The anti-IRA demonstrators began singing 'Go home you bums' to the tune of 'Auld Lang Syne'. Others chanted 'IRA out'. A bottle, followed by several bags of flour, was hurled at the hearse, but there were no hits.

The coffin was loaded quickly into a waiting hearse. The mourners clambered hastily into three waiting funeral cars and then the little procession sped away, escorted by four police cars. As they moved off, scuffling broke out between the two groups of demonstrators and there were several arrests. As the funeral cars sped past the anti-IRA demonstrators, one of the mourners was seen to make a V-sign.

On arrival at Birmingham's Elmdon Airport, McDade's coffin was loaded aboard a British Airways Viscount, scheduled to take off for Belfast at 6.30. The twenty-two mourners who were accompanying the remains to Belfast took their seats on the plane. Soon, however, it became apparent that all was not well.

From Belfast word came that airport workers would refuse to handle the coffin following threats of assassination from Protestant para-military groups. There was a delay while British Airways officials tried unsuccessfully to persuade the Belfast airport workers to change their minds. When this failed, the coffin was unloaded and the Sinn Fein mourners were transferred to a passenger lounge. Security was tight. Eight hundred policemen surrounded the airport and the Sinn Fein mourners were kept well away from the public.

There was a further delay when ground staff at Birmingham walked out after hearing that a bomb threat had been made against them. Eventually the Viscount took off – without McDade and his mourners.

Brendan McGill went to negotiate with the pilot of an Aer Lingus flight bound for Dublin. The pilot agreed to take the coffin and preparations were made for the Sinn Fein party to board. It was after eight o'clock and the atmosphere at the airport was tense.

By now, the five Irishmen were speeding towards Crewe. At Crewe they would have to change on to the London-Heysham train. From Heysham they would take the ferry for Belfast.

British Rail guard Rab Nawaz remembered checking their tickets just after Stafford. He later described them as being in a jolly mood. One of them, he thought, was slightly drunk, but he could not be sure. He noticed that they had Irish accents.

They reached Crewe at 8.50 and went into the buffet for a cup of tea. Paddy Hill bought a steak and kidney pie which broke up while he was eating it, causing gravy to dribble over his hands. While the others were in the buffet, Gerry Hunter again went to telephone his mother's neighbour, Felix Doherty, to confirm that Diddler Dunlop would be waiting in his car to meet them when the ferry arrived in Belfast. Doherty confirmed the arrangement. The London-Heysham train arrived on time, at 9.15, and they boarded without incident.

After seeing his friends off at New Street station, Hughie Callaghan went back to the Taurus Bar to finish his drink. When he got there, however, he found that his glass had been cleared away. He decided to go on to Yates' Wine Lodge in search of the man who owed him £12.50. He left

New Street station by the front entrance, skirted the left-hand side of the Bull Ring and went into New Street. As he did so, he passed within three feet of the Mulberry Bush public house which was by now crowded with customers – some of whom had only minutes to live.

At Birmingham airport the Sinn Fein passengers were preparing to board the Aer Lingus flight for Dublin. Police and airport authorities heaved a sigh of relief that McDade would shortly be off their hands. Assistant Chief Constable Maurice Buck was chatting to journalists when a police-man called him to one side and said that there was an important telephone call.

When word that bombs had gone off reached the journalists, they scrambled for their cars and raced into town. In his haste one reporter left a bag behind and triggered off a bomb scare which led to the evacuation of the airport buildings.

Of the Sinn Fein mourners, only Birmingham organiser George Lynch knew what had happened. As they were about to board the plane, he was called to a telephone. It was his wife, Phyllis, ringing to say that she had got home safely from the Coventry mortuary. As she was speaking, news of the bombings flashed on to the television. She relayed the contents to her husband. Lynch went back to the airport lounge and shortly afterward they boarded the Aer Lingus Boeing 727 without his breathing a word to any of his colleagues. Through the aeroplane window he watched as six policemen loaded McDade's coffin into the cargo hold.

Chief Superintendent Harry Robinson, head of West Midlands CID, was in his office at Lloyd House when news of the bombings came through. His deputy, Superintendent Pat Cooney, and Superintendent Andrew Crawford, head of Special Branch, were with him. It had been a long day and the three men were looking forward to going home. Robin-son was checking through some last minute paperwork when the phone rang. Crawford answered. 'There's been a bomb go off,' he said. There had been a lot of bombs in Birmingham that year. Robinson thought his leg was being pulled. 'I told you,' he said, 'as soon as I've finished this, I'm going home.' Before Crawford had a chance to explain, the phone rang again. A second bomb had gone off. For a moment Robinson still thought Crawford was joking until he saw from Crawford's face that it was no joke. The three men raced for their cars. They were on the scene by 8.30.

Nine miles away, at police headquarters in Walsall, Detective Superintendent George Reade was also thinking about going home for the night, when the phone rang. It was his wife, Pat. There had been more bombings she said. Big ones. Many dead. It had just been on the TV. 'See you when I see you,' said Reade, replacing the phone. And, with that, he rounded up every available CID officer and set off for Birmingham. In his time George Reade had handled some big cases, but this was to be his finest hour.

At the airport, the Aer Lingus Boeing was still on the tarmac. On board, the Sinn Fein mourners and their fellow passengers waited impatiently for take-off. Only George Lynch knew the reason for the latest delay. Through the plane windows they could see policemen and officials scurrying back and forth. Eventually Special Branch officers came on board and took away two Sinn Fein men, Michael Holden and John Higgins. They had not returned by the time the pilot was given the all clear for take-off and the plane left without them. It was 9.15.

Lynch kept his secret all the way to Dublin. The friends of James McDade would be among the last to learn of the terrible retribution that attended his departure from Birmingham.

As the plane carrying McDade's remains took off, the five Irishmen were boarding the train for Heysham. They sat at a table in an almost empty compartment. Four of them sat round the table and one perched on the arm of the opposite seat. Gerry Hunter produced a pack of cards and they started playing Don, a popular card game in Birmingham's Irish pubs.

The only other passengers in the compartment were Linda Jones, a market trader from Blackburn, and her mother. They were returning from a day's shopping spree in London. Linda Jones remembered the men getting in at Crewe. She later recalled that one of them – it must have been Paddy Hill – was shorter than the others. He was carrying a case which, because of his height, he had difficulty putting on the luggage rack. Ms Jones noticed nothing about the men except that they had Irish accents. They were still playing cards when she and her mother left the train at Preston.

Soon after arriving at the scene of the bombings, Chief Superintendent Harry Robinson ordered a watch to be kept on all ports and airports.

Telex messages went out from Lloyd House alerting police and port authorities around the country to be on the look-out for suspicious passengers travelling from Birmingham. When the booking clerk at New Street reported that he had sold return tickets to Belfast to a group of Irishmen not long before the explosions, the Birmingham police immediately contacted the British Transport Police at Heysham.

Sergeant Alan Dickie took the call. Bombs had gone off in Birmingham, he was told. A number of people had been killed. A party of Irishmen were on their way from Birmingham New Street to Heysham. There was nothing necessarily to connect them with the bombings, but they should be questioned on arrival.

The only train they could possibly be on was the Ulster Express from London Euston. It had three stops before arriving at Heysham – Crewe, Preston and Lancaster – and it was due in at 10.45. There was plenty of time to prepare. Dickie stationed a dog handler, Constable Gerald Baines, at the end of the platform so that no one could escape down the track. Another officer was deputed to board the train to make sure everyone got off. Special Branch officer David Watson was stationed near the barrier and the ticket collector, sixty-four year old Arnold Taylor, was warned to be on the look-out for passengers with tickets issued at Birmingham New Street.

The Ulster Express arrived on time. There were about three hundred people on board, all bound for Ireland. Mr Taylor looked carefully at each ticket. The returns he tore in half, keeping the used portion. The singles he kept. It was not hard to spot the men from Birmingham. Four men with Irish accents were walking together and three had return tickets to Belfast. The fifth, Paddy Hill, was some way ahead of the others. Each ticket was numbered consecutively and each had been issued earlier that evening at New Street station. Taylor immediately pointed out the four men to Detective Constable Watson. By now they were standing by the Special Branch tables having their bags checked before boarding the *Duke of Lancaster* ferry to Belfast.

Less than three hours had passed since the explosion. Already the police had their first big break.

6

Paddy Hill was walking ahead of the other four. It was some time before the Special Branch officers realised he was travelling with the others. The officer on duty at the Special Branch tables was Detective Constable Fred Willoughby of the Morecambe police. He asked Hill to step into a tiny office behind the table and asked for his name, address and destination. Only routine, he explained. No mention was made of the bombs that had gone off at Birmingham.

Hill gave Willoughby his name and address and said that he was going to see his grandmother and an aunt who lived at Brumpton Park, Belfast. He made no mention of McDade's funeral. He was then asked to open his case and Willoughby glanced at the contents. It contained only a change of clothes. Willoughby told Hill he was free to board.

As Hill went towards the ferry, he noticed a man staring at him. Hill went over and asked the man who he was staring at. The man laughed and said 'Don't you recognise me?' It was Whisky McGill, a childhood friend from the Ardoyne. Hill had last seen McGill fifteen years earlier when he left home to join the Merchant Navy. McGill now worked on the ferry. He told Hill to go down to the bar, mention his name to the barman and he would be all right for a drink. Hill went down to the bar and ordered a Harp lager. After a while he began to wonder where the others were. He went back up to the deck and asked McGill to keep an eye out for the others. Then he went back to the bar to finish his lager. He assumed McGill would tell the others where to find him, but half an hour later there was no sign of them.

Walker, McIlkenny, Hunter and Power passed the ticket barrier together. McIlkenny showed his own ticket and Walker's and put them both in his pocket. Power was wearing the overcoat that Hunter was taking back to his friend in Belfast.

Detective Sergeant Donald Bell was on duty at the Special Branch tables and Constable Michael Walker of the British Rail police was standing nearby. 'Have you lads all travelled from Birmingham?' asked Bell.

'Yes,' they replied in unison.

'Are you travelling together?'

'Yes,' again in unison.

Bell told them to wait on one side while the other passengers were checked through. He then asked them to go with D C Willoughby (who had by now finished interviewing Paddy Hill) and Constable Walker to the office of the railway police which was back through the ticket barrier. Constable Gerald Baines and his Alsatian went with them. Baines remained at the door of the office while the interviews were in progress.

Hunter and Power were interviewed in a back room by a British Transport policeman, Fred Hulmes. Hulmes wanted their names, addresses, dates of birth, and places of work. Both gave their occupations as unemployed painters and both were asked when and where they had last worked. Hunter said he had last worked for Carness and Pearson in Handsworth. Power said he had last worked for Horricks of Hockley. They were asked for proof of identity. Hunter produced his N H S card. Neither man had any luggage (Power had put the brown paper bag containing his change of clothes in Walker's case). They were asked to turn out their pockets and to take off their shoes and socks. Asked why they were going to Belfast neither man mentioned McDade. Hunter said he was going to see his mother. Power said he was going to bring his younger brother back to England. Asked later why they had not mentioned McDade, Hunter said, 'I thought if I told them they would be awkward with us and hold us up so that we would miss the funeral.'

Walker and McIlkenny were interviewed in the front office by D C Willoughby and Constable Walker. The questions were the same. Name, address, place of work and proof of identity. Willoughby asked to see inside their bags. He glanced quickly at the contents. McIlkenny's suit, a shirt and tie. In Walker's maroon hold-all there was a change of clothes, the Granny Smith apples and the sandwiches made by his daughter, and two pairs of socks belonging to Gerry Hunter.

Walker and McIlkenny said later that they were asked to turn out their pockets and that Willoughby saw the mass cards and said, 'For McDade's funeral?' To which Walker said he replied, 'Yes.' Willoughby had no recollection of seeing the mass cards. Had he done so, he said, his suspicions would immediately have been aroused. He asked where they were staying in Belfast. McIlkenny said they would be staying with his mother. According to Willoughby, McDade was not mentioned.

Questions over, the four men were told to wait outside. They waited by the ticket barrier, unguarded except for Constable Baines and his dog at a discreet distance. While they were waiting, a Scots detective approached

Gerry Hunter and asked after his wife and children. Hunter was astonished and asked how he knew about his family. The detective said he remembered seeing Hunter, his wife and children pass through in August. (They had been on their way to visit Hunter's dying father.) The little girl, he remembered, had long red hair. While they were chatting, another police officer came over and said that bombs had gone off in Birmingham and that people had been killed. It was the first they knew about the bombings.

Nearby, in the Special Branch office, Bell and Willoughby were checking out the identity of the four men. They were also checking to see if any of them featured on Special Branch files. Within minutes the answer came back that the names and addresses were accurate and that the West Midlands Special Branch had nothing on them – which was surprising in view of what was later alleged.

By now it was past 11.30. The ferry was due to sail at 11.45. Sergeant Bell was all set to let them go. Then the phone rang. It was the head of Lancashire CID, Joe Mounsey. Bell mentioned that he had detained four Irishmen and asked what he should do with them. Without hesitating, Mounsey replied, 'Take them to Morecambe and call in Frank Skuse.' Skuse was a scientist from the North West Forensic Science Laboratory at Chorley. The die was cast.

Hughie Callaghan's wife, Eileen, celebrated her birthday alone in her Erdington council flat. Her sixteen year old daughter, Geraldine, was out with a friend. Hughie had been out all day and had not returned. He had promised to bring home the social security money, but instead appeared to be blowing it on drink. Eileen Callaghan was angry with him.

At nine o'clock she turned on the television and saw that bombs had gone off in the centre of Birmingham. She began to worry. Geraldine could have been in one of these pubs. For the next hour and a half she sat at home alone, worrying. At 10.30 the door bell rang. It was Bill Dawe and his daughter, Anne Marie, good friends of the Callaghans. Hughie and Eileen were Anne Marie's godparents, and she and her father had come to wish Eileen a happy birthday.

But Eileen was far from happy. The minutes ticked by but there was no sign of Hughie or Geraldine. She rang her daughter's friend and was told that Geraldine was on her way home. She wondered whether she might have been caught up in the bombing and rang the emergency number being given out on the television for relatives of victims to telephone. There was no reply. At about 11.15 she went out to look for Hughie, leaving the Dawes waiting in the living-room. A few minutes after she had gone out, Geraldine arrived home safely. Hughie turned up ten minutes later.

Eileen was angry when she got home. 'Where have you been all day?' she shouted. Hughie gave a confused account of his movements. He said he had been seeing Dick McIlkenny and the others off at the station. Then he started to cry and said he was lucky to be alive. At one point Anne Marie thought she understood him to say he had been in the Tavern when it had exploded. There were glasses and bodies everywhere, he said.

After the Dawes departed and Geraldine had gone to bed, Eileen demanded to know what had become of her housekeeping money. She searched his pockets and found £11. She also found the social security book and saw that he had received £17. 'You'd better find the rest of the money,' she said, as she went to bed. She left Hughie on the settee repeating to himself that he was lucky to be alive.

Hughie Callaghan later gave a more coherent account of his movements that night. After waving his friends off at New Street station, he had gone to Yates' Wine Lodge in Corporation Street. He often went to Yates' in search of casual work and it was here he hoped to meet the sub-contractor who owed him £12.50. Instead he ran into a friend he had not seen for years, John Fannon, a painter and decorator who lived in Hockley. Fannon bought Hughie a drink and they started chatting about old times.

They did not hear either of the explosions, but after they had been talking for about ten minutes, the lights went out and it was announced there had been a bomb scare. The barman asked everyone to leave. Callaghan and Fannon made their way out by a back entrance, still carrying their drinks. They crossed Cannon Street and, drinks in hand, went in to the Windsor pub. Callaghan bought another round and after they had been drinking for several minutes police officers arrived and said that a bomb had exploded in the Tavern in the Town. They ordered everyone to drink up quickly and leave.

When they got outside, Fannon suggested they go and see what had happened. They walked down Corporation Street to the corner with New Street, less than one hundred yards from the Tavern in the Town. There they stood for five minutes watching rescue workers carrying bodies from the ruins. Then they went their separate ways – Fannon to the Locarno Ballroom via another public house, the Fox in Hurst Street.

Callaghan indicated that he was going home and set off back up Corporation Street in search of a bus stop, but on the bus he ran into another acquaintance. They got off at Sixways, Aston, and went to Lozell's Working Men's Club, another of Callaghan's favourite haunts. The Club was packed and everyone was talking about the explosions. Callaghan described vividly to his friend the scenes he had witnessed outside the Tavern in the Town.

At around ten o'clock he and his friend left Lozell's and caught a 5A bus. The other man got off at the Wyrley Birch Estate and Callaghan travelled on to the Crossways on College Road. He arrived just in time for last orders and whiled away the next half hour talking about the bombings. It was 11.30 when he finally went home.

The four Irishmen were kept waiting by the ticket barrier at Heysham for about twenty minutes. They did not know that Paddy Hill was already on board the ferry, but assumed that he was still being interviewed in the Special Branch office and that, as soon as he rejoined them, they would be allowed to board. The ferry was only yards away. Through the glass windows of the covered tunnel that led from the ticket barrier to the quayside, they could see passengers looking down at them from the deck of the *Duke of Lancaster*.

With about ten minutes to go before the ferry sailed, Sergeant Bell called them into the Special Branch office and told them that bombs had gone off in the centre of Birmingham. He asked them to go with him to Morecambe police station for forensic tests so that they could be eliminated from inquiries. He apologised for the inconvenience. They could catch the ferry tomorrow night, he said.

'What about our mate?' they asked.

'What mate?' said Bell.

Until then the police had not realised that Paddy Hill was with the others.

Hill was standing by the bar when he felt a tap on the shoulder. He turned round to see DC Fred Willoughby. Constable Gerald Baines and his Alsatian were a few paces behind. Willoughby said the sergeant would

like to see him. He finished his drink, picked up his case and followed
Willoughby off the boat.

Sergeant Bell later testified that he cautioned the five Irishmen, told them
that they were being detained and that they made no rely. The men testified that he neither cautioned them nor said that they were being
detained. Only that he asked them to go to Morecambe police station for
tests. The distinction is academic, but from this point on there was to be a
marked divergence between the men's account of what happened to them
and the story told by the police.

7

Morecambe police station is situated in a quiet road about three hundred yards from the sea front. It is a squarish, modern building, made mainly of prefabricated concrete interrupted by long narrow windows which run from floor to ceiling. The windows are permanently sealed because the building is air conditioned.

Entrance for the public is through glass doors at the front. The cells are on the ground floor to the right of reception. CID offices are on the first floor and consist of a large, open-plan room with interview rooms leading off it. The walls are thin and sound carries. The top floor of the station is given over to living quarters for unmarried officers.

At the rear there is a large yard, off which a door leads directly to the cells, enabling prisoners to be loaded and unloaded without being seen from the street.

On most nights, Morecambe police station is unlikely to see any officers above the rank of inspector. In the early hours of November 22, 1974, however, Morecambe suddenly hit the headlines.

Soon after midnight, Hunter, McIlkenny, Power and Walker were brought four miles from Heysham to Morecambe in a police transit van. According to one of the men who detained them, they seemed calm and made no attempt to run away although, to begin with, they were lightly guarded. Sergeant Bell travelled with them in the transit van.

Paddy Hill followed in a police car. DC Watson was driving and DC Willoughby sat in the back with Hill. Like the others, Hill also appeared relaxed. He even offered to return to Birmingham to assist with inquiries until Sergeant Bell explained that this would not be necessary.

Inspector Ken Brown was the officer in charge of Morecambe police station when the men arrived. He ordered each to be placed in separate cells with a police officer outside each one to make sure there was no communication. Since the men were only suspects, the cell doors were left open.

There weren't enough cells to go round. Hunter, Walker and McIlkenny had a cell each. Power was put in the female jailer's room, known as matron's room, and Hill was lodged in the charge room at the end of the cell corridor. DC Willoughby sat with him for most of the night. A Scots detective sat outside Hunter's cell. For a while they chatted, about football mainly. Hunter had cigarettes with him but no lighter. He had to keep asking the detective for a light.

By now the wires out of Morecambe were humming. Superintendent Roy Lenton, Head of Morecambe sub-division, was called in to take charge of the station. Detective Superintendent Bernard Ibison, was called in to take charge of the Lancashire end of the investigation. Other senior officers also got in on the act. Chief Superintendent Alf Collins and Assistant Chief Constable Tommy Watkinson turned up in evening dress. They had come from a Rotary Club dinner in Lancaster.

The forensic scientist, Dr Frank Skuse, arrived from his home in Wigan in the early hours. He was lodged in the medical room at the end of the cell corridor where he set about preparing to test the men for contact with nitroglycerine. He needed a supply of ether for his tests and someone was sent to find an all-night chemist. Skuse was scrupulous in his preparations. He declined to shake hands with Superintendent Lenton to avoid allegations of contamination. When he needed to use the telephone he insisted on using one at the top of the building that had not been handled by officers connected with the enquiry. Before commencing the tests he washed his hands in distilled water and ether. Then he tested his hands, using exactly the test he was about to use on the five suspects. According to Skuse's record, which is disputed, he had been on the premises for the best part of three hours before he was ready to commence.

Meanwhile the Irishmen were interviewed again. They repeated their earlier stories. Hill was going to see his sick aunt. Walker and McIlkenny were going to stay with McIlkenny's mother. Power was going to collect his younger brother. Hunter was going to see his recently widowed mother. Of McDade's funeral there was no mention.

At Lloyd House in Birmingham there was chaos. Reports of bomb scares were coming in from all over the West Midlands and each had to be treated seriously. The bomb at Hagley Road had been defused and there was every reason to suppose there might be more. Shortly after the pub bombs had exploded, there was a false alarm at New Street station and this caused a major diversion of precious resources. Harry Robinson,

Andrew Crawford and Cyril Cooney, the three policemen leading the investigation, were at New Street until nearly midnight.

When they got back to Lloyd House they found it crowded with off-duty police officers who, on hearing of the explosions, had not waited to be called in. Among them was Superintendent George Reade from Walsall.

Information about suspects was coming in from all over the country and so the news that five Irishmen had been detained at Morecambe was not, initially, treated with the seriousness it deserved. According to Superintendent Alf Collins, 'At first the West Midlands police did not seem very interested. We were surprised.'

By about one o'clock however, Harry Robinson decided that the men detained at Morecambe were worth taking a look at. He ordered that a team of CID men be sent up the motorway to check out the suspects and, if necessary, to bring them back to Birmingham. The man chosen to lead the team was George Reade.

Reade and his men set off just after one o'clock. The drive up the M6 motorway took about two hours. He took with him three CID crews and Detective Inspector John Moore of the West Midlands Serious Crimes Squad.

They went in three cars. Reade travelled with Detective Sergeant Ray Bennett and Detective Constable John Brand.

Inspector Moore travelled with Detective Sergeant Alan Watson, Detective Constable Michael French and Police Constable Keith Ingram, who was driving.

The third car contained Detective Sergeant James Kelly and Detective Constable Tom Sutcliffe. The driver was Police Constable George Cole.

At least five of the men were carrying revolvers. Thirty .38 Smith and Wesson Model Ten revolvers had been issued earlier that night from the armoury at Lloyd House. Inspector Moore was wearing his revolver in a holster around his waist. PC Cole and DC Brand were also armed.

Most of the detectives knew each other. The Serious Crimes Squad was an élite who worked together and socialised together. George Reade was the odd man out. He knew Inspector Moore fairly well. DS Bennett and DC French he knew by sight. The others were complete strangers. It was quite by chance that a Walsall officer should find himself in charge of a posse of Birmingham-based policemen. Over two hundred off-duty officers had shown up at Lloyd House that night to volunteer their services. George Reade happened to be one of them. As Andy Crawford, the head of the Special Branch, put it: 'It wasn't a question of "We want George Reade". George had come in and he was available.'

George Reade liked to think of himself as a copper of the old school. He wasn't one of those policeman who got promoted by taking courses or by shifting from one force to another. He had spent most of his police career in the Black Country and he knew it like the back of his hand. Detective work, he believed, was knowing people. Nothing glorious about it. Just hard work and a bit of basic psychology.

After being demobbed from the army in 1948 Reade had gone to work as a railway fireman at the Bescot Locomotive Depot in Walsall. In November, 1950, he left the railway and joined the Walsall police force. He later joked to his friends that he only signed up to qualify for a police house and to get away from his mother-in-law, with whom he was living at the time. Officially, he said that the railways did not provide sufficient opportunity for advancement.

In the police force, Reade's advancement was steady. In 1955 he was attached to the CID. He was appointed Detective Sergeant in 1958, Detective Inspector in 1966, Detective Chief Inspector in 1967 and in April 1974 – six months before the pub bombings – he became Detective Superintendent in charge of H Division based in his old stamping ground, Walsall. By now Reade was a very experienced detective. He had a string of successful murder inquiries under his belt, of which the best known is the arrest, in 1968, of Raymond Leslie Morris for the murder of Christine Darby in Cannock Chase.

Reade's career had its dark side, however. In 1968 his wife, Brenda, died of cancer leaving him with three daughters, the youngest aged eleven.

In 1971 Reade married again. His second wife, Pat, was a nurse in a Walsall Borough Council home. The marriage did not last, however.

In the tightly knit world of the West Midlands CID Reade had friends all the way to the top. Former Chief Constable Edwin Solomon and Deputy Chief Constable Gerry Baumber had been among his close friends. Even among the criminal fraternity he was respected. 'We'd be out for a drink,' says someone who was once a close friend of Reade's, 'and some bloke would come up and buy George a drink. I'd say "Who was that?" and George would say "I locked him up ten years ago."'

Although Reade cultivated an image of bluntness he was, to those who knew him, a man who possessed reserves of charm and humour. He was a fan of Nat King Cole, keen on cricket, rarely missing a Test at Edgbaston. But to those who came up against him there was another side to George Reade. 'Be careful how you approach George,' said one of his friends, 'he's got a very bad temper.'

Reade and his men arrived at Morecambe at 3.15. They were met by Superintendent Ibison who gave them the use of the conference room on the first floor. It was a large room with several tables separated by a passage from the general CID office. Ibison insisted that Birmingham officers were to have no contact with the prisoners until after the forensic tests had been completed. This was to avoid allegations of contamination. This led to a row. According to Superintendent Lenton, 'The Birmingham Police were very upset to find they could not start questioning immediately. After a while, however, we managed to calm them down.'

To this day, Bernard Ibison and Roy Lenton insist that the Birmingham officers had no contact with the prisoners until the forensic tests were complete at around 9.30. George Reade and his officers say the same. They say they spent the next six hours in and around the CID conference room on the first floor of Morecambe police station and that none of them went near the cells or had any contact with the prisoners. The prisoners, however, tell a different story.

8

Dick McIlkenny was in the women's cell, opposite the medical room where Dr Skuse carried out his tests. Like the others, his door was open and a policeman sat with him. A detective came, asked questions and wrote down the answers. He wanted to know McIlkenny's movements of the previous day, why he was going to Belfast and where he would be staying. McIlkenny stuck to the story he had told at Heysham. He was going to visit his mother. He was coming back in two days. In time for work on Monday. By the end the detective seemed satisfied. 'You'll be able to get the boat tomorrow,' he said as he went out.

Soon afterwards, Superintendent Ibison took McIlkenny to see Skuse. There is a dispute about the time. McIlkenny testified that it was around three o'clock in the morning.[1] He said he remembered the time because he had a watch. Skuse put the time he saw McIlkenny as 5.50.[2] McIlkenny had his hands tested first. A stout man in a white coat, Skuse was seated behind a table when McIlkenny came in. On the table were three small white bowls and a pad of cotton wool. A police officer was also present. He sat at the table beside Skuse and said nothing.

Skuse asked McIlkenny if he had any objection to having his hands tested. McIlkenny said he had none. Skuse then produced a bottle of liquid which he said was ether. He poured the ether on to the cotton wool and swabbed each of McIlkenny's hands. Then, using a pair of tweezers and a smaller piece of cotton wool, he swabbed behind McIlkenny's fingernails. The process took only a few minutes. McIlkenny was then returned to his cell. Later he saw the others being taken in to see Skuse. Hunter was next. Then Power. Then Hill. Walker was last.

Gerry Hunter was taken to see Skuse at 6.10, according to Skuse. Hunter told the court that the time was much earlier, but conceded this was only a guess. The procedure was the same. Each hand was swabbed with cotton wool and then the fingernails. Skuse remarked on Hunter's bitten fingernails.

Billy Power was under the impression he was taken to see Skuse at three or four in the morning but there was no way he could be sure. Skuse put the time at 6.35. Power's hands were swabbed twice. Once with ether, once with water. Billy Power did not yet know, but he was in deep trouble.

Skuse used a simple test named after a chemist called Greiss. Greiss had invented what many scientists then believed was a foolproof method of detecting nitroglycerine.

After swabbing each hand, Skuse squeezed the ether out of the cotton wool and into the first of the three white bowls. He then added more ether and divided the sample into three more or less equal parts, using the other two bowls.

Next he added caustic soda to the first bowl, followed by Greiss reagent, a clear liquid kept in a bottle. If nitroglycerine or another organic compound is present, say the scientists, the sample should turn pink within ten seconds. If he obtained a positive reading from the first sample, Skuse would then pour only Greiss reagent into the second bowl. If nitroglycerine is present, this time the liquid should stay clear. Or so the scientists say. Skuse later testified that, if he obtained these results, he was ninety-nine per cent certain that the suspect had been in contact with nitroglycerine. There was, he said, only one other known substance that could produce a similar result and that, too, was a constituent of explosives.

If he obtained positives from the first two tests, Skuse would then take away with him the contents of the third bowl and subject these to more sophisticated laboratory tests. He would also swab the suspect's hands again. This time with water to test for the presence of ammonium and nitrate ion. By themselves the presence of ammonium and nitrate ion proved nothing since they are commonly found in a wide variety of innocent substances such as food preservatives, but taken together with a positive Greiss test, such evidence would be damning.

The Greiss test on Richard McIlkenny's hands proved negative. So did those on Gerry Hunter. The sample from Billy Power's left hand was negative. The samples from under his nails were negative. The sample from his right hand, however, turned pink immediately. Skuse then applied the Greiss reagent to the second bowl. This time without the caustic soda. The solution remained clear. As far as Dr Skuse was concerned there was only one possible explanation. Bill Power had recently handled explosives.

He then swabbed both of Power's hands with water. The swab on Power's right hand also proved positive for ammonium and nitrate.

45

Paddy Hill was next. He had spent the night on a bench in the charge room. DC Willoughby had sat with him until five in the morning. Another Lancashire detective had quizzed him on his movements the previous day. Willoughby offered Hill his tobacco tin and Hill took enough for two or three roll-ups. Someone found him a book to read – *Bear Island* by Alastair McLean. Towards dawn, Hill asked if he could use the toilet. The officer who took him told him not to wash his hands as he would shortly be going for forensic tests.

Hill later testified that he was taken to see Dr Skuse by a Birmingham detective who he later came to know as Detective Sergeant Ray Bennett.[3] The police denied this. Superintendent Ibison told the court that it was he who took each of the men to see Skuse and Skuse confirmed this. DS Bennett testified that he was not in the cell area at this time.

According to Skuse's notes, he saw Hill at 7.05. Hill said that Skuse remarked on his greasy hands and he told him about the meat pie he had eaten at Crewe.

Skuse testified that he obtained a strong positive reaction from Hill's right hand. From then on he was ninety-nine per cent certain that Hill, too, had been in recent contact with explosives. Skuse did not, however, go on to test the sample from Hill's left hand. He was anxious, he said, to preserve as much of the sample as possible so that he would have enough for further tests back at his laboratory. He, therefore, took the sample from Hill's left hand and the sample in the third bowl away with him. When he later did a Greiss test on the sample from Hill's left hand, the result was negative.

There now occurs an unexplained gap in the timings offered by Dr Skuse. According to his records, he had seen McIlkenny, Hunter, Power and Hill. The first test on Hill would be over by 7.20 at latest, and yet, says Skuse, he did not see Walker until 8.55. After which he had Hill back for a second test with the water swab.

It is unclear why an hour and a half should elapse between seeing Hill and Walker. There may be a perfectly simple explanation but, since the Home Office will not permit Skuse to be interviewed, we are obliged to rely upon guesswork. One possibility is that this is the point at which Skuse ran out of ether and had to send out for more. Another is that he adjourned for breakfast. Or perhaps he went upstairs to inform Superintendent Reade and the Birmingham officers of his findings. However, in court the defence alleged that the tests on Walker were carried out much before 8.55 and that the Birmingham officers had begun to interrogate the suspects much before 9.30 – the time they later claimed to have taken over the investigation.[4]

According to Superintendent Roy Lenton, the officer in charge of Morecambe police station that night, the results of each test were being communicated to the Birmingham officers waiting impatiently in the CID conference room upstairs. This means that, even on Dr Skuse's disputed timings, the Birmingham officers would be aware by about seven in the morning that the tests on Billy Power had proved positive. If Skuse's times are right, by about 7.30 they would also have known that tests on Hill proved positive. Maybe Skuse waited until 7.30 before communicating his ninety-nine per cent certainty about the results on both men. Perhaps that explains the long gap between the tests on Hill and Walker. One thing is certain: from at least 7.30, and maybe earlier, every detective in Morecambe police station believed that the men downstairs were the Birmingham pub bombers.

George Reade spent a frustrating night in the conference room at Morecambe. He was itching to start questioning the prisoners but Bernard Ibison had flatly refused to let him. As the results of the forensic tests became known, it was clear that these were the men. Reade spent most of the night drinking tea and telephoning Lloyd House. By the time dawn broke he knew that raids on the men's houses had yielded little in the way of incriminating evidence. The only exception was Johnny Walker's house where police had found receipts for radios, lamps, glassware and, most curious of all, clocks.

Breakfast was served sometime between 7.30 and 8.00. Probably by Ron Buckley, the sergeant in charge of the cells who had come on duty at 7.00. It consisted of a slice of fried bread dipped in fat and a cup of tea. Hunter drank the tea, but left the food. Soon, Hunter testified, he heard someone screaming.[5] It was Paddy Hill.

Dick McIlkenny didn't think much of the breakfast either. Like Hunter, he drank the tea, but left the food. Soon afterwards he was taken to a room where two young officers, later identified as PC Brian Pinder from Morecambe and PC Keith Ingram from Birmingham, told him to undress. He was given a light blue jacket, trousers and a white shirt. No socks, shoes or underwear. Pinder and Ingram listed each item of clothing and put it in a plastic bag. They did the same with the contents of his hold-all. McIlkenny was then taken barefoot back to his cell. Soon afterwards, he later testified, he heard Paddy Hill shouting, 'Let go of my arm. You're breaking my arm.' About the same time he heard other raised voices. They seemed to be coming from upstairs. One sounded like Billy Power.[6]

After seeing Skuse, Hill was taken back to the bench in the chargeroom. He had not been there more than five minutes when he was taken to have his clothes changed. 'Don't fuck about, get stripped,' was how P C Ingram put it, according to Hill. They gave him a jacket, trousers and a shirt. No shoes, socks or underwear. The clothes did not fit well. The trousers were too long and too tight for Hill's round frame and the sleeves of the jacket came halfway over his hands. Dressed like this, Hill was taken to see Skuse for a second time. Skuse said he was going to do a water test. Hill said that was alright with him. His hands were swabbed again. Skuse thanked him and said that would be all.

Outside, according to Hill, DS Bennett and another Birmingham detective (later identified as D C John Brand) were waiting. Hill alleged in court that they told him to stand by the wall, Bennett then grabbed his right arm and tried to twist it up his back. Hill pushed him away and asked what the rough stuff was for. 'You'll find out in a few minutes, you little Irish fuck-pig,' said Bennett in a low voice. Then the other officer said something to Bennett and the two men moved away.[7]

A few minutes later Skuse emerged from the medical room and went off down the corridor. As soon as they were out of sight, said Hill, Bennett and Brand bundled him into the medical room. As he went through the door one of them punched him on the back of the head and he went flying forward. They came in after him, slapping, punching and kicking. 'They were screaming at me. Calling me an Irish bastard, cunt, fuck-pig, animal. They said I had more gelly on me than Judith Ward.* That I was covered in gelignite from head to toe.'[8]

Hill said, 'I told Bennett he was a liar. That I'd never seen a bomb in my life. He said, "It's not me who says it, it's the scientist." He went on, "You're one of the bastards that planted those bombs and you're going to make a statement admitting it." I told him I was making no statements. I was saying nothing.'[9]

* The woman convicted of the M62 coach bombing.

48

After his hands had been swabbed Billy Power was taken back to the matron's room and given a magazine to read. On the way, he testified, he noticed a man standing in the corridor whom he would soon come to know as Detective Sergeant Alan Watson of the West Midlands Police.[10] Some time later, Watson and another Birmingham detective, DC Michael French, collected Power from the matron's room and told him they were taking him upstairs. From this point onwards, the police account of what went on in Morecambe police station and that of the men themselves diverges dramatically. The only point upon which everyone is agreed is that, by lunchtime that day, Billy Power had signed a six-page confession describing how he and the others had carried out the bombings.

9

There are two versions of how Billy Power confessed so readily. The police say he was overcome by remorse and owned up with very little prompting. Power says that the police – literally – beat the shit out of him. This is the story Billy Power told in court.

Watson and French took Power up a staircase leading from the cell block to the CID rooms on the first floor. Power was still wearing his own clothes and carrying the overcoat loaned to him by Gerry Hunter.

At the top of the stairs they turned right into a corridor, past the CID general office and then right again through what Power described as a small, windowless room, with a door at each end. They then found themselves in a room with a window reaching from floor to ceiling and a mirror on the wall. Watson entered first, then Power, then French. This, Power told the court, is what happened next: 'As I walked through the door French punched me on the back of the head.[1] I stumbled forward and they both set about me. They threw one or two punches at my face but I managed to block them with the overcoat I was carrying. Watson grabbed the coat and flung it in a corner. I was then pushed into a chair. They were shouting "You dirty, murdering IRA bastard. You got gelly on your hands." I was also punched in the chest and arms.'[2]

The room was about ten feet by six. There was a table and three or four chairs. The table was against a wall, away from the window. There was a chair on each side of the table and one at the end. Power said his jacket was torn off and he was pushed into a chair at the end of the table with his back to a wall. Watson sat on his right, French on his left. They shouted, 'We're going to do you, you bastard.' As they did so they jabbed him in the ribs, punched his arms and kicked him under the table.

Power said he repeatedly denied being a member of the IRA. 'They asked me to explain the gelly on my hands. I said "There's no gelly." They said, "The forensic expert says there is." They told me they had been to the scene of the bombings and they were going to do me for it.' Power testified that French made him put his hands palm down on the table and look at Watson while Watson described the scene of the bombing. French had taken out a pair of handcuffs and put them on his own

50

hand like a knuckleduster.[3] Whenever Power tried to protest his innocence, French would rap him on the back of his right hand with the handcuffs. 'Shut up and listen,' he said. Power testified that he was hit six or
seven times with the handcuffs, then the door opened and an older detective came in.[4] He had dark wavy hair and his sideboards were greying.
He shouted something at Power and punched him on the left side of the
head. The blow half knocked him off the chair and he steadied himself
with his hand on the floor. The man who struck the blow went out again,
before Power could get a look at him. Watson and French lifted him back
onto the chair and started questioning him about his movements the previous day. What time had he left home? What time had he arrived at New
Street station? When had the others arrived? Power told them he had
arrived at about 6.30 and waited for the others. He had been intending to
catch the 6.55, but the others had not turned up on time. They asked him
what the others were carrying. He told them a grip bag and a case. They
asked what these were made of. Power said he thought it was a kind of
plastic. 'At this they started on me again, saying I had told them that the
others had been carrying plastic bags. When I said I hadn't, I was
punched and told that both of them heard me. That there were two of
them and only one of me. Their word would be believed.

'They asked me what happened next. I told them we got our tickets and
went for a drink. They started on me again shouting, "What pub did you
go to?" I said we never went to a pub. We went to the bar inside the
station. They shouted that I had said we went to a pub just outside the
station. I kept telling them I hadn't. They said there were two of them and
they had heard me say the pub.

'Then they asked, "Do you know the pub just outside the station?" I
said "Do you mean the Mulberry Bush?" They punched me again on the
arm and the side of the head shouting that I even knew which pub had
been blown up. They kept telling me they had enough on me, saying I had
told them that the others had carried plastic bags into the station, I had
gone to the Mulberry Bush and they had an expert who was going to say
there was gelly on my hands and on Hill's. They kept saying, "That's the
truth, isn't it?" and I kept denying it.'

At some point Watson left the room. French said he would not hit
Power while he was away. Instead he told Power that even if he had not
done it they would make it look as though he had. They would not hit his
face. Just his body. No broken bones, just cuts and bruises. French said
he had twenty years experience.[5] 'He started telling me that he could

even make it look like I was in the IRA and had squealed on the others. Even the IRA, he said, would believe it.' Power said the IRA would know he wasn't one of them. French replied that the IRA didn't know all its members.

Then, according to Power, French changed tack. They would do Power in, he said. They would put handcuffs on him and throw him out of the car on the way back to Birmingham. They would get away with it by saying he had been trying to escape. No one would care, said French. In fact they would probably get a medal for it.[6]

When Watson returned, he said they had found the mass cards for McDade in Walker's bag. 'He asked if I knew McDade and was I going to his funeral? I did not reply. Then they started telling me there was a mob outside my home ready to lynch my wife and children. All that was saving them was the police who were searching it. They said the police would not stay for ever and that the only way to save my wife and children was to tell them what they wanted to know.'

The man with the greying sideboards came back and asked Watson and French to hand Power over. They declined and the man left, pausing only to punch Power again on the side of the head. French said, 'If we give them to you now, they will make us look like angels.'[7]

While Power was allegedly being punched and slapped Watson, looked out of the window and saw a photographer pointing a camera. He shouted to French, 'Quick, run down and catch him.'

'He couldn't take photos from down there,' said French.

But Watson insisted. 'He's got a long lens.'

French put the chairs one on top of the other against the window and ran out of the room. Watson pushed Power into a corner away from the window. While French was out, Watson told Power that he knew he was only on the fringes. Why didn't he tell the truth and save his wife and kids?

When French came back they started on again about plastic bags. Then they told him that, if he told them which of the others had planted the bombs, they would only charge him with conspiracy and he would get out in five or ten years. Power said that none of them had planted the bombs. 'In that case,' they asked, 'how come your hands are covered in gelly?'

The man with greying sideboards returned. One of them said, 'You might as well have him now,' whereupon the man grabbed Power by his hair and dragged him to the windowless room through which they had entered. Someone shouted, 'You're dead whatever happens. You might as well save your wife and children.'

It was dark in the room save for the light from the two doors which were slightly ajar. Power guesses there were about half a dozen men in the room. One by each of the doors, the older officer and perhaps three others. He was subsequently unable to identify any of them. Power said later, 'The officer who had me by the hair with my head pulled downwards let go and then from all sides I was being punched, hit and kicked. I doubled up and slid down the wall toward the floor. I was dragged up by the hair and again punched systematically. I was kicked in the stomach and was sliding down the wall. Then I was kicked in the legs. I was then dragged up again by the hair. This was repeated three or four times.' It was at this stage, said Power, that he fouled his trousers. After about ten minutes, he went on, someone shouted, 'Hold it.' He was spreadeagled against the wall and then a voice said, 'Stretch his balls.' Someone put his mouth close to Power's ear and bellowed, 'You'll never have sex with your wife again.' This was the point at which Power surrendered. 'I screamed "okay, okay". I had to say something to stop them. I couldn't take any more.'[8]

Power testified that the detective with greying sideboards then grabbed him by the throat and dragged him back into the interview room. This left a mark which was still visible when he was photographed two days later. Someone shouted, 'Who was the sixth man?'

'What sixth man?' asked Power. He then received a punch in the mouth which cut his lip.

An officer said, 'The man who stayed behind.'

'Oh,' said Power, 'you mean Hughie?'

'Why yes, we mean Hughie. What was his second name?'

'I can't remember.'

Someone said, 'Throw him through the fucking window.' At this they started clearing the chairs away from the window and dragged him towards it. Power was not to know, but the windows were sealed shut and could not be opened. Someone said, 'If the fall doesn't kill him, the crowd will.'

By this time Power was hysterical. 'I'll tell you anything you want me to say,' he screamed.

Watson and French then took him to a third, larger room and for the first time started to take notes. By now, Power was sitting in his own excreta.

'They made me repeat what they had claimed earlier on about plastic bags. They took me through the statement putting words into my mouth and correcting me every time I said something with which they did not agree.'[9] Once he refused to answer and they grabbed him and threatened to take him back to the other room for more treatment. One detective – Power could not remember whether it was Watson or French – took notes. French then read them back to Watson while Watson wrote. Power just sat there in a daze. When he had finished, Watson looked up at Power and said, ' "Jesus, I'm sorry", isn't that right?' Power just looked blankly at him. French pulled out the handcuffs and Power nodded. Watson shouted, 'Well say it then,' and Power said, 'Jesus, I'm sorry.'[10]

They then pushed the papers in front of him and indicated where he should sign. Power hesitated and they made as if to take him back to the small room. At the top of the first page was Power's name and address and the date. Then there was a paragraph headed CAUTION. It read: '*I, William Power, wish to make a statement. I want you to write down what I say. I have been told I need not say anything unless I wish to do so and that whatever I say may be given in evidence.*' They indicated that he should sign this and he signed. They then indicated a place at the bottom of the page and he signed that too. There were six pages in all and Power was told to sign the bottom of each one. In a couple of places he was told to initial words that had been crossed out. At the end, Watson dictated: '*I have read the above statement and I have been told that I can correct, alter or add anything I wish. This statement is true. I have made it of my own free will.*' Power says he was in such a state that they had to spell out every word for him. They then told him to sign again and he signed. It was 12.55 on the afternoon of November 22, 1974. Billy Power had just confessed to the biggest murder in British history.

Detective Sergeant Alan Watson and DC French offered an entirely different version of the events leading up to Billy Power's confession. Watson testified that the interview began at 9.30 and not a minute before; that Power had by this time exchanged his own clothes for clothes supplied by the police; that he had not fouled his trousers during the interview, but earlier while still in the matron's room and still wearing his own clothes. Watson said that Power was asked to account for his movements the previous evening. Power told them he had arrived at New Street around 6.30; that Gerry Hunter, Johnny Walker and someone called Hughie had shown up just before seven and Dick McIlkenny had arrived shortly after. Paddy Hill had shown up later. They asked who Hughie was and Power said he didn't know Hughie's second name.

Asked why he was going to Belfast, Power stuck to the story about collecting his brother. Asked why the others were going he said, 'They had their own reasons.' Asked if he was going to McDade's funeral, he said, 'No, I wouldn't have anything to do with that.' Told that Dr Skuse had found traces of explosives on his hand, he is supposed to have said, 'Oh my God, Jesus. That can't be. Not these hands.' After that he is said to have broken down and was given a cup of tea to calm him down. By 10.10, after just forty minutes, he had confessed. At this point, said Watson, he and French went to report their success to Superintendent Reade, leaving Power alone with a Morecambe detective whose name Watson could not recall. It was forty minutes before they returned and, when they did, Power dictated his confession without further prompting.

Billy Power's confession was a very thin document. Later it would be found to contain many inconsistencies. It amounted to no more than nine hundred words. It began, *'I'm glad it's all come out... It all started with the death of James McDade.'* The first two pages consisted of a more or less accurate account of Power's movements over the previous week. Gerry Hunter and Johnny Walker were both said to be in the IRA. Walker was said to have arrived at New Street station carrying two white plastic bags in addition to his maroon hold-all and Hunter was said to have arrived with three plastic bags and Hugh Callaghan was said to be carrying one. Six in all. At the station they were said to have shared out the bags so that Walker, Hunter and Power had two each. The statement goes on, *'I said to them all, "I'm not taking these." I just knew what they were. They were bombs and I didn't want to take them.'* But Callaghan is said to have insisted. He is quoted as saying to Power, *'You have to take them to the pub at the side of the Rotunda.'*

The statement continues: *'I went out of the station and past the taxi rank. I looked back and saw Hunter and Walker coming out behind me carrying two bags each. I walked straight round to* (sic) *the Rotunda to the Mulberry Bush. I walked in from the left hand side... I turned right inside and down a couple of steps. There were quite a few people in so I walked over to the bar and put the bags down at my feet because I was going to have a drink... I started to walk out and*

55

then I put the two bags down by the juke box and then I walked . . . straight back to the station the way I came.'

Power's statement says he arrived back at the station before the others. *'A few minutes later Walker and Hunter returned. They weren't carrying anything this time. Then Richard (McIlkenny) and Hill came back in from the other entrance . . . Hughie didn't come back at all.'*

There was no mention of drinking in the Taurus Bar. The statement simply says: *'We all went to platform nine together and got on the train . . . There were other people in the carriage and we didn't want to talk much. We just had a game of cards. I was in a daze and couldn't take anything in because of what I had done.'*

Power's statement concludes, *'Jesus, I'm sorry. I wish this day had never come.'*

Paddy Hill's story[1] was similar to Billy Power's. The police, however, disputed almost every detail. This is what Hill told the court happened after he was pushed into the medical room by DS Bennett and DC Brand.

'They were asking me how the gelignite gets to England, how it comes in, who sends it, who picks it up, how it was brought into Birmingham, who looks after it. Every question they asked me, I answered "I don't know".'

Hill said they told him, '"You are going to make a statement admitting you planted those bombs". I told them I wasn't. They said, if I didn't make one, they would kick it out of me.'

There was a chair in the room. He was told to sit down. No sooner had he done so than Brand punched him on the back of the head, knocking him off the chair.

According to Hill, Bennett then grabbed him by the hair and started dragging him round the floor. Brand and Bennett left the room at intervals, but one or the other was with him throughout. From time to time he could hear the others screaming. Once – he guessed it was around two in the afternoon – another officer put his head round the door and told them to keep the noise down because there was a visitor in the police station.

At one stage, said Hill, Bennett and Brand told him that the purpose of his visit to Walker's house on the afternoon of the bombing had been to see if the bombs had arrived. Hill replied that he had his two year old son with him when he visited Walker. At this, he said, 'I was kicked and punched and called a liar. They said I went there with another bloke to see if the bombs had arrived for that night.

'They said that if I didn't make a statement they had plenty of experience and they would get me thirty years no matter what way they done it. Sergeant Bennett told me not to ask to see anyone, as I might never see anyone again. He told me not to ask for anything as I was not going to receive anything. He said that if I signed a statement admitting I had planted the bombs I would have something to eat, drink and smoke and there would be no more beating up.'

Later, they talked about shooting him and dumping him on the motorway on the way back to Birmingham. 'They said nobody would know, as nobody knew I was in police custody.'

According to Hill, this treatment continued for most of the day. Unlike Billy Power, however, Paddy Hill did not confess. Not then. Not ever.

Detective Sergeant Bennett later gave his account of the interview with Hill. He agreed that it took place in the medical room, but said that it did not start until 10.45, at least an hour after Dr Skuse had completed his tests. DC Brand had taken notes throughout. To begin with there was no mention of Dr Skuse's findings. Hill was cautioned and told he did not have to say anything, if he chose not to. They asked why he was going to Belfast. To see his aunt, said Hill. When had he decided to go? At six o'clock the previous evening when he had finally succeeded in borrowing the fare from Sister Bridget at the convent. After that he had gone to the Crossways and then caught a bus to the station.

Bennett said that Hill was asked if he had seen anyone he knew at the station. According to Bennett, Hill's story was that he was travelling alone. He had read a newspaper on the train. At this point Inspector Moore came in. Hill was asked if he knew any of the others. He is said to have replied that he had never seen any of them before. He was asked if he had ever handled explosives and he said he had not. Still, according to Bennett, there was no mention of Dr Skuse's findings. What did he think of McDade's death? 'I was very upset. I've known him all my life. We went to school together.' Still, however, he is said to have insisted that the purpose of his journey was to visit his sick aunt. The interview, said Bennett, ended at around noon.

Bennett said he returned – along with DC Brand and Inspector Moore – in the afternoon at one twenty-five. It was then that they, for the first time, revealed to Hill the findings of Dr Skuse. Hill repeated that he had never had any contact with explosives. He was asked again about Walker. Wasn't it true that he had been to see Walker only the previous afternoon? Hill then conceded that he did know Walker. He was told that Billy Power had made a statement. He then conceded that he knew the others, but knew nothing about bombs. Power's statement was read to him and he said, 'It's all lies.' The interview ended at two thirty. At three o'clock. Brand and Moore returned and told Hill they were arresting him. At this, Hill is said to have put his head in his hands and started whimpering.

Johnny Walker was the last to have his hands tested. Skuse says he saw

Walker at 8.55. In court Walker estimated that he saw Skuse around 6.30.[2] He accepted that this was only a guess but said it was definitely before breakfast which was served sometime after seven thirty.

Before testing Walker, Skuse first tested his own hands to make sure he was not contaminated as a result of his contact with Hill. The Greiss test on his hands was negative. The Greiss test on Walker's hands was also negative, but when Skuse swabbed Walker's hands with water he found faint positives for the presence of ammonium and nitrate. Skuse also found faint positives for nitrate on his own hands. As far as the nitrate went, there was slim chance that he could have contaminated Walker. The same could not be said for the ammonium. Skuse later testified that in his view contact between Walker and an ingredient of explosives could have occurred.

After seeing Skuse, Walker was taken to change his clothes. He later identified the officers who escorted him as DC Kelly and DC Sutcliffe of the West Midlands police. Kelly and Sutcliffe deny they were anywhere near Walker at this time.

While Walker was changing, PCs Ingram and Pinder went through the contents of his pockets and hold-all, listing every item and putting them into a plastic bag. It was at this point that the mass cards for McDade were discovered.

Walker said he was then taken to another room on the ground floor by the two officers he identified as Kelly and Sutcliffe. They walked on either side of him, each having hold of an arm.

'As I entered the room somebody else behind kicked me on the base of the spine. I yelled out. There were three officers in the room and they all started hitting me with their fists and kicking me. I was pushed and kicked from one officer to the other. One of them said, "I've a good mind to throw your fucking body in the Irish Sea."' Walker later identified the third officer – the one who kicked him in the spine – as PC George Cole, one of the drivers from Birmingham.[3] Walker said he was at this point asked no questions. The three policemen pushed and kicked him from one to the other. At some stage his shirt came open and they saw the scar on his stomach caused by an operation for ulcers. From then on they started punching him in the stomach on or about the scar. Today Walker has a large lump in the centre of the stomach which, he says, was caused by what happened in police custody at Morecambe and, later, Birmingham.

At some stage, Walker alleged, Cole took out his gun and Kelly said, 'Let's shoot the bastard.' Walker was sitting on a wooden bench. Cole pointed the gun at Walker's head and they put a blanket over his head. Someone else said, "Give him a few minutes with his maker." Cole put the gun to Walker's head. He could feel the barrel through the blanket. Suddenly there was a clap. For a moment Walker thought he had been shot. They took the blanket off his head and for a couple of seconds there was dead silence. Then they started laughing at him.[4]

As soon as the blanket was off his head, Walker was jerked to his feet and they started hitting him again. After a while DS Kelly noticed that Walker had a blister on the big toe of his right foot. It had been caused by new shoes he had been wearing. Kelly, Walker maintained, lit a cigarette and pushed it into the blister, causing Walker to scream. To this day, Walker has a scar on the big toe of his right foot.[5]

According to Walker, this treatment went on most of the day. 'They didn't so much ask questions as keep saying, "You planted the bombs." I became completely deranged and it is difficult to remember exactly what happened.'

At some stage Walker remembers Kelly leaving the cell and returning with one of the mass cards for McDade. Kelly held the card up to Walker's face and said, 'You knew this bastard, didn't you?' Walker replied, 'Yes, I knew him.'

At one point, Walker said, he was told to stand on one leg with his hands on his head. Each time he lost balance he would receive a kick in the genitals or on the legs. Later, DS Kelly stamped on his feet causing them to swell so badly that, when his shoes were eventually returned, they no longer fitted.[6]

Walker said he lost all track of time and eventually blacked out. When he came to he found himself lying on the cold stone floor of his cell. He revived himself by flushing the toilet in the cell and dousing his face with the water.

Sergeant Kelly gave a different version of the interview. PC Cole denied that he had been present. The interview began, said Kelly, at 10.55. He and DC Sutcliffe did not take notes, but they made up their notes together soon after the interview, at 12.40. They asked Walker's name, address, where he was born, how long he had lived in England, whether he had any religious beliefs. To this last question Walker replied that he had none. He was asked if he had any sympathy towards the IRA. He replied, 'Not me, sir, I was a British soldier and I've a brother who's a sergeant in the British Army.' He was asked why he was going to Belfast. He replied that he was going for a holiday. 'It was Dick McIlkenny's idea. His aunty is sick.' He was asked if he knew McIlkenny's aunt. He replied that he didn't. He was asked if all five of them were going to see McIlkenny's aunt and he replied, 'No.'

Walker was then asked to account for his movements the previous evening. He told them that Dick McIlkenny had called for him. They had then called for Gerry Hunter. The three of them caught a bus to New Street station. Then they had met Billy Power and gone for a drink in the railway bar. Paddy Hill had turned up later.

Kelly stated that he asked Walker if he had ever met James McDade. Walker replied, 'No, sir.' He was asked if he knew anyone associated with McDade or the IRA. He replied, 'No, sir, I wouldn't have anything to do with any of them at all.' He was told that receipts for alarm clocks had been found at his house. He replied that these were for raffles. He was asked what charity he ran the raffles for and he replied, 'I do it for myself.' He was asked whom he sold the tickets to and he replied, 'To the fellas at work and in the Crossways.' What did he tell them about the purpose of the raffles. 'I make something up.'

Kelly told Walker he didn't believe him. 'I think you collect for the IRA.' According to Kelly, Walker then held his head in his hands and said, 'I do, sir. I just collect.' Kelly then produced the mass cards for McDade at which point Walker admitted they were all going to McDade's funeral. Kelly said he then told Walker that traces of explosives had been found on the hands of two of his friends, and added, 'Do you realise the serious position you are in? All leaving Birmingham at 7.55, just before the bombs went off... You're going to McDade's funeral. You now admit you are a member of the IRA and members of your party have positive explosive tests on their hands. Articles found in your house are ingredients for making bombs.'

By this time Walker is said to have been shaking. He put his head in his hands and said, 'Oh God, they've taken me for a right cunt. What have I got myself into, the bastards.'

Kelly asked, 'Did you plant any bombs?'

'No sir, no sir. I'm telling you the truth. I'm telling you the truth.'

At this point Superintendent Reade entered and told Walker that Power had admitted planting bombs.

'I don't believe it,' said Walker.

On this note the interview is said to have terminated. It was 12.25 and had lasted one and a half hours.

Shortly after Gerry Hunter had heard the commotion coming from the medical room where Paddy Hill was being interviewed, two plain clothes officers took him to have his clothes changed. Pinder or Ingram threw him a polythene bag and told him to empty his pockets. They took note of every item as he put it into the bag. Then they told him to strip. When he was naked, they put the clothes into the plastic bag and gave him a shirt and a suit to put on. Hunter remembers the suit was serge blue. Like the others he was given no shoes, socks or underwear.

He was then taken to a cell different from the one he had been in. Here, some time elapsed before he was interviewed by two officers whom he later identified as Inspector Moore and Superintendent Reade. Moore, he recalled, had a gun in a holster strapped to his hip. Hunter said they first asked him to account for his movements the previous day, then they started punching and slapping him. Reade grabbed his hair and banged his head against the wall of the cell. At some stage he fell on the floor and Moore kicked him in the stomach.[7]

Reade and Moore later gave a different version of the same incident. They said they interviewed Hunter at about 10.45. The interview lasted about twenty minutes. They questioned Hunter about his movements the previous day during the course of which Hunter referred to Hughie. 'Who's Hughie?' asked Moore. Hunter replied, 'Hughie Callaghan. He went to New Street with me and Johnny.' Hunter gave them Callaghan's address. Reade and Moore then asked why he was going to Belfast. Hunter is said to have replied that he was going to bring his recently widowed mother back to England. They then asked about McDade. According to Reade, the conversation went like this.

'Who's McDade?'
'He was a friend.'
'How much of a friend.'
'Bloody questions, I'm fed up with them.'
'We're trying to get at the truth. How well did you know McDade?'
'He was a good friend.'
'Did you know he was a member of the IRA?'
'If I did I wouldn't tell you, but you know anyway.'
They then asked about the mass cards. Was it true he was going to Belfast for McDade's funeral and not to bring his mother back. Hunter is

62

said to have replied, 'I have told you why I was going.'

Towards the end, the interview took a more controversial turn. Moore and Reade asked if he had been involved in organising raffles for the IRA. Hunter is said to have answered, 'Find out. I'm not saying anything else. I am just about fed up with you.'

To which Reade says he replied, 'The fact that you are fed up does not interest me. What we are concerned with is that last night between fifteen and twenty people were killed by two bomb explosions. You have already told me that you have been friendly with a known IRA man who blew himself to pieces while carrying a bomb.' At this point Hunter is said to have interrupted, 'Why bring that up again? He was a good man, Jamie. Don't be so bloody cruel.' Hunter is said to have added that even if more people had been killed, they would not make up for Jamie. 'Did I hear you right?' asked Reade.

At this point, according to Moore and Reade, Hunter spat at Reade and shouted, 'That's what I said, there should have been a bloody lot more. It's a bloody pity a better job wasn't made.'

Reade said later, 'I pushed him away with my right hand and, as I did so, he seemed to lose complete control of himself. Hunter struck out at me with his right hand. I caught hold of him and stood up facing him. He was lying back on the cell bench. Inspector Moore stood up and moved toward him as well. Hunter kicked out with both feet at the same time. He was shouting, "You killed Jamie, you killed Jamie.' His right foot caught me on the left side over my ribs and I staggered back towards the cell door.'

Reade and Moore's version of events was supported by Ronald Buckley, the Morecambe police sergeant in charge of the cells. Buckley later testified that he saw Hunter kick Reade and then saw all three men – Reade, Moore and Hunter – collapse into a scrum on the floor.

Hunter denied shouting 'You killed Jamie.' He also denied suggesting that even more deaths wouldn't have made up for Jamie. According to Hunter, after being kicked in the stomach and knocked to the floor, he was left on his own with Reade. 'He continued to pull my hair, and then, holding my hair, shook my head and kept hitting me with his open hand across my head and across my body. He kept telling me to admit that I'd planted the bombs.'

After a few minutes Reade left saying he was going for his dinner. When he came back he expected Hunter to start talking.

By the time Richard McIlkenny's turn came he was a very worried man. He could hear the noise coming from Hill's interrogation which was taking place in a room exactly opposite the women's cell where he was lodged. He could also hear the sounds coming from Power upstairs. An officer whom he later identifed as DS Kelly came in. Another officer stood at the door. Kelly asked McIlkenny who he was. Kelly then asked who Hughie was and, McIlkenny testified, when he hesitated Kelly slapped him several times across the face. Kelly said, 'My mate's coming in a minute. He's got someone belonging to him who was in that pub and he's really mad.'[8]

At this point a man came in whom McIlkenny later identified as Inspector John Moore. 'He asked Kelly who I was and then said, "You are an Irish Catholic bastard."' With that, said McIlkenny, who was seated on a low wooden bench, Moore aimed a kick which caught him in the chest just under the left shoulder. 'It was an extremely painful blow and eventually left me with a big black and blue bruise on my chest. I fell down and Moore jumped on top of me and held a blanket over my face. He held it very tight and I was unable to breathe. I was coughing and choking. He was a big man. Too heavy for me to shake off. I just went limp on him. He just got up and walked out. They left me alone after that.'[9]

According to McIlkenny this was his only contact with the West Midlands detectives at Morecambe. The West Midlands men, however, tell a different story. DS Colin Morris and DC Terence Woodwiss later testified that they had spent an hour interviewing McIlkenny in Morecambe. Morris and Woodwiss had not been among the original three CID crews to arrive in the early hours. They were reinforcements summoned by Reade earlier that morning. Together with two other officers in a separate squad car, they had left Birmingham at 9.30 that morning and arrived in Morecambe around noon. Within half an hour of arrival they were, they said, interviewing McIlkenny. Morris's notes were not made in a notebook but on separate foolscap sheets. He recorded a bizarre interview with McIlkenny, during the course of which McIlkenny is said to have claimed not to know the other four Irishmen, only to have met them on the train.

When it was pointed out to McIlkenny that Johnny Walker worked for the same firm as himself he is said to have replied, 'A lot of Irishmen work for the same firm.' McIlkenny is said to have gone on denying that he knew the others, even when it was pointed out that he drank in the same pubs as the others and that they all had consecutively numbered railway tickets.

To this day, McIlkenny denies that any such interview took place at Morecambe. It is hard to see why it should be in his interests to deny being interviewed by Morris and Woodwiss. Equally it is hard to see why Morris and Woodwiss should go to the trouble of constructing an interview that never took place. The episode is one of the unsolved mysteries of the case. What no one disputes, however, is that over the course of the next few days, McIlkenny, Morris and Woodwiss would get to know each other very well indeed.

When he heard that Power had confessed, Chief Superintendent Alf Collins opened the drinks cupboard. It was a little early in the day for a drink – not later than eleven in the morning – but it was not every day that the Lancashire force captured an IRA terrorist unit.

Among those to whom Collins offered a drink was Fred Willoughby, the detective constable who had first intercepted the men as they were about to board the ferry at Heysham. Willoughby was the hero of the hour. He should have clocked off duty many hours earlier, having sat with Hill in the charge room until the day shift arrived. Instead, he hung around, watching the coming and going and recounting the events of the previous night.

By now the normal work of Morecambe police station was severely disrupted. Superintendent Ibison had formally handed over the investigation to George Reade at 9.30 and the West Midlands detectives had the run of the first floor and the cell area. Civilian employees were kept away from their offices on the first floor on the orders of Superintendent Lenton.

The station was swarming with top brass. Superintendents Collins, Ibison and Lenton were to remain on the premises all that day. They had been joined by the head of the Lancashire Special Branch, Superintendent Frank Taylor.

All these men spent the morning in and around the CID offices on the first floor. Billy Power's interrogation took place just across the corridor. The walls are very thin. Had there been violence on the scale alleged, no one could have avoided hearing what was going on.

Gradually, very gradually, the outside world was becoming aware that something big was happening in Morecambe. Bob Satchwell, chief reporter on the *Lancashire Evening Post* at Preston, first suspected something when he rang Superintendent Frank Taylor's office on a routine security matter. Taylor wasn't there. He's in Morecambe, they said. Satchwell rang Morecambe police station and was eventually put through. He had known Taylor for several years and regarded him as a down-to-earth, open man. This morning, however, Taylor sounded very cagey.

'What's up, Frank?'

'Can't tell you.'

'Is it worth my coming over?'

'Yes.'

Satchwell leapt in his car and raced over to Morecambe. He arrived just after 11.30, little more than an hour after Billy Power started confessing. Almost immediately he spotted Superintendents Taylor and Ibison in the street outside the station. They were tight lipped. 'We can't say anything.'

'Is it to do with the Birmingham job?'

'Can't say.'

There was an irritating young journalist who kept pressing them. The more he pressed the more they clammed up. Satchwell gave the young journalist a couple of pounds and sent him to buy fish and chips four times. When the young man was out of sight, Taylor and Ibison relaxed slightly. 'When's your deadline?' they asked.

'Two o'clock.'

'We'll see what we can do.' With that they disappeared back into the station. The young journalist came back with four lots of fish and chips. 'What do I do with these?'

'Stuff them,' said Satchwell.

By two o'clock the word was out. Journalists, photographers and television crews were beginning to crowd the street outside the police station. Shortly after two, Ibison appeared. He invited reporters into the station and read a bland little statement. It said: *'Five men were detained at Heysham harbour at 10.40 last night. They are being interviewed by senior CID officers from the West Midlands in connection with last night's bombing incidents in Birmingham. They will be escorted to Birmingham later this afternoon.'*

Even before he had arrived at Morecambe, George Reade had decided
he would bring the prisoners back to Birmingham. 'I make no bones
about it,' he says. 'I'd have brought them back whatever the forensic tests
had said.'

By Friday afternoon the investigation was going better than he could
ever have hoped. Forensic tests had proved positive against three of the
suspects, Power, Hill and Walker. They had the name and address of the
sixth man, Hughie Callaghan. Power's confession was in the bag. It was
only a question of time.

By five o'clock on the Friday afternoon Reade was ready to depart. He
had sent back to Birmingham for reinforcements, and two more squad
cars and four more detectives (DS David Millichamp, DC Douglas Bell,
DC Colin Morris and DC Terence Woodwiss) had arrived around noon.
Several other West Midlands officers had arrived to take charge of the
security of the convoy.

By now the whole world knew that five men had been arrested at Heysham. The crowd of reporters, photographers and curious members of
the public outside Morecambe police station was growing by the hour. To
throw the press off the scent, a dummy convoy was organised. Police
cadets and officers with blankets over their heads were loaded into transit
vans. Photographers and television cameramen were permitted to take
pictures from the rear gate. A careful study of press photographs that
appeared next day will show that the 'prisoners' were all wearing police
boots and trousers. The dummy convoy then sped off through Morecambe to Lancaster where it drove into the police station and dispersed.
This stunt worked a treat. The press gave chase to the dummy convoy
allowing Reade and his prisoners to escape unseen. Just after five the
Irishmen were brought from the cells. Their heads covered, their feet still
bare. Each was handcuffed and guided by two detectives, one holding the
end of the handcuffs. Billy Power was brought out by French and
Watson, the two officers who had taken his confession. He had been
given a change of clothes and allowed to clean himself up. He spent the
afternoon alone listening to the others being interrogated. As he was

loaded into a car, he heard someone in another car screaming. He couldn't recognise the voice, but said he heard a detective say, 'Put a bullet through the bastard.'

Walker remembers being handcuffed by DS Kelly. A coat was put over his head and he was led down a corridor. He said he was kicked and punched as he went. All he could see from under the coat was legs and feet kicking him. He was put in the back seat of the car and handcuffed to the strap above the door so that his arm was in the air. Kelly got in next to him. 'I've hit you so much, my hands are sore,' he is alleged to have told Walker.[1]

McIlkenny was taken out with a coat over his head. On the way he walked into a wall. They put him in the back of a car and left him for about a minute. An older man came along whom the others referred to as 'Chief'. It must have been Reade. He looked at McIlkenny. 'Who's that?' he asked.

'That's McIlkenny,' said the detective in the front seat.

'Get him out of there,' said Reade, 'I want Hunter.'

Hunter was taken out barefoot with a coat over his head. It had been raining and they made him stand in a puddle. They put him in the back of a car and he sat there for a minute or two. A box of clothing was put in with him. Presumably the clothes they had been stripped of earlier that day. After a couple of minutes he was taken out and bundled into the back of another car. He found himself sitting next to George Reade. He recognised Reade as one of the men who had questioned him that morning. There was another officer in the front passenger seat whom he had not seen before. Hunter later identified him as DS Millichamp. The driver was DC Bell. According to Hunter, as soon as he was in the car Reade started slapping and punching him. 'I had one hand strapped to the passenger grip above the door and I was screaming. Reade's breath smelled of drink. He scratched me with his nails, grabbing handfuls of flesh and then squeezing. He seemed to enjoy it because he laughed a lot. Millichamp asked him to stop as there were reporters outside.'

As the car moved off, Hunter said, Reade grabbed his hair and forced his head downwards, slapping him lightly on the back of the head. After a while Reade grew tired of this and went to sleep with his head resting on Millichamp's coat. From then on Hunter was left alone. He noticed that red diagonal marks had developed across his chest where Reade had scratched him.[2]

Paddy Hill was given DC Brand's zip-up windcheater and told to put it over his head. Then he was handcuffed and taken out. Like the others he was also barefoot. His right arm was handcuffed to the passenger grip over the rear door.

They waited for about five minutes. The younger of the two detectives who had charge of him – John Brand – told him to keep his mouth shut and to keep the windcheater over his head. Another officer came. He looked at Hill and said, 'This is the bastard I want.' Bennett then uncuffed Hill's right arm and moved him over to the other side of the back seat, cuffing his left arm to the other passenger grip. He then got in beside Hill. Inspector Moore climbed into the front passenger seat. Brand was the driver. A couple of minutes later the convoy moved off.

Billy Power had an easy ride down the motorway. He had confessed and the worst was over. For the others the worst was yet to come.

According to Johnny Walker, his ride was more eventful. He was on the back seat with DS Kelly. DC Sutcliffe was in the front passenger seat. PC Cole was driving. After a while, said Walker, Kelly removed the coat from his head and started slapping him. Once Kelly pulled him close and butted him in the face with his head. Walker said he could smell drink on Kelly's breath.[3] After a while Kelly said he was going to get some sleep. Sutcliffe turned round and kneeled up in the front seat. He said to Kelly, 'Put the coat back over his head before you go to sleep.' Kelly did this and said to Walker, 'Don't you be going to sleep under that coat.'

'Don't worry, I'll make sure of that,' said Sutcliffe. With that he hit Walker in the face. Walker, whose head was covered, said he blacked out. The next thing he remembered, he was in a cell in Queen's Road.[4]

McIlkenny's journey was uneventful. He was on his own in the back of the car. DS Morris was in the passenger seat. DC Woodwiss was driving. McIlkenny says they left him alone.

Paddy Hill is alleged to have had the roughest ride. He testified that, soon after they set off from Morecambe, Sergeant Bennett told him to sit on the front of the seat and keep his legs wide open. According to Hill, Bennett rammed a police truncheon between his legs. Then he whipped Hill in the testicles with the leather thong on the handle of the truncheon.

69

Later in the journey, Hill alleged, Bennett stubbed a lighted cigarette on his bare feet.[5]

Inspector Moore, meanwhile, was seated in the front passenger seat. From time to time, Hill alleged, Moore would turn round and punch him on the head. Eventually Moore took out his revolver and told Hill to open his mouth. Hill testified: 'He shoved the muzzle in my mouth and told me he was going to blow my fucking head off.' There was a click as Moore pulled the trigger. Then the inspector started laughing. 'He took the gun out of my mouth and passed a comment to the other two that there must have been something wrong with the ammunition. He said, 'I'll try again', and he put the gun back in my mouth.' According to Hill, Moore pulled the trigger again, but still nothing happened. 'Moore said I must have a charmed life, but third time lucky. He put the gun against my eye and pulled the trigger again.'[6]

They arrived at Queen's Road police station between 7.30 and 8.00. It was a modern building, just off the Aston Expressway, a few hundred yards from Spaghetti Junction. At that time it was the only station in Birmingham with an exercise yard.

Entrance for the public is through glass doors at the front of the building. Prisoners usually enter through gates to the right of the station, on the same side as the cell block.

The cells are built in a square. There are three male cells on one side and on the other a female cell and a juvenile cell. In the middle there are showers and washrooms. The cell block is connected to the main police station by a passage-way leading from the main reception. The station sergeant's desk is at the entrance to the passage-way and he alone has the keys to the cell block and to the individual cells. He is also responsible for maintaining what is known as the 'Person in Custody' sheet which should record details of every visit made to the prisoners. The station sergeant on duty when the five Irishmen were admitted was Sergeant John Wilkinson. Later, at 9.30, he was relieved by Sergeant Dennis Holt. Sergeant Holt was relieved at 5.30 the following morning by Sergeant Eric Holland. Between them the three men were on duty for the whole period that the men were held at Queen's Road.

Sergeant Wilkinson was having his dinner break when the men arrived. He later testified that when he returned he visited each of them in turn. He could see no sign of injury on any of them except Walker, who had a mark under one eye. None made any complaint.

Billy Power's first visitors at Queen's Road were DS Watson and DC French, his interrogators at Morecambe. According to Power, French said they were taking him to their boss and that he should stick to what he had said in his statement.[7] They took him out of the cells to an upstairs room where he was introduced to an older man with a thin moustache. This was Chief Superintendent Harry Robinson, the man in overall charge of the inquiry. He told Power to sit beside him.

Robinson said the police had been following Walker on the evening of the explosions, but had lost him in town. He had a copy of Power's statement on the desk in front of him. According to Power, he offered to tear it up if Power would tell him where the explosives and other bomb-making materials were. Power said he knew nothing about any explosives. 'You know why I signed,' he said.

From the room next door there came the sound of a commotion. According to Power, someone was being beaten up.[8]

Power did not get much sleep that night. He tried to lie down, but he said, his body ached from the beating he had received at Morecambe. Throughout the night he was visited at intervals of about twenty minutes by officers who ordered him alternately to stand up or to sit. He heard Gerry Hunter screaming, 'Leave me alone, leave me alone.'

As soon as he arrived at Queen's Road, Hunter was questioned by two of the officers who had brought him from Morecambe, DS Millichamp and DC Bell. 'They started to hit me. I was hit across the mouth and fell onto a bench. Another officer came in and said, "Let me get at him, I haven't fucking touched him yet."[9] He jumped on top of me and threw me onto the bench and kicked me twice in the back. He told me to stand up. He hit me with his fist across my face again. They kept calling me names and telling me I had killed lots of people. Every time I denied it, they hit me.'

Hunter was then handcuffed and shut in his cell. The handcuffs were done up so tight they cut into his wrists. After about half an hour they were taken off but he was not allowed to sleep. The lights kept going on and off. He was told to stand up and, if he sat, someone would come in or shout through the door telling him to stand. Like the others, he was still barefoot. His feet were freezing and he wrapped them in a blanket but he was told to take it off.[10]

McIlkenny does not seem to have been questioned further during the night though he, too, testified that they were not allowed to sleep. 'We were kept awake all night by a uniformed sergeant going around continually telling me to stand up.' In court McIlkenny identified the Sergeant as Dennis Holt.[11]

Walker said he was made to stand to attention most of the night. His feet were freezing. 'There was lots of shouting and bawling. Someone would shout, "Sit down." Then another would shout "Stand up!"[12] I didn't know where I was,' said Walker.

Paddy Hill's recollection of arrival at Queen's Road is the most vivid. 'I was dragged out of the car and into the police station. There was an untold number of police officers running around with shotguns and handguns. The police station was like a mini-fortress. It was sealed off for about a hundred yards around.

'I was taken to a cell. The handcuffs were taken off and an officer gave me a punch in the jaw. I fell into a corner and he kicked me. "We haven't started on you yet," he said.'

It was later established that there were two officers on security duty in the cell block that night from about 9.30 in the evening until 10.00 the following morning: DC Fred Jennings and PC William Coffey. Both men were also on security duty the following night, Saturday to Sunday, and again on Sunday to Monday at Central Lock-up in Steelhouse Lane, to which the men had by that time been transferred. DC Jennings was armed with a shotgun and a revolver. PC Coffey was armed only with a revolver. They both denied making any of the alleged threats. The sergeant in charge of the cells from 9.30 each evening until 5.30 the following morning was Dennis Holt. He later testified that he had visited each of the men several times over the two nights and that none complained. He too, denied harrassing the prisoners.

Among the senior officers who would have been in and out of Queen's Road (though not necessarily in the cell area) during the forty-eight hours in which the men were held there were Assistant Chief Constable Maurice Buck, Chief Superintendent Harry Robinson and Superintendent George Reade. The duty inspector was Ronald Chapman. He was on the premises from 5.30 in the morning until 2.00 in the afternoon on both the Saturday and the Sunday.

The officer in charge of Queen's Road police station – though not involved in the investigation – was Superintendent Joe Matthews. He was on the premises day and night throughout the period the men were held there. He saw the prisoners on Saturday morning and later confirmed that some were standing rigidly to attention. He put this down to their IRA training. 'They had discipline,' he said.[13]

12

Nora Power had been playing bingo at the Hardy Spicer Social Club when she heard that bombs had gone off in the centre of Birmingham. Her first thought was for Billy. 'Oh Christ, Billy's gone back to Ireland. I hope he's got away all right.' She got home about eleven. Her brother Eddie, who lodged with her and Billy, paid a pound to the babysitter, and they went to bed. It was a stormy night and at first the thunder kept her awake. Sometime in the early hours she was awakened by a loud banging at her front door. She went downstairs and found half a dozen policemen on the doorstep. One was a woman, another had an Alsatian on a lead. (Later Nora Power learned that the police had broken down the door of a house two doors away mistaking it for hers.) She let the policemen into the hallway. 'Where's your husband,' they demanded. They must have known the answer.

'Gone to Belfast.'

'What for?'

'To a funeral.'

'Whose funeral?'

'James McDade's.' She added hastily. 'And to bring back his mum.'

The police then searched the house but not very thoroughly. They opened cupboards. Looked in saucepans. They looked in the children's bedroom and in her brother Eddie's. A couple of the police officers lingered over a store of girlie magazines they found under Eddie's bed. They stayed about half an hour. They were civil except for one young officer, a thin, blond man, who said to Nora, 'You'll never see your husband again.'

Sandra Hunter's council house in Erdington received a rather more thorough going over. She counted eight officers including a woman. One of the policemen had a dog.

'Where's your husband?'

'Gone to Belfast. To Jamsie McDade's funeral.'

They searched the house. Seamus McLoughlin's seven year old daughter was staying because McLoughlin had gone back to Ireland on the plane with McDade's body and his wife, Mary, had been to Coventry for the service. McLoughlin's daughter was sharing a bed with Tracey Hunter. The two girls were tipped out of bed and their room searched. In Sandra's bedroom the police broke open the wardrobe and examined the Christmas presents. Sandra had prepared early for Christmas: the presents were already wrapped. They asked her what was in them but did not open them. They gathered up Gerry's clothes and said they were taking them away to be examined. They looked in the garden shed and in the fridge. One of the policemen noticed a phial of phenobarbitone. 'Who's that for?'

'My daughter, Tracey. The doctor prescribed it.'

They opened the dustbag in the hoover and took away the dust. They asked what she thought about the bombings and Sandra said she thought they were terrible. 'Is your husband an IRA sympathiser?' they asked. Sandra said they must make up their own minds. One said, 'We know he is a sympathiser, but he's not in the IRA?' They asked when he was coming home. 'On Sunday,' said Sandra. 'Tell him to come down to the police station when he gets back. We just want to check him out.' Never once did they mention that Gerry was already in custody. Sandra was not unduly worried. 'I thought it was normal for Irish families to be raided after a bombing.' She went back to bed and slept like a log.

Johnny Walker's house was also thoroughly searched. His eldest daughter, Bernadette, recalls, 'There were five or six policemen. Some were in plain clothes. One was a woman. There was also a dog. They came about three in the morning. Wrecked the house. They took the back off the television, threw everything out of the cupboards. All the time they kept asking, "Where's your father?" They never said they were holding him.' It would be another three days before Bernadette Walker discovered what had become of her father.

Paddy Hill's wife, Pat, was awakened in the early hours of Friday morning by her seven year old daughter, Michelle. 'Someone's kicking the front door,' she said. Mrs Hill got out of bed and went downstairs. 'Who is it?' she called.

'Police,' said a voice.

She let them in. There were a good few, maybe ten. All in plain clothes except for a policewoman. Three or four of them took her into the living-room. They were all firing questions at her at once. She asked them to slow down.

'Where's your husband?' they demanded.

'Gone to Belfast.'

'What for?'

'To see his aunt. She's had a stroke.

'When will he be back?'

'Monday or Tuesday.'

'Where did he get the money for his fare?'

She told them about Sister Bridget at the Convent.

Kate McIlkenny had seen the news of the bombings on television on Thursday evening. 'Murdering gits,' she said to her daughter Anne. She added, 'The Irish homes will be getting pulled apart tonight.'

When the knock came at the door at about four in the morning she knew at once it was a raid. She could hear a police dog barking. She opened the door to them and a man started reading from a piece of paper he held in his hand. 'Don't waste your time. Come in,' she said.

About half a dozen of them started searching the house. 'Where's your husband?' they wanted to know.

'Gone to Belfast, for the funeral of James McDade.'

'When will he be back?'

'Sunday.'

'What have we got here,' one of them shouted downstairs. He was holding up a black bag containing kitchen utensils from the factory where she worked. They were rejects given to her by the foreman, but the policeman thought they were stolen.

'We'll do you for that,' he said.

'You can't find anything on my husband so you're going to do me, is that it?'

'Shut your mouth,' he said.

The search lasted about twenty minutes. They took away a *Daily Mirror* with a picture of James McDade, two copies of *Republican News* and a *Morning Star*. 'It was the *Morning Star* which seemed to upset them most,' she recalled. They also took her young son, Sean's, Boy's Brigade uniform, a piece of wood with fuse wire wrapped round it and a few bits of electrical wire.

'When your husband comes back, tell him to report to the police station,' they said as they left.

Back home in his Erdington council house, Hughie Callaghan got out of

76

bed on Friday morning feeling slightly the worse for wear. Eileen had already gone out to work by the time he surfaced. She was still angry with him for staying out the previous day.

The news on the radio was dominated by the bombings. There was a report that five men were in custody at Morecambe, but Hughie did not connect it with his friends. They would all be safely back in Belfast by now. It occurred to Callaghan that Sandra Hunter might be worried about Gerry being in town when the bombs had gone off. He decided to pop round and tell her that Gerry and the others were safely away.

Sandra Hunter got up that morning around 7.30. She too heard on the radio that five men were being questioned. She took her children and Seamus McLoughlin's daughter to school and came home again. Looking out of the window she saw the street was full of policemen. They were questioning her neighbours. It was then that she started to worry. A few minutes later there was a knock at the back door. It was Hughie Callaghan.

'Hughie, I thought you'd gone to Ireland.'

'No, I only went to see them off. Don't worry Sandra, they got away safely. I saw them on to the train.'

Sandra told him about the raid and about the policemen questioning the neighbours. Even as they sat there the street was full of policemen.

By now the mood in Birmingham was growing ugly. The wave of revenge attacks on Irish property had begun four hours after the bombing, with the petrol bombing of the Irish Community Centre at Digbeth. The Centre's president, Father Brendan O'Malley, spent Friday answering threatening phone calls. The phone at the Irish Welfare and Information Centre, next to the home of the Catholic Archbishop, began ringing less than two hours after the bombings. Father Paddy Sheridan, the priest who ran the Centre, said people just seemed to be looking up Irish organisations in the telephone directory and abusing whoever answered the phone.

Many Irish people in Birmingham were afraid to go into work. At British Leyland's Longbridge plant hundreds of workers downed tools and took to the streets. They carried placards depicting gallows and bearing slogans like 'Hang the IRA'.

Later that day, Assistant Chief Constable Maurice Buck appealed for calm. Revenge attacks would, he said, only hinder the hunt for the bombers.

The police knew they had to get results quickly, if serious violence was to be avoided.

Hughie Callaghan did not go home after leaving Sandra Hunter. He met a friend, Charlie Sloane, at a bus stop and they went for a drink at the Aston Tavern, by the football ground. They talked in muted tones about the bombing – about how Hughie had been down there when it happened, and about the lads who had gone to Ireland on the train. They were getting strange looks from the other customers because of their Irish accents. Eventually they left and went to Lozell's Working Men's Club in Witton Road. Callaghan was well known there. He often used to spend a day at the club playing snooker. Here, too, the mood was ugly. It was not a good day to be an Irishman in Birmingham.

Eileen Callaghan had a terrifying experience when she arrived home from work at about four o'clock. It was getting dark. She opened the front door and pushed open the door to the living-room. As she did so, a man caught her by the arm. There were four men in the living-room. They all had guns in holsters, and said they were policemen. 'Where's your husband?' they asked. Eileen said she had no idea. 'Act normally,' they said. 'Put the lights on, draw the curtains, switch on the television.' Later they said, 'This is serious. Act normally or someone might get shot.'

The men stayed all evening. There was a policewoman too. Eileen kept making cups of tea. She was terrified. Her daughter, Geraldine, came home. They told her the same. 'Act normally,' they said. At around eight a friend came to the door. They took him away for questioning. Eileen was crying now. So was Geraldine.

'He's going to be charged,' said the head policeman. 'He'll be in court on Monday or Tuesday.'

It was past closing time when Hughie rolled in. He did not see the armed policemen hiding behind neighbours' hedges as he came up Stanwell Grove. He opened the front door. A man pulled him inside and stuck a gun to his head. Someone frisked him. Eileen and Geraldine screamed. 'I haven't done anything,' said Hughie.

'We know different,' they are alleged to have said, and then took him away.

78

13

Hughie Callaghan was arrested at 10.45 on Friday night. He was taken first to Queen's Road police station, where the others were being held. He was driven there by DS Peter Higgins and DC Alan Buxton. They arrived at eleven o'clock. On arrival, Callaghan was taken upstairs to the finger-print room. He was not told of the presence of his five friends.

According to the police, his clothes were taken from him and he remained for about thirty minutes wrapped in a blanket until fresh clothes were brought from home. Callaghan's recollection is different. He says his clothes were not taken until the following afternoon.

Half an hour after midnight, Callaghan was interviewed by Chief Inspector Colin Powell, DS Higgins and DC Buxton. According to Higgins, Callaghan was distraught.

Inspector Powell cautioned Callaghan and told him he had reason to believe he had been involved in the pub bombings. Callaghan replied, 'I'm not in the IRA.' Powell then asked Callaghan about his movements on Thursday. Callaghan described how he had met up with the other men and they had gone to New Street station. They were going to McDade's funeral and he had seen them on to the train. He had then gone to Yates' Wine Lodge.

When Powell told Callaghan that five of his friends had been detained Callaghan is said to have put his head in his hands and started sobbing, saying, 'Oh no, oh no.' Powell asked Callaghan what part he had played in the bombings and Callaghan, still sobbing, said, 'I've told you, I've nothing to do with the movement.' According to Powell, Callaghan kept saying, 'Can you help me? Can you help me?' Powell said he then asked Callaghan how well he knew McDade. He replied that he knew McDade's family in Ardoyne and he had known McDade since he was a boy. With this the interview ended. It had lasted no longer than ten minutes.

Callaghan's recollection of the interview was vague. He was, by his own account, shocked and confused. He could identify only Higgins, but conceded that Powell and Buxton may have been present. He was under the impression that Higgins had asked most of the questions. Once, he said,

Higgins slapped his face.[1] They kept insisting he was involved in the bombing. He denied it. When the interview ended, Callaghan says he was given a cup of coffee. Higgins and Buxton then drove him to Sutton Coldfield police station, apparently because there was no space for him in the cells at Queen's Road. They departed at 1.45 in the morning. The drive to Sutton Coldfield took about twenty minutes.

At Sutton Coldfield, Callaghan said, he was again taken to an interview room and questioned by DS Higgins and DC Buxton. According to Callaghan, he was again asked for an account of his movements on the day of the bombing. It took him about half an hour to recount his movements and at this stage he was not assaulted.

At some point, according to Callaghan, one of the officers left the room and returned with a copy of Billy Power's statement. He put it down on the table in front of Callaghan who glanced at it but did not read it. 'They said that all the others involved me and that I was the last to make a statement.' Callaghan said Power's statement could not be true.

DS Higgins and DC Buxton later told the court that this interview did not take place.

Callaghan's account of his night in the cells at Sutton Coldfield is much the same as that of the men detained at Queen's Road. 'They would not let me lie down and each time I started dozing off they would wake me. An officer sat in the cell all night and stared at me. Whenever I started to drop off to sleep the officer would shout at me, "Are you sleeping, wake up." This happened four or five times. Eventually they did let me sleep for a while, but all the time an Alsatian dog was wandering in and out of the cell (the door was open). The handler stayed outside and said, "If you move, that dog will eat you." I slept only fitfully.' Callaghan's next appointment with DS Higgins was at 11.20 on Saturday morning.

Sometime on Saturday two police officers came to fetch Billy Power from his cell. Power had not seen either of them before. They took him upstairs to a room where Gerry Hunter was being interrogated. At first, Power said, he hardly recognised Hunter. His skin looked yellow and his face was puffed up. One of the officers said, 'Who's that?' At first Power did not answer. The officer repeated the question. Eventually Power answered, 'That's Gerry Hunter.'

'Tell us what he was carrying when he arrived at the station.'

'Nothing,' said Power.

The detective thrust a copy of Power's statement in front of him. 'It says here that he was carrying plastic bags.'

'I know what it says there,' said Power, 'but he was not carrying anything.'

At this, according to Power, the detective pushed him against the wall. Power thought they were going to start beating him again. He said, 'I can't take no more.'

'Take him away,' said someone. With that, Power was taken out by the two officers who had brought him up. One said to the other, 'That was a great help, wasn't it.'

Before they were interviewed at Queen's Road on Saturday morning most of the men say they were finger-printed and photographed. The finger-printing took place in an office on the first floor. The photographs were taken in a room in the cell block so that prisoners only had to walk a few paces and were usually taken by one of the arresting officers. They were poor quality black and white polaroids which show the beginnings of Walker's black eye and an apparent split lip on Hill. They do not, to the untrained eye, show many other obvious signs of injury. However, the distinguished forensic doctor, David Paul, was later to argue that signs of injury could be seen in these photos. Many of the alleged injuries were, of course, to the men's bodies and no photographic record of these exists. The timing of the photographs may be important since, on the Saturday morning, except in Power's case, many of the alleged injuries had yet to be inflicted. Police witnesses later testified that all the photographs were taken on Sunday morning, just before the men were charged. Hill, Hunter, McIlkenny and Walker all claimed that they were photographed as they were finger-printed, on Saturday morning. McIlkenny said he was photographed twice, once on Saturday morning and again on Sunday morning, after being given a change of clothes. He also said that his first set of clothes were stained with blood from a nose-bleed inflicted on Saturday night.

On Saturday morning, after being finger-printed and, according to him, photographed, Hunter had a coat put over his head and was taken down a corridor to an interview room – the superintendent's clerk's office on the first floor. As he walked, looking down at the ground, he could see the feet of policemen and women trying to trip him or kick his ankles. The interviewing officers were DS Millichamp and DC Bell, who had driven Hunter from Morecambe the previous evening.

As the interview started, said Hunter, DC Bell appeared to be doodling on a piece of paper. He showed Hunter what he had drawn. It was a tombstone with "Gerry Hunter Rest in Peace" written on it.[2]

Millichamp opened the proceedings. He asked Hunter to account for his movements on the day of the bombing. DC Bell took notes. Hunter told them how he and Billy Power had called at Seamus McLoughlin's house to pay their respects to McDade's widow. How they had gone to the Irish Centre at Digbeth in search of free transport to the mortuary at Coventry. How, on finding no transport, they had whiled away the early part of the afternoon in a pub and a couple of betting shops in Digbeth. How they had then split up and arranged to meet at New Street. Eventually Millichamp became impatient. 'This is no fucking good,' he said. He said he knew Hunter had done the bombing because two of his mates were covered in gelignite. Hunter denied any knowledge of the bombing and later said that, every time he did so, he was hit across the face.[3] Millichamp also kept threatening to bring the gaffer, presumably Superintendent Reade, down on Hunter.

According to Hunter, seven or eight detectives took part in his interrogation at different times of the day. Each time Millichamp and Bell left the room other detectives would take over. One, a short, fat detective with gingerish hair, who Hunter identified as DC Roger Ball, said he had searched Hunter's house early on Friday morning. He knew Hunter's daughter, Tracey, was on phenobarbitone because he had seen it in the fridge. Another detective, identified by Hunter as DS Morris, asked, 'Don't you love your wife and children?'

'Of course,' said Hunter.

'Don't you know your house is surrounded by a screaming mob which is dying to get at them?'[4] According to Hunter, Morris said that if he cooperated, his family would be given police protection. When Millichamp was out of the room, Morris told Hunter he did not believe in hitting people and Morris did not assault him. At lunchtime, Morris went to buy food. Millichamp gave him a pound. As he reached the door, Morris said, 'What about our friend?'

'Give him fuck all,' said Millichamp.[5]

When Morris came back, they sat eating pie and chips in front of Hunter. It was forty hours since he had last eaten. It was around teatime, Hunter guessed, when Billy Power was brought in. He had still not recovered from his interrogation at Morecambe. 'He was in a terrible state and being held up by a police officer. They called his name, *'Power'* and he jumped. They told him to tell me that he had made a statement. At first Power didn't answer and they repeated the question. He said, 'I signed, didn't I? Leave me alone.' Then they took him away.'

The more Hunter denied, the more he alleged he was hit. On one occasion, he was sitting with his hands on the table.

Millichamp jumped up and brought his fist down on them.[6]

On another occasion, Inspector Moore came in. 'He went round the back of my chair, grabbed my hair and started beating my head on the table. He was screaming at me, "You mass murderer."'[7]

Somehow the conversation came round to dogs. They must have noticed his reaction to the dogs in the cells the previous night. One of the detectives said, 'You don't like dogs, do you, Gerry?'

'No.'

At that point, the door opened and in came an Alsatian held on a lead by a uniformed policeman. The constable shouted, 'Get him, get him,' and the dog started growling, barking and straining at its leash. They let it come within six inches of him and then took it out.[8]

Later they had a visit from Chief Superintendent Robinson. He was accompanied by an unidentified senior officer. According to Hunter, they told him they had known quite a few murderers in their time. At first, they said, murderers convince themselves they haven't killed anyone. They put their crime at the back of their minds. Then, in three months time, they realise what they've done and go mad.' Still Hunter declined to confess.

Eventually, long after dark, Hunter was taken back to his cell. A uniformed sergeant gave him a pork pie and a glass of water. He was also allowed for the first time to wash. While he was washing, the sergeant noticed the marks on his chest. He asked what had happened. Hunter said he had fallen. There was blood on his lip. It had congealed and he chipped it away with his fingernail.

Hunter estimated that the interview on Saturday lasted from ten in the morning until ten at night. Twelve hours. The police version was different. According to the notebooks of DS Millichamp and DC Bell, the interview began at 10.15 in the morning and continued until 12.30, when there was a break for lunch. It resumed at 2.00 and finished at 4.30, then continued between 5.40 and 7.00. A total of less than seven hours.

Millichamp and Bell had a somewhat different recollection of what took place.

The two detectives agreed that the first part of the interview consisted of a lengthy account of Hunter's movements on the day of the bombing. This took until 12.30 when they went to lunch. They denied that either of them laid a finger on Hunter. They denied, too, that D S Morris or D C Ball had taken part in the interview or that Morris had gone out to buy pie and chips. They denied making any reference to Hunter's family and denied that Inspector Moore had banged Hunter's head on the table. Or that the incident with the police dog had occurred.

In the afternoon, said Millichamp and Bell, they asked Hunter if he sympathised with the I R A. He is said to have replied, 'I do not agree with bombing in this country. Shooting soldiers in Belfast is fair game.'

They showed him a copy of Billy Power's statement and he replied, 'He's just said this to save getting a good hiding. It's all lies.' Millichamp and Bell, however, denied bringing Power to confront Hunter. They said that Hunter became excited at this point and they gave him a cup of coffee to calm him down. When the interview resumed Hunter is said to have volunteered that Walker was connected with the I R A. He told them that the proceeds of Walker's raffles went to the Prisoner's Defence (sic) Fund.

'I think we are getting a little nearer the truth now, Gerry,' said Millichamp.

Hunter is supposed to have replied, 'I'm not saying any more. You know that I can't, for my family's sake.'

By now it was 4.30 and Millichamp and Bell said they again adjourned to make up their notes. The interview resumed forty minutes later. They gave him a copy of McIlkenny's statement and he began to shake and cry. He said, 'Please leave me alone for a few minutes. Let me think about it.'

Millichamp and Bell said they left him alone for another forty minutes, until 6.20. When they went back, George Reade came with them. Hunter was still shaking and crying. 'Just settle down, Gerry,' Millichamp is supposed to have said. He then asked about McDade and Hunter replied, 'Now please don't bring that up again, you know it upsets me.'

'All right,' said Millichamp, 'we will let that pass for the moment.'

Reade then told him that Walker had also signed a statement admitting the bombings. 'he has put you right in it up to your neck.'

Then, said Millichamp, they gave Hunter a copy of Walker's statement. Hunter read it two or three times and said, 'Oh no, this is terrible, oh no.'

'Now don't start getting upset again,' said Reade.

They told him that Callaghan had also confessed and Hunter is then said to have blurted out, 'Please, please you must believe me. This was never meant to be. I don't know why I had anything to do with it. Please God forgive me.'

'That is a matter for you and your conscience,' said Millichamp, 'but you are in a position to stop any further killings.'

'How can I do that? I have got to think of my wife and children. I know I am finished.'

Reade is then said to have asked where the bombs were made and Hunter is said to have replied, 'I can't tell you. I must think of my family. I can't tell you anything.'

'Do you want to make a statement? You don't have to if you don't want to. It's up to you.'

'I can't, I can't. I can't believe this has happened. I wish I could turn the clock back. I am not going to say any more.'

On that note, said Millichamp, the interview ended.

14

Walker's interview at Queen's Road began at 11.15. According to DS Kelly and DC Sutcliffe, the officers who conducted the interview, it took place in three stages. The first lasted only twenty minutes and finished at 11.35. The second commenced at 11.55 and finished at 12.15. The third started at 1.30 and culminated with Walker signing a statement confessing that he had placed the bomb in the Tavern in the Town. Kelly and Sutcliffe said they did not take notes during the first two interviews. Their account is based on notes prepared around 12.40.

Kelly agreed that by then Walker had the beginnings of a black eye and he said that this was caused when Walker had accidentally hit his head while getting into a car at Morecambe. Kelly testified that he opened the first interview by telling Walker that the death toll had now risen to nineteen and that Billy Power had made a statement admitting that he had planted a bomb in the Mulberry Bush and implicating Walker. 'Walker said, 'He's telling lies, sir. I don't believe in bombs. I wouldn't have anything to do with them.'

Kelly then showed Walker a copy of Power's statement. Walker is said to have remarked, 'I only look after things. Somebody brought me things to look after.' What kind of stuff? 'Batteries, wire and watches.'

'Do you realise,' Kelly is said to have asked, 'that these are essential ingredients in the making of a bomb?'

'They have been using me as a cunt.'

'Did you have any explosives in your house?'

'I don't know. They could have given me anything. I trusted them and I didn't care really. I must have had explosives in the house. Me, with seven kids.' Then, according to Kelly, he started to cry and said, Please leave me.' At which point, said Kelly, they gave Walker a cup of tea and left him in the care of another officer. When Kelly and Sutcliffe returned twenty minutes later, Walker insisted that he and the others had not left New Street station, and Sutcliffe said, 'You didn't tell the truth to begin with. Why should we believe you are telling the truth now?'

'I am sir, oh I am, sir. I've brought shame on my family. I wish I was dead.'

86

At this point, said Kelly and Sutcliffe, they went for lunch. They left Walker at about 12.15 and returned at 1.30. This time Superintendent Reade was with them. Reade told Walker that McIlkenny had now confessed his part in planting the bombs. He then left the room. DS Kelly gave Walker a photostat of McIlkenny's statement. Walker read it and said nothing. Kelly said, 'John, I am now going to remind you what Billy Power said in his statement.'

'You don't need to remind me, I can remember.'

'You remember what he said or is it that you remember what happened on Thursday night?'

There was a long pause and then, according to Kelly, Walker said, 'I can remember because it's true.'

'You are telling me now that you did plant the bombs?'

Walker is said to have become agitated. 'Not all of them,' he said.

'Where did you plant your bombs?'

'In New Street.'

Kelly then gave Walker a piece of paper and asked him to draw a diagram. Walker drew lines representing Colmore Row where he, McIlkenny, Callaghan and Hunter had got off the bus. He then indicated their route to New Street station: across Temple Row, down Needless Alley and into the station.

'Show me where you put the bomb,' said Kelly.

To this Walker is alleged to have replied, 'Jimmy, say they're parcels. It makes me feel sick when you mention bombs.'

'Okay, parcels. Where did you put your parcel?'

'In a pub in New Street. Down the steps.'

'What pub?'

'I don't know, sir.'

'You must know.'

'I think it was the Tavern.'

Kelly then asked him to mark the Tavern on the plan and Walker made a cross in the bottom left-hand corner of the paper. 'Sign it,' said Kelly and Walker signed.

That, according to DS Kelly and DC Sutcliffe, is how Walker came to dictate his confession. Walker told a rather different story.

After being photographed and finger-printed, said Walker, he was taken back to his cell. Soon afterwards, PC Cole, the driver of the car in which Walker travelled from Morecambe, came to collect him. He put a coat over Walker's head and took him upstairs, still barefoot, to be interviewed. DS Kelly and DC Sutcliffe were waiting for him. They asked his name, address, how long he had been in England, where he was born. To this last question, Walker replied, 'Derry.'

Kelly slapped his face. 'There's no such place,' he said.

'Beg your pardon?'

'It's Londonderry.'[1]

Walker claimed they gave him a few more slaps, and Cole congratulated Sutcliffe on his ability to throw a punch. Walker took this to be a reference to the blow that had knocked him out in the car yesterday on the way down from Morecambe, which, he says, was the cause of his black eye.[2]

Kelly left the room briefly and came back with Power's statement. They read bits of it to him. A senior officer with greying hair came in with a piece of paper. There was a crude drawing on it. He showed it to Walker and said, 'That's how you make a bomb, isn't it?' The drawing was to crop up later in the evidence of Thomas Watt, the workmate of Walker's who alleged that Walker had sketched out a diagram of a bomb on the back of a cigarette packet and had given it to him. At some stage, Kelly and Sutcliffe went out and two other officers came in. Walker later identified one of them as Detective Sergeant Roger Ball. The other he was unable to identify. Walker was shaking and Ball offered him a cigarette. At first he seemed to be playing the nice guy. He said, 'I don't believe in beating people up. You don't have to put up with all this. Why not make a statement.'

'I never done anything,' said Walker.

Ball asked him to move his chair closer. Walker moved closer. Ball said again, 'Are you going to make a statement?'

'No.'

At which point, according to Walker, Ball suddenly made a grab for his testicles.[3] Meanwhile, the other officer was standing behind Walker. He took Walker's two thumbs and drew them to the back of his neck, Walker alleged. Then he pressed them in. Hard. 'Watch his eyes,' he is supposed to have said to Ball. For a moment Walker seemed to be paralysed. He had the impression he was lifted clear off the chair. Then the man released him and he fell on to the floor. The man picked up the chair, ready to hit him, but Ball stopped him.[4]

Later, the young detective, the one Walker could not identify, spread a newspaper on the table. The paper showed pictures of the bombings. As

88

Walker bent forward to look at it, the detective smashed his head forward on to the table.

When Kelly and Sutcliffe came back they told Walker that his wife had made a statement saying he was responsible for the bombings. They said there was a mob outside his home.[5] Kelly produced a handful of bullets. He said, 'We're taking you to the firing range for target practice.'[6] With that, says Walker, they all started laying in to him. There were four of them. Kelly, Sutcliffe, Ball and the unidentified detective.

One of them, Walker said, kneed him in the groin. Kelly broke his cuff-link hitting Walker. He cursed, picked up a ruler from the table, a big ruler with a metal edge, and hit Walker repeatedly behind the ears.[7] From then on, said Walker, he was bounced around the room.

Walker says he suffered permanent damage. He now sleeps on a wooden bed because of injuries to his back, caused, he believes, by the anonymous detective who applied pressure to his neck. He is unable to say when the interview ended or the precise form of much of the later violence. He dimly remembers sketching a diagram of his route from the bus stop in Colmore Row to New Street. He remembers that typed papers were put in front of him and that he was told to sign. He did not know what was in the document and he did not care. 'I just wanted to stop the beating,' he told the court. He signed in several places. His hand was shaking so much that he could hardly write. Sutcliffe came round behind and steadied his hand. After that they left him alone.

Walker's confession is a little less than one thousand words long. According to DS Kelly and DC Sutcliffe, it was dictated by Walker in their presence between 1.00 and 3.10 on the Saturday afternoon. It begins: '*About four years ago I began to work for the IRA. My part in the Army was to collect money for the fund to buy weapons to fight the British.*' It then goes on to describe more or less accurately his activities running raffles at the Crossways Public House, the Kingstanding Ex-Servicemen's Club and at his workplace, the Forging and Pressworks at Witton. It says that he and his wife had attended an IRA meeting at the White Horse pub in the Nechells area of Birmingham about eighteen months previously. '*My wife done her nut and said she wouldn't go back there again.*'

It goes on: '*James McDade asked me if I would keep some stuff for him, wire, batteries, tape, drawing pins and some pocket watches, and some other stuff. It looked like explosives. There was no detonators as far as I know but ... they could have given me anything. It was always James McDade that brought the parcels to my house.'*

The confession then describes a Sinn Fein man who came to Walker's to collect the parcels. *'He was 30 to 40 years, about 5 foot 10 inches, well built, always wore a cap . . . very well spoken.'* The man was said to come in an 1100 car, green with four doors. He always came between 9.00 and 9.45 in the evening. Always rang in advance to say he was coming. *'There was no particular day he came. I only know there was always an explosion afterwards.'*

The confession then gives a more or less accurate account of Walker's movements on the day of the bombing. When McIlkenny and Callaghan called round at Walker's house that evening, the confession says, *'I had my "parcel" ready.'* They went to Gerry Hunter's. *'He had his "parcel" ready as well.'* They then went to New Street where they had a drink in the railway bar. *'I was shitting myself now . . . But Billy Power was more scared than me.'* Paddy Hill turned up. He had his 'parcel' too.

The planting of the bombs is described in just eighty-seven words. *'Gerry and me went to a pub in New Street near the Odeon. I don't know. I think it's called the Tavern. I know we went down lots of stairs, it was packed. It was not dark but the lights were sort of low and you couldn't see when you went in. We went straight to the bar. I was shaking by now. I just wanted out. Gerry wanted a drink. I said let's get out. We put the parcel down. I cannot remember what happened then.'*

The confession concludes: *'They have used me as a cunt. I want to apologise for all the damage and injury I have caused. I have brought complete shame on my family. I am full of sorrow and remorse.'*

At the end, in Walker's writing, are the words: *'I have read the above statement and been told that I can correct, alter or add anything I wish. This statement is true and I have made it of my own free will.'*

Even allowing for the lack of circumstantial detail, there are problems with Walker's confession. It offers no clue as to where Walker and the others obtained their 'parcels'. It makes no mention of priming the bombs, essential if they were to explode. It is not specific about where in the Tavern in the Town the bomb was placed. It makes no attempt to describe what the bombs were contained in.

When it is compared to the confession signed by Billy Power, the problems multiply. Power's confession states there were a total of six bombs. Walker has only three.

Power says the bombs were carried to New Street by Walker (two bombs), Hunter (three) and Callaghan (one). Walker's bombs were brought to New Street by Hunter, Hill and himself, each carrying only one.

Walker's confession makes no mention of Power going off to put his bomb or bombs in the Mulberry Bush. It says only that he and Hunter took one bomb between them to the Tavern. Billy Power, by contrast, has Walker and Hunter going off together with four bombs between them.

Someone had done his sums wrong.

15

According to the police, Richard McIlkenny confessed within little more than an hour of being interviewed on the Saturday morning. McIlkenny testified that the interview took place in two stages and that it lasted until late at night. He said that during the interval he was taken to the cells to be photographed and finger-printed. (He also said that at one stage he and his interrogators moved office because of the sound of violence coming from the next door room.)

McIlkenny's confession was allegedly dictated to DC Terence Woodwiss and witnessed by DS Colin Morris and DC Rex Langford. Woodwiss and Morris were the officers who had brought McIlkenny from Morecambe the previous day.

According to Woodwiss, the interview began at 10.10, in the woman inspector's office on the first floor. Morris opened the conversation by stating that McIlkenny had lied in the interview they had had with him the previous day (which McIlkenny denied took place). He had claimed not to know the other men but the police had now interviewed the other men and their families and were satisfied that McIlkenny did know the others. To this McIlkenny is said to have replied, 'All right, I know them, but what does that prove?' He was then asked for an account of his movements on the Thursday.

McIlkenny told them that Hughie Callaghan had called at about four in the afternoon to return a pound that he owed. Callaghan stayed playing with the children and McIlkenny told him that he and the others were going to Belfast. They left about six and walked to Walker's house. Walker had a maroon hold-all. He went with them to Hunter's house. They were there about fifteen minutes and then caught a bus into town. They met Billy Power at the station and went for a drink in the railway bar. Hunter went out to make a telephone call. Hill turned up just as they were getting ready to leave. They had boarded the train at about 7.45.

'Nobody planted any bombs?' asked Morris.

'No, sir, I couldn't do that.'

Morris then produced Power's statement. Woodwiss read it out to McIlkenny. McIlkenny then asked to see it. He read it and said nothing.

'What have you got to say?' asked Morris.

At this point, McIlkenny is said to have responded, 'It was a mistake. Nobody should have been killed. There should have been a warning. I don't know what went wrong.' He is then said to have started crying.

'Compose yourself, Dick,' said Morris, 'and I'll get some tea.' He went out. He reappeared a few minutes later followed shortly by DC Langford with tea.

'Sit down a minute, Rex,' Morris is supposed to have said to Langford. And then to McIlkenny, 'Dick, let's have some tea and while you are drinking it let's get it straight. Are you telling us that you helped plant the bombs?'

'Yes. May God forgive me. It all went wrong.'

'Why?'

'We should have sent a warning. There should have been a phone call.'

'Where did you put your bomb?'

'In an alcove. We only stopped for a few minutes. I wanted to get out so we acted as though we couldn't get a drink and left.'

'Who was with you.

'Paddy Joe Hill.'

'What happened then?'

'We went back to the station and met the others. Then we caught the train.'

That, according to Woodwiss, Morris and Langford, is how McIlkenny came to unburden himself. He started dictating his confession at 11.20 that morning and had finished by 12.05.

Richard McIlkenny's account of his interrogation is dramatically different. Like the others he was taken from his cell to an upstairs interview room. He had not slept since he came off nightshift on Thursday morning, nearly forty-eight hours earlier. All the previous night he had been kept awake by a uniformed sergeant who, he said, had kept shouting every fifteen minutes, 'Stand up. Who told you to sit?'

DS Morris and DC Woodwiss were waiting for him in the interview room. They asked him to account for his movements on Thursday and he told them. Morris said he didn't believe him. Morris then left the room and came back with several sheets of paper which he said was Billy Power's statement. McIlkenny said he refused to touch it and so Morris told him what was in it.

'If Power signed that,' said McIlkenny, 'he must be cracking up.' McIlkenny said that he then refused to answer any more questions and so

Morris slapped his face.[1] After Morris had slapped him a couple of times, Superintendent Reade put his head round the door. He looked at Morris and Woodwiss and they shook their heads. Reade then rushed up to McIlkenny, grabbed him by the jacket, smacked his face and punched him in the chest. He then tried to kick McIlkenny's legs, but mostly hit the leg of the chair.[2] Reade departed and Morris resumed questioning. He said he wanted a statement from McIlkenny similar to the one Billy Power had signed. McIlkenny said he was signing nothing and on that note the interview ended. According to McIlkenny, it lasted two or three hours.

McIlkenny said he was then returned to the cells for several hours. At about 3.00 or 3.30 in the afternoon, he was taken out, finger-printed and photographed. He was then left until sometime in the evening. He guessed it might have been around 8.00. He was then taken back to the inspector's office where Morris and Woodwiss again pressed him to make a statement admitting that he helped plant the bombs. Again he refused to answer and again Morris slapped his face. Once, he said, Morris punched him and his nose started to bleed.[3] The blood dripped on to his shirt. Reade put his head round the door three times. After Reade left the third time, Woodwiss got up and went out. He came back with a revolver strapped to his waist. According to McIlkenny, he said, 'It's all right to shoot him. The Home Office has given permission. We can always say he was shot trying to escape.' He had bullets in his hand and was throwing them up and catching them. They took him to a room at the back of the police station. Seven or eight officers had gathered around the doorway. George Reade was the only one McIlkenny said he recognised.

The room was about twelve feet long and there didn't seem to be a window. He was taken inside and the other officers followed, closing the door behind them. Reade came close and punched him on the chest. They put him up against a wall. Woodwiss backed away about ten feet. 'Are you going to sign,' he asked. McIlkenny made no reply. Woodwiss took the gun and held it with both hands at arm's length. He seemed to be pointing at McIlkenny's head or just below. He pulled the trigger. There was a click and nothing happened. Woodwiss turned away cursing. He appeared to be fiddling with the gun. 'I've fixed it,' he said, 'it will be all right this time.'

Again he asked if McIlkenny was going to sign. Again McIlkenny said nothing. Woodwiss pointed the gun again. McIlkenny's heart was thump-

16

Detective Constable John Brand came back for Hill on Saturday morning. By now they knew each other well. Brand and DS Raymond Bennett had interviewed Hill at Morecambe. Brand had also been the driver of the car that had delivered Hill to Queen's Road the previous evening.

Hill testified that Brand first took him to be photographed, and then to the juvenile detention room on the first floor. Sergeant Bennett was there. So, according to Bennett and Brand, was Inspector Moore. Hill said Moore was not there. The police said that the interview began at 11.15. Hill put it much earlier. He said he could hear the rattle of milk bottles being delivered as he went upstairs.

Bennett asked the questions. Brand took notes. According to Brand, the conversation went as follows.

Bennett cautioned Hill and told him the police had taken statements from his wife. She had said he had been a member of the IRA for more than two years and that, together with McIlkenny, Walker and Hunter, he had been raising money for the IRA by running totes.

'Let me see that,' said Hill.

'You'll see it in due course,' said Bennett. 'Is it true?'

'The part about collecting money is true. But I'm not in the IRA.'

It was put to Hill that he and the others had been going to McDade's funeral. His wife had also said that he had attended IRA meetings at the White Horse pub in Nechells and the Crossways in College Road, Erdington.

According to Bennett and Brand, Hill had up to this time maintained that he did not know the other four men arrested with him at Heysham. They had now learned from Hill's wife – and from Walker – that he had been at Walker's house on Thursday afternoon only a few hours before they set off for Belfast. To this Hill is supposed to have replied, 'Oh my God, has she said all that? We've had it, we've had it. If I tell you the truth, what will you do for me?'

'Just tell the truth,' said Bennett, 'we are making no promises.'

At this point, according to Bennett and Brand, Hill started talking. The explosives, he said, had been at Walker's house. They planned to put the bombs in the pubs and then get on the train. Walker was to meet up with Hunter at Hunter's house. 'We were to go to the station separately to stop anyone suspecting us.'

'What was your part in the plan?' asked Bennett.

'It was nothing to do with me. Walker and Hunter were in charge. It was up to them.'

'If you didn't plant the bombs, how did you get nitroglycerine on your hands?'

'I don't know. Honest to God, I don't.'

'I don't believe you,' said Bennett.

'Jesus, Mary, I don't know what to say.'

'Why don't you admit responsibility?'

'I've told you everything I can. Just leave me alone. I've got enough on my mind.'

There was then an interval. DS Bennett left the room and came back with cups of tea for himself and Brand. Inspector Moore also went out and returned a few minutes later. When he came back, Bennett again cautioned Hill (he said that he cautioned Hill before each interview) and the interrogation resumed.

Bennett began by reading McIlkenny's confession which said that Hill had had a bomb in his case. To this, Hill is supposed to have responded, 'He's told you the truth. I never thought he'd make a statement. He's a bastard like Hunter. You don't cross them.'

'McIlkenny says that you and he left your bombs in the Tavern in the Town,' said Bennett.

'We left them in the downstairs bar. I was that scared all I wanted to do was get out and get away.'

'Where did you leave the explosives?'

'Over the left-hand side of the bar under the seats.'

Inspector Moore is said to have asked how Hill's hands came to be contaminated with gelignite. Hill is said to have replied, 'It must have been when I was at Walker's house.'

'How many bombs were there?'

'I don't know, honest to God, I don't.'

Moore asked Hill why he had got involved in the bombings. Hill replied, 'It's obvious isn't it? I'm in the IRA. We all are and this was because of Jamsie and everything he died for. You wouldn't understand, but I never thought it would come to this. There was supposed to be a warning.'

'Who was supposed to give the warning?'

'That was nothing to do with me. It was all arranged before.'

At this point, Bennett is said to have asked Hill if he wanted to make a written statement. Hill replied, 'I have told you what I know, surely you have got enough. Dick has said it all and I just want to forget it. For God's sake leave me alone.'

On this note the interview is said to have ended. It was 1.10. It had lasted nearly two hours. The police said there were no further interviews with Hill. Since he signed no statement we have only the word of the three policemen, Brand, Bennett and Moore that this is an accurate record of what took place. Hill's position, then and now, is that this account was entirely fabricated.

According to Hill, only Sergeant Bennett was present when he and DC Brand arrived at the juvenile detention room. Inspector Moore was not there. The only other officer involved in the interview was DC Michael French, one of the two detectives alleged to have beaten a confession out of Power at Morecambe the previous day. Bennett opened the proceedings by asking if Hill was going to make a statement. Hill said he was not. Then Bennett said, 'You can have it the easy way or the hard way. If you don't make a statement, you are going round the walls again.'[1]

At some point, they were joined by DC French. He came over to Hill and put his hand on Hill's shoulder. He asked if Hill knew why they had been so long leaving Morecambe.

'No,' said Hill.

'Well I'll tell you. It was because Billy Power was finishing off his statement and I made him a promise.' French said he had promised to take Power's wife and children to a safe house outside Birmingham. He had just been fulfilling that promise. That was why he was late coming on duty. He would do the same for Hill's wife and children if Hill would confess. French is alleged to have said there was a crowd outside Hill's house and that, if he did not make a statement, the police would call off the officers who were protecting Hill's family.[2]

'I told him I was signing nothing,' said Hill. At this, French is said to have punched Hill on the back of the head and kicked him. French then left the room and Hill did not see him again.[3]

When French had gone, Bennett is supposed to have said, 'Around the walls again.' With that, said Hill, they began punching him in the chest and upper arms. Constable Brand kneed him in the thigh. They told him, 'We're going to get a statement out of you or kick you to death.'[4]

Eventually Bennett said it was lunchtime. He told Brand to take Hill back to the cell. Hill was given nothing to eat or drink.

Brand and Bennett came back for Hill in the afternoon. Bennett had some papers in his hand which, he said, put Hill in it up to his neck. The first was said to be Billy Power's confession. Bennett would not show it to Hill but he read extracts. There were references to bombs in plastic bags. Hill was supposed to have planted one of them. Hill said it was lies.

Bennett is then said to have produced two statements from Hill's wife, Pat. He showed Hill the signature. He read what he said were extracts, but he would not show them to Hill. In one of them Hill's wife was supposed to have said that he was in the IRA and that he had attended IRA meetings in the White Horse pub.

According to Hill, they then started abusing his wife and children. They called his wife an IRA whore and his children IRA bastards. They said that his daughters would grow up to be IRA whores. Hill had the impression that they were trying to provoke him. Brand is supposed to have said, 'Go on, You're getting mad, Take a dig at me.' The chair was on the floor where, Hill said, he had been knocked off it. He was told to pick it up. One of them then accused him of threatening a police officer.[5]

According to Hill, they told him that everyone else had made a statement, that the others were putting the blame on him, saying that he was the brains behind the organisation and the one who had made the bombs. 'Bennett said I should get my bit in now and put the blame on them.' They said he would ease his conscience by making a statement. Hill declined and was taken back to his cell.[6]

Billy Power was in the next-door cell and they were able to communicate. It was the first chance he had to talk with any of the others since the interrogation began. Power said he had been forced to make a statement admitting to planting the bombs. Hill said he had made no statement and had no intention of doing so.

It was dark when they came back for him. Bennett told Hill they had arrested Hughie Callaghan and that he had also confessed. This was the first he knew of Callaghan's arrest. Hill estimated that this third interview lasted about three-quarters of an hour and said he was again punched and slapped.[7] When this had no effect he was returned to the cells and offered a pork pie and half a cup of water. According to Hill, the abuse and threats went on all night. For most of the time sleep was impossible.

17

Hughie Callaghan was brought up from the cells at Sutton Coldfield at
11.20 on Saturday morning. His hands were swabbed by a forensic scientist and he was briefly interviewed by DS Higgins and DC Buxton.
According to Higgins, Callaghan described how he and the others met at
New Street, then he went very quiet and started to sob. 'He put his head
in his hands and said, "Listen, I shall need help. God forgive me. God
forgive me."' Higgins said he told Callaghan to compose himself and told
him arrangements had been made for him to be interviewed later that
afternoon.

Callaghan told the court a different story. Buxton, he said, sat at a desk
opposite him. Higgins was seated at a table some distance away. Buxton
took down his name, address and asked how long he had lived in
Birmingham. 'All the time he was doing this he was kicking me under the
table, in the shins on both legs, but mainly on the right leg. He kicked me
about a dozen times in all. When I examined my leg next morning it was
yellow and black.'[1]
    Callaghan said it was at this interview that he told them he suffered
from a duodenal ulcer and had to eat regularly. Higgins and Buxton said
he made no mention of the ulcer.
    The interview lasted only ten minutes.

Three officers came to interview Callaghan that afternoon. They were
Detective Sergeant Michael Hornby, Detective Sergeant Richard Bryant
and Detective Constable Davies. According to Hornby, it was a touching
scene. 'Callaghan said, "I want to confess. Mary, Mother of Jesus, help
me and forgive me." He then threw his arms around DC Davies and
sobbed on his shoulder. After some minutes I was able to console him.'
Then, according to DS Hornby, Callaghan sat down and dictated his
confession.

Callaghan recalled it differently. First, he said, he was told to take off his
clothes. (According to the police, this had happened the previous evening.) At first he was naked except for a blanket. Then they gave him the

clothes they had brought from his home and he put them on. Callaghan said that while he was still clad in the blanket one of the officers held a fist close to his face and shouted, 'You are going to make a statement.' At this Callaghan broke down and started to cry. 'I kept repeating to them, "Please don't beat me up. Please don't beat me up."'

'Not half,' the detective is alleged to have replied.

According to Callaghan, Hornby was shouting like a lunatic. 'If you don't make a statement, you'll get bashed around the cell.'[2] He mentioned Callaghan's daughter. 'Did you know your daughter uses the Mulberry Bush? You could have killed your own daughter,' Hornby is supposed to have shouted.

Later, said Callaghan, Hornby asked where he had put the plastic bags. He repeated the question two or three times, pushing Callaghan hard against the wall. One of the other detectives appeared to sympathise. 'That's not the way to treat him,' he said. He put his arm around Callaghan's shoulder and said, 'You'll tell me everything, won't you? I'm not like the others.'

Hornby then took a pen and paper and Callaghan started to ramble. 'I was in a state of shock. I do not know what I said. They said things to me, I agreed and they wrote it down. This must have gone on for about three-quarters of an hour. At the end, one of the officers put a pen in my right hand, placed it over the paper and guided my hand as I signed.'[3]

Callaghan's confession is just over one thousand words. The first part is an accurate account of his movements up to the time he and the others met in the Taurus Bar on New Street station. Up to here, the only part that Callaghan denied was saying that Johnny Walker was an IRA sympathiser and that he ran a tote for the IRA.

The confession goes on. *'Whilst I was in the bar I noticed that Walker and Hunter had got some white plastic bags. I hadn't seen them before this. When we were about to leave the bar Hunter gave us all a plastic bag with a bomb in and told me to go to the Mulberry Bush with him. I put my bomb on the main road side of the Mulberry Bush. That's the side where you can walk out of New Street station. Gerry took his and put it round the other side. After this Gerry and me went back to the station.'*

After this, according to Callaghan's confession, he went back to the bar in search of his drink. Finding it had gone, he went out again and saw Hunter going through the barrier. Callaghan bought a platform ticket and went with him to the platform. *'After a short while the other four came on to the platform. The train came and the others got on it and I waved them off.'*

The confession then lapses back into what Callaghan agreed was an accurate account of his movements. It concludes: *'When Gerry gave me the bomb he only told me to put it down. He didn't tell me to do anything else with it. I didn't want to kill anybody. I am sorry. I've never done anything like this before. I'm not even a member of the IRA.'*

There were now four confessions and each one added to the confusion. Like all the other confessions, except Walker's, Callaghan's said the bombs were in plastic bags, which conflicted with the testimony of the forensic scientists.

Callaghan was not specific about the number of bombs, but he suggested there were six. McIlkenny's and Walker's confessions said there were three.

Callaghan said that he and Hunter placed their bombs at different places outside the Mulberry Bush. Forensic evidence would later show that, if there were two bombs at the Mulberry Bush, they must have been placed next to each other. What is more, forensic evidence showed clearly that the bomb had been placed inside, not outside, the pub.

Power had confessed that it was he who planted the Mulberry Bush bomb. Callaghan said it was Hunter and himself. Walker said that Hunter was with him bombing the Tavern.

Gerry Hunter, it seems, was in two places at once.

18

On Sunday morning, Hughie Callaghan was collected from Sutton Coldfield police station and driven to Queen's Road. DS Hornby was driving. Callaghan sat in the back between DS Bryant and DC Davies.

For the second night running, Callaghan had hardly slept. At around ten o'clock other people had been brought into the cells. Sometime in the early hours of the morning he was ordered out of his cell and told to sit in a chair in the corridor. At one end of the corridor there was a barred door and beyond that two uniformed police officers. According to Callaghan, they kept him awake by shouting at regular intervals to the people in the other cells. Callaghan could not be sure, but he had the impression that the other 'prisoners' were also police officers and that they were trying to keep him awake.

Callaghan stated that there were four officers in the car, all in plain clothes. It was a Sunday morning, there wasn't much traffic. During the journey, Callaghan claimed, he said, 'You can't use that statement. I have been forced to involve myself and Gerry Hunter in something we didn't do.'

At this, according to Callaghan, Hornby slammed on the brakes. The officer in the front passenger seat whom Callaghan was unable to identify turned round and pulled a gun from under his jacket. He leaned over the seat and stuck it in Callaghan's stomach. 'You stick to that statement,' he said. According to Callaghan, they had pulled up near Salford Park which runs under Spaghetti Junction. There is a lake in the park. 'Let's throw him in the lake,' shouted Hornby.[1]

Hornby, however, told a different story. He said there were three officers, not four. None had a gun and the passenger seat in the car was unoccupied. During the journey to Aston, which took about fifteen minutes, there was no conversation and the route they took went nowhere near Salford Park. DS Bryant confirmed DS Hornby's account. DC Davies did not give evidence.

On arrival at Queen's Road, Callaghan was taken to an interview room and handcuffed to a chair. He asked for a biscuit and a cup of tea but this was refused. He had not eaten since before his arrest on Friday and the ulcer in his stomach was causing him pain.

Later, he was visited by two officers he had not seen before. They turned out to be DS Roger Ball and DS Raymond Bennett. Callaghan said he told them that the statement he had made was not true. They took no notice of this and asked, 'Who are the head men in all this, the captains, the brigadiers and so forth?'

'This is silly,' said Callaghan. 'We're not even in the IRA.' All he knew was that Walker and McIlkenny collected money and sold raffle tickets for the Irish Prisoners' Dependents' Fund. Callaghan stated he was not threatened during this interview but claimed he was out of his mind with worry and eventually agreed with Ball and Bennett that Walker was a brigadier in the IRA, that McIlkenny was a captain and the others were lieutenants.

On Sunday morning Paddy Hill also found himself being interviewed by two officers he had not seen before, DS Roy Bunn and DC Paul Matthews. As before, there is an absolute difference of opinion between Hill and his interrogators as to what took place. The following is DS Bunn's account.

According to Bunn, he introduced himself and DS Matthews, and told Hill they had come to ask him about his associates in the Crossways and White Horse public house. To this, Hill is said to have replied, 'Yes, sir, there is no point in telling any more lies I couldn't sleep last night through thinking about it.'

Bunn then asked about an IRA meeting at the White Horse. Could Hill remember who else had been there? Hill is supposed to have named James McDade, Gerry Young, Martin Coughlan, Johnny Walker and Dick McIlkenny. Young and Coughlan had been in custody since August, charged with earlier bombings.

Bunn asked who organised the raffles and dances held at the pub and Hill is said to have named Johnny Walker and 'Big Mick'.* He said he didn't know Big Mick's second name, only that he was high up in the IRA. He believed Big Mick worked with Johnny Walker. Hill is also said to have named another man called Mick† a six-footer, slim and in his late forties.

* A reference to Mick Murray who would be arrested later.
† A reference to Mick Sheehan also arrested later.

Bunn said he then asked Hill when he had last been to Ireland. Hill said he had not been back since 1960, whereupon Bunn reminded him that he had gone to Dublin in June to attend the Bodenstown celebration in commemoration of the Irish nationalist, Wolfe Tone. The trip had been organised by Sinn Fein. Hill is then said to have named others who had been on that trip who by this time were in custody, charged with causing explosions.

According to Bunn, the interview ended with Bunn asking the whereabouts of arms and ammunition. Hill is supposed to have replied 'I don't know, sir. That was always kept by Johnny Walker.' He was asked about the bomb which had been recovered intact at Hagley Road on the night of the pub bombings. To this Hill is alleged to have replied, 'Honest to God, I don't know nothing about that one. All I did was the one in the town.'

Hill, however, said that none of the conversation recounted by DS Bunn took place. Instead, Bunn showed Hill a statement made by Callaghan. Hill read it and said it was lies. Bunn said he wasn't going to kick Hill around the way the others had been doing. Hill insisted he knew nothing about the bombings, whereupon, according to Hill, Bunn's patience snapped. He grabbed Hill by the lapels and said, 'If you don't want to make a statement, just say so. But if I hear you say one more time you know nothing about the bombings, I will kick the fuck out of you.'[2] And there said Hill, his interrogation ended.

On Sunday morning, Billy Power received a visit from DC French who took him to be photographed. DS Watson took the photo. Power said French told him that the police now had enough to 'do' them: everyone except Hill had confessed and that Hill would in the end. He also said that the others were saying that Power had put the bomb in the Tavern.

Power was returned to his cell until two o'clock that afternoon.

Richard McIlkenny said he was taken upstairs on Sunday morning by DS Morris and DC Woodwiss. The clothes he had been given at Morecambe were stained with blood from his nose-bleed the previous day. Morris and Woodwiss produced fresh clothes – a sports jacket, dark blue trousers, a white shirt and a pair of shoes. Then they took him to be photographed. The police denied that he was photographed twice.

Hunter said he was taken upstairs by DS Millichamp and DC Bell, the two officers who had spent the previous day interviewing him. By now he was exhausted. It had been another bad night. He had been allowed to sleep only in short snatches. Each time he dropped off someone would bang on the door and he was told to stand up. Millichamp and Bell took him to an interview room upstairs. He was shown a copy of that day's *Sunday Mercury* and told to read it. It was full of pictures of Thursday's carnage. They then waved papers in front of him which they said was Callaghan's confesson. They said that all the others had made statements and they had landed Hunter up to his neck in it. They were saying he was the leader. According to Hunter, they were joined at some stage by Chief Superintendent Robinson, who said, 'Now young man, I want your word there will be no trouble in court in the morning.'

Hunter asked what he meant. Robinson said, 'The last lot we brought to court started playing to the gallery and turned their backs on the court.'* Hunter said he would recognise the court, but Millichamp seemed to misunderstand. He leapt to his feet and shouted, 'What did you say?' Hunter repeated he would recognise the court.

He was then taken back to the cells.

D S Millichamp agreed that there was a copy of the *Sunday Mercury* in the room. He said that, on seeing it, Hunter started to shake and cry. 'This was never meant to be,' he said. 'It has all gone wrong.'

As for the conversation with Harry Robinson. Millichamp – and Robinson – said that it did not take place. Robinson testified that the only time he had seen Hunter on Sunday was when Hunter was charged. Millichamp said he asked Hunter whether he would recognise the court and Hunter had replied, 'We can't. No I R A man can.'

Nora Power was cutting her nine year old daughter Breda's hair when the news broke. It was six o'clock on the Sunday evening. The television was in the corner of the room. On the news they heard that six men had been charged. Then the names were read out. Breda started screaming. That was how Nora Power learned that her husband had been charged with the Birmingham pub bombings.

All weekend Sandra Hunter had been hearing on the radio that five men were being questioned. She told herself it couldn't be Gerry and his

* A reference to the I R A men arrested in August.

friends. There were only four of them. She didn't know that Paddy Hill had gone too.

Sandra had not been completely straightforward with the police when they had questioned her on Friday. She had told them that Gerry had gone to Ireland on his own. She said later that she didn't want to involve anyone else.

It was not until the news appeared on television on Sunday evening that Sandra realised. Her mother-in-law rushed over and took care of their children while Sandra's brother, Trevor, took her to the McIlkennys' house.

Kate McIlkenny had not seen the television news. When Sandra and her brother arrived, they found Kate still waiting for Richard to walk through the door.

After the police raid on Friday morning, Kate had not gone back to bed. Just after seven, Johnny Walker's oldest daughter, Bernadette, had called to say that their house had been raided, too. At 8.30, Kate had called to see Theresa Walker. She found her being questioned by detectives, one of whom claimed to be head of the Bomb Squad. They ordered her into the bathroom where she was searched by a policewoman. That evening they had come to her house and taken a statement. Did she know Gerry Hunter, they asked.

'Yes.'

'Did she know Patrick Hill?'

'Yes.'

'What type is he?'

'A bit long in the mouth.'

'What's that supposed to mean?'

'You hear him before you see him.'

Did she know William Power? 'No.' Did she know James Callaghan? 'No.' (She didn't realise they meant Hughie.)

When the detective had finished the questions, she asked, 'Is my husband one of the men you are holding?'

'I honestly couldn't say,' he replied.

When Kate McIlkenny went shopping on the Saturday she noticed she was being followed. She was followed again when she went to mass on Sunday. That evening Sandra came with the awful news.

The police were back at Pat Hill's house on the Friday evening. They questioned Danny, the lodger. Where was he from? Scotland, he said. What part? Barrhead. What religion was he? 'I am an Orangeman,' he said. How long had he lodged with the Hills. 'Two years. These people have been very good to me.' But they weren't satisfied. Where had he been on Thursday night? Bridgwater in Somerset, he said. When they were satisfied with his alibi, they turned back to Pat. Did Paddy know James McDade? 'Yes.' Would he have gone to the funeral? 'Probably.' What would you say if I said your husband is in the IRA. 'I don't know.'

'That's not the answer I want.'

'Well I'm not as brainy as you.'

After they left, Paddy's mother rang. She wanted to know what was going on. 'Meet me at the Crossways,' said Pat. They met at about 10.15. Paddy's brother and two sisters came too. No sooner had they arrived than the police swooped. 'We want you,' they said to Pat. A police car was waiting outside. As Pat got in, one of the policemen put two fingers close to her eyes. 'We've picked up your husband with two sticks of gelignite,' he said. 'You'd better tell us everything or we'll kick it out of you.'

At the station, they told her, 'Your husband is in the IRA.' They asked if she knew the others. Johnny Walker was the only name she recognised. When they let her go a big detective came to the door with her. 'He's going down for thirty years,' he said.

At Lloyd House that evening, Assistant Chief Constable Maurice Buck addressed a crowded press conference. He was bleary-eyed from lack of sleep. 'I am satisfied,' he told the assembled journalists, 'that we have captured the men primarily responsible.'

19

The black maria carrying the prisoners to the Central Lock-up sped out of Queen's Road at 3.10 on Sunday afternoon. An officer with a shotgun sat in the narrow corridor between the cells in the back of the van. Car-loads of armed detectives travelled before and aft. Sirens wailed.

The convoy turned right onto the Lichfield Road, then joined the Aston Expressway and went down to Steelhouse Lane. The journey took only ten minutes and, before they knew where they were, the six Irishmen were being bundled into cells in the basement of Steelhouse Lane police station, which adjoins Birmingham magistrates' courts.

Chief Inspector Anthony Rawsthorne was the officer in charge of the Central Lock-up. A tall, balding man in his mid fifties. He should have been off duty that day, but had come in specially to supervise the arrival of the most important prisoners of his career. Security was tight. Raws-thorne said later, 'It was frightening. There were so many people wander-ing around with guns, including shotguns. I remember thinking, 'If one goes off, it could kill a lot of people.'

Rawsthorne ordered the men to be placed in individual cells, each sep-arated by an empty cell to make communication impossible. He said he also ordered that the six men be stripped so that their clothing could be searched. It was standard procedure for new arrivals at the Lock-up.

Chief Inspector Rawsthorne's evidence would be important. He was the first person to see the Irishmen after they emerged from three days in-terrogation at the hands of the CID. He said about them, 'They were absolutely terrified. I have never seen men so frightened.' On the other hand, he saw no obvious sign of injury except on one man, Walker, who had the beginnings of a black eye. 'I saw them all naked. I did not go into the cells and, okay, the light was not bright, but I am almost certain I could not have made a mistake. Except for the man whose eye was bruised, I could see no sign of injury.'[1]

In court the men insisted that Rawsthorne did not see them naked. They testified that they were not stripped on arrival at Steelhouse Lane and that, had they been, their injuries would have been obvious.

Billy Power said his lower lip was cut and swollen. There was a large

Such was the level of police understanding of the Irish Republican movement in Birmingham in the winter of 1973.

The IRA's mainland bombing campaign began in February, 1972, about a month after Bloody Sunday. A bomb exploded outside the officer's mess at the headquarters of the Parachute Regiment at Aldershot. Seven people were killed.

In March, 1973, four massive car bombs exploded in London. Two, parked outside the Home Office and Scotland Yard, were found and defused. The other two, outside the Old Bailey and the army's main recruiting depot in Great Scotland Yard, exploded. Forty-five minutes before the first explosion a voice with an Irish accent had telephoned a warning to *The Times* giving the registration number and location of all four cars. The Old Bailey bomb was not discovered until four minutes before it exploded – 147 people were injured, one later died.

To begin with, the police were highly successful in their hunt for the bombers. The suspect cars had been spotted entering the country and, even before the bombs exploded, ten suspected bombers had been arrested at Heathrow boarding flights to Dublin.

In April, the police scored another success. In Coventry they arrested a Catholic priest, Father Patrick Fell, and six other men, five from Coventry and one from Birmingham. It was the first sign that the IRA's bombing campaign was about to move to the West Midlands. It was also the first sign that apparently respectable citizens living and working in England were involved. Father Fell and three of the men arrested with him were later convicted of conspiring to cause explosions at arms factories in Coventry.

In mid-August, two small fire bombs ignited at Harrods. The IRA claimed responsibility and announced that others were on the way. On August 21, nine incendiaries were discovered at shops in and around Oxford Street. Only one exploded but central London was reduced to chaos.

The IRA's West Midlands campaign opened on August 29, 1973. A bomb exploded in the doorway of Lloyds Bank in Poplar Road, Solihull. Simultaneously another went off nearby, at the offices of the Burnley Building Society.

The next day incendiary bombs ignited at three shops in New Street. One – Freeman, Hardy & Willis – was gutted.

mark on his throat where, he said, he was half throttled at Morecambe by the unidentified officer with greying sideboards. He said his chest and stomach were marked by red blotches where he had been kicked. He had two bruises and several red marks on his arms where, he said, he had been punched and a large bruise on the back of his right hand where he alleged DC French had hit him with handcuffs.[2] He said there were large bruises on each hip, the one on the left being about nine inches long. His legs, he said, were also marked.

Paddy Hill said his head was bruised where it had been banged against the partition at Queen's Road. He had dried blood on his face which next morning he was told to wash off before going into court. His left ear was swollen and had been bleeding. His chest and upper arms, he said, were covered in bruises, and his right hip was marked. His testicles were sore from repeated kicking. His legs, particularly the left one, were marked below the knee and his right foot was blistered where, he alleged DS Bennett had stubbed his cigarette on the journey from Morecambe. These last injuries later turned septic.

Gerry Hunter alleged that his chest was marked from his shoulder to his waist by scratches caused by George Reade in the car as they were leaving Morecambe. He also said he had bruising under his right eye and a swollen lower lip.

Richard McIlkenny said that the upper part of his body, from his left shoulder across his chest, was covered by black and blue bruises.

Johnny Walker told the court that, apart from his black eye, he had marks on his chest and on his feet. On his right foot there was a blister where, he said, DS Kelly had stubbed a cigarette. His back ached from the kicks he had received, but he did not know whether it was marked.

Callaghan said he had bruises on his right shin where he had been kicked.

It was to be another sleepless night. Rawsthorne's deputy, Inspector Ray Cartwright, was in charge of the Lock-up until 9.30. The same team, DC Jennings and PC Coffey, were on overnight security duty. As at Queen's Road, Jennings had a shotgun and a .38 revolver, and Coffey had a revolver.

According to the prisoners, both men were in the habit of pointing their guns through the flaps on the cell doors. Hunter testified that every time he lay down he was ordered to get up and stand in the middle of the floor. Sometime in the early hours PC Coffey told him to stand on tip-toe with arms outstretched; 'I'm going to crucify you tonight,' Coffey is alleged to have said. Every time Hunter relaxed, Coffey would point his gun through the flap in the door and say, 'If you don't get back on your toes, I'll blow your fucking head off.' Later, said Hunter, Coffey made a noose from a piece of string and hung it above the hatch in the door. He ordered Hunter to bend forward, hands on knees, and keep his eyes on the noose.[3] For breakfast, they were given a sandwich and a cup of tea. Callaghan said there was urine in his.

DC Jennings and PC Coffey told a different story. Jennings said he visited the prisoners every half hour. He heard no threats or abuse and offered none. He denied threatening to crucify Hunter or making him stand with his arms outstretched. He said that, when a prisoner was awake, he always asked if there was anything he wanted and always the answer was 'No'. Coffey denied threatening Hunter with his gun. He also denied all knowledge of a noose.

At 8.00 on Monday morning the prisoners received a visit from duty solicitors, Ian Gold and Anthony Curtis. It was the prisoners' first contact with anyone from the outside world.

Gold and Curtis were young Birmingham solicitors. Gold was in practice on his own. He had qualified less than three years earlier. Curtis worked in his father's practice. Much of their work involved small-time criminal cases picked up through the legal aid scheme. Along with other young solicitors, they took turns to visit the cells at Steelhouse Lane first thing in the morning to offer their services to whoever happened to be in custody. It was quite by chance that they found themselves representing the persons charged with the pub bombings.

Gold and Curtis divided the prisoners between them. Gold took Callaghan, Hill and Power. Curtis took Hunter, Walker and McIlkenny.

Curtis saw Hunter first. The cell was dimly lit. The walls were a dirty yellow colour. Armed police officers stood guard in the corridor. Hunter was standing to attention when Curtis entered. Curtis said he was a solicitor and produced a legal aid form. He asked Hunter for his name, address, occupation and details of his income. As Curtis filled in the answers, Hunter unbuttoned his shirt and indicated his chest. Curtis could see a number of red marks running diagonally between Hunter's chest and navel. He asked what had caused them. Hunter said he had been beaten by the police. The police, he said later in court, had been trying to get him to make a statement. Curtis did not look closely at Hunter's injuries. Instead, he promised to arrange for Hunter to be seen by a doctor. Curtis completed the legal aid form and left. The interview had lasted less than ten minutes.

Next, Curtis saw McIlkenny. McIlkenny said, 'My chest is marked,' and made to unbutton his shirt.

'I haven't got time to see that now,' said Curtis, 'I'll get a doctor to examine you later.' He completed the legal aid form and left without seeing McIlkenny's chest.

Walker was Curtis's final call. 'This one's the brigadier,' said the policeman outside the cell. Walker was standing rigidly to attention and staring straight ahead. Curtis noticed at once that he had a black eye. When he saw Curtis, Walker became agitated and insisted that the policeman who had opened the door, remain in the cell. Curtis asked how Walker came by his black eye and Walker said, 'I fell down.' There was no point in probing further with a police officer present, so Curtis completed the legal aid form and left. At the time, Walker seemed to Curtis a very strange man. 'However,' Curtis later testified, 'at subsequent interviews, Walker appeared to be completely different from the man I interviewed that Monday morning.'

Walker said of that first meeting with Curtis, 'I thought he was a policeman come to give me another beating. I wouldn't talk to him.'

Gold spent only five or six minutes each with Callaghan, Hill and Power. All three complained of being beaten by the police. Hill and Power unbuttoned their shirts and showed him their chests, but Gold was too busy completing legal aid forms.

All he could say afterwards was 'I glanced momentarily at their chests and saw some discoloration'.

Just after ten o'clock, the six men were taken one by one before the stipendiary magistrate and remanded in custody to Winson Green prison. Each were accompanied into the dock by a CID officer. DC French escorted Power, holding him tightly by the arm. 'Don't start making a fuss,' he said as they walked up the steps to the dock. A fuss was the last thing on Billy Power's mind.

The court was crowded but, apart from Walker's black eye, no one noticed any sign of injury. Michael Posner, a reporter from the Midland News Association, was seated on the left-hand side of the dock. He had a clear view of each defendant and later testified that none bore any sign of facial injury. He did not notice Walker's black eye. George Clark, a court usher, was seated to the right of the dock. He did see Walker's eye, but saw no other sign of injury on any of the men. Everyone who saw them agrees they looked dishevelled, unshaven and dejected but in the circumstances that was hardly surprising.

Walker claimed he did try to show his injuries to the magistrate. 'I was in such a state I could hardly walk up the stairs,' he said. 'I tried to open my shirt and show the beatings, but they didn't want to know. The magistrate just said, "Take him away" and they nearly threw me downstairs.'

The hearing was over in a matter of minutes. Neither Gold nor Curtis attempted to place on record the alleged injuries to their clients. In the light of what was about to happen, this was a crucial error.

Outside the court a crowd had gathered, baying for blood. Women carried home-made placards saying, 'Lynch them' and 'Hang the IRA.' Chief Inspector Rawsthorne had to send out two dummy runs before he felt safe in letting the black maria with the six men leave the Lock-up. As the dummy convoys left, women rushed the van beating on the sides with their fists. There would be no hope of a fair trial in Birmingham.

As the six Irishmen were about to discover, their ordeal was by no means over. Already they had a hint of what was to come. Callaghan says that, as they stood in line earlier that morning, waiting to be taken up to Number One Court, a detective whispered, 'We've set up a good reception for you at the Green.'

LIEUTENANT JAMES PATRICK McDADE

Birmingham Battalion, Oglaigh na h-Eireann

Died on active service,
on enemy soil,
in the cause of Irish freedom
14th NOVEMBER, 1974

✝

Mother Ireland I have loved you with a love that showed no fear.

1. *Above* James McDade, who blew himself up planting a bomb outside Coventry telephone exchange on 14 November 1974. *Top* His funeral cortège leaves the mortuary in Coventry under heavy police escort. *Right* A funeral card commemorating McDade's death.

2. *Above* The Mulberry Bush after the bombing; ten people died there. *Right* The same pub before the bombing.

3. *Above* The Tavern in the Town after the bombing; eleven people died there. *Right* The same pub before the bombing.

4. *Above* Rescue workers carry a body from the ruins of one of the pubs. *Below* Roy Jenkins, the Home Secretary at the time, at the scene of the bombings the next day.

5. Photographs of the six convicted men taken before their arrest. *Left to right from the top* Hill, Callaghan, Walker, McIlkenny, Hunter, Power.

6. Photographs of the six convicted men taken on the second or third day in police custody. *Left to right from the top* Hill, Callaghan, Walker, McIlkenny, Hunter, Power. According to David Paul, a distinguished forensic doctor, all the men show sign of injuries.

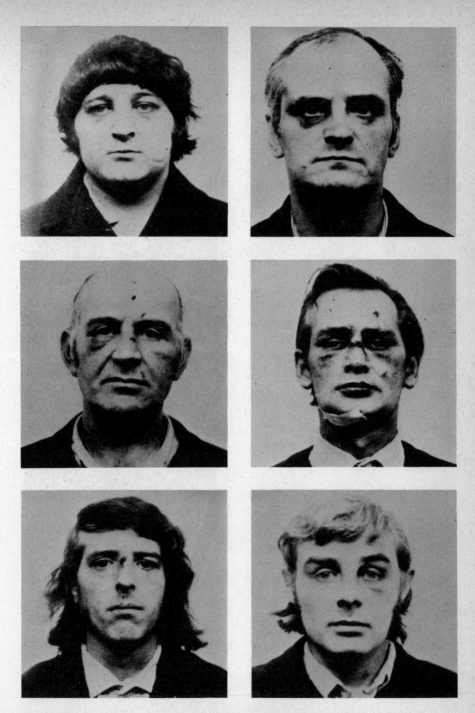

7. Photographs of the six convicted men taken three days after their admission to Birmingham's Winson Green prison. *Left to right from the top* Hill, Callaghan, Walker, McIlkenny, Hunter, Power. Fourteen prison warders were later put on trial for inflicting the injuries, but all were found not guilty.

8. *Above* On the day after the bombings factory workers in Birmingham staged walk-outs with placards calling for the bombers to be hanged. Some Irish workers had to be sent home from work for their own safety, and there were revenge attacks on Irish property. *Below* The scene outside Birmingham Law Courts as a van containing the six suspects leaves for Winson Green prison.

9. *Above* Detective Superintendent George Reade, the officer who led the investigation and interrogation of the six suspects. He has always denied allegations of ill treatment. *Below* Mr Justice Bridge, the judge who presided at the forty-five day trial. In his summing up he made no secret of his belief that the men were guilty.

10. *Above* Dr Frank Skuse, the forensic scientist who swabbed the men's hands at Morecambe police station hours after they were arrested. He later testified that his tests showed that at least two of the men had recently handled nitroglycerine. *Below left* Dr Hugh Black, who testified that Dr Skuse's tests proved nothing of the sort. His evidence was disbelieved by the jury. *Below right* Dr Brian Caddy, head of the forensic science unit at the University of Strathclyde. In 1985 he conducted new tests which proved that Dr Black had been right all along.

20

The atmosphere at Winson Green was electric. On the day after the explosions, eight Irish prisoners awaiting trial on bombing charges had been attacked by other prisoners while returning from exercise. Prison officers were also alleged to have taken part in the assaults. Solicitors Charles Royle and George Jonas had gone at once to the prison and seen the assistant governor, Donald Vuller. They reminded Mr Vuller that their clients were entitled to protection. Vuller had replied that the situation in the prison was very serious and the discipline of prison officers could not be relied upon. He said he had heard that several men had been arrested for the pub bombings. He hoped they would be taken elsewhere. According to Charles Royle, Mr Vuller went so far as to say that, if the men charged with the pub bombings were to come to Winson Green, troops might be needed to maintain order at the prison.

That was on the Friday. On the Monday morning at about ten o'clock Ivor Vincent, the officer in charge of security at Winson Green, was told to expect the six men charged with the pub bombings within the hour.

All weekend Principal Officer Vincent had been trying to convince his superiors that special arrangements should be made for prisoners charged with bombings. He suggested that two landings in D Wing should be cleared and used only to house alleged IRA prisoners. No one, however, would accept responsibility for clearing D Wing.

By Monday morning it seemed almost certain that the men charged with the pub bombings would be remanded to Winson Green. PO Vincent tried again. He cornered Deputy Governor John Jones and Assistant Governor Vuller and argued that two landings in D Wing should be cleared as a matter of urgency. Vincent's advice was not accepted. Prison routine must go on, he was told. All that Deputy Governor Jones would agree to authorise was the clearing of half a landing in D Wing. No sooner had this been agreed than PO Vincent received a call from the police at

* This account of what happened at Winson Green is based on allegations made by the six prisoners and on statements given by the prison officers to their solicitors. These statements were not made available to the court and their contents have not been published before. See also chapter 33 p. 213.

Steelhouse Lane to say that the men accused of the bombings would soon be on their way. Because of the angry crowd outside the court, a dummy convoy would be sent first.

Vincent immediately ordered that the reception area in D Wing be cleared. A group of fifteen prisoners awaiting transfer were locked in a large cell overlooking the reception area. Several prisoners engaged in cleaning duties were ordered to put out brown prison uniforms for the men and then they, too, were locked up. Only one prisoner remained free in reception – James Murphy, a 'trusty' serving nine months for car stealing, who was helping to collect the clothes of incoming prisoners in the reception office.

Outside P O Vincent ordered that the prison drive-way be kept clear. He then stationed three officers with dogs at intervals along the drive near the entrance to the D Wing reception.

A dummy convoy arrived at 10.30. There was then a wait of more than half an hour for the real thing.

The prison van carrying the six Irishmen swept through the gates of Winson Green at 11.07. It was accompanied by six carloads of armed detectives, two marked police cars with uniformed officers, and motorcycle outriders. Another five detectives rode in the back of the van, two armed with shotguns. The motorcycle escort and the marked police cars halted at the gates of the prison while the rest of the convoy drove through. George Reade's deputy, Inspector John Moore was in charge of the escort.

P O Vincent was waiting just inside the gate and he followed the convoy on foot as it made its way round to the reception wing. The prison van drew up parallel to the reception building and then backed up to within ten feet of the entrance. Detectives piled out of their cars and lined up to form a narrow corridor between the rear of the van and the nine steps leading up to reception.

By now P O Vincent was standing at the back of the van, behind the two rows of detectives. He was joined by Inspector Moore. The prison officers with dogs were standing nearby. A plump police officer in uniform had climbed down from the front of the van and disappeared up the steps into reception. This was P C Edwin Payne, know to his colleagues as Chunky Payne. He was the custodian of the committal warrants, documents which accompany every prisoner. If a prisoner is seen to be injured on arrival at a prison, the prison officer in reception makes a note of the injuries on the back of the warrant which the police officer would then be expected to endorse. PC Payne was also responsible for the Body Receipt Book which should be signed by the prison reception officer and in which any injuries would also be noted. On this occasion, however, neither the committal warrants nor the Body Receipt Book were signed, and in due course Chunky Payne would have some explaining to do.

The rear door of the van opened to reveal a policeman armed with a shotgun. It was unbroken and the detective held it pointing upwards with his finger on the trigger. 'I was speechless,' PO Vincent said later, 'I had never before seen a shotgun in a prison.' At the sight of the shotgun the dogs, who had been trained to react to guns, went wild, barking and straining at their leads. It was all the handlers could do to restrain them.

There was a pause. The detectives stood waiting in their two lines. The dog handlers were struggling with their dogs. Then someone gave the order to unlock the prisoners, and the first of the six Irishmen appeared at the back of the van. It was Paddy Hill. He was not handcuffed but, according to PO Vincent, left the van at speed. The prisoners were released one at a time. As one reached the top of the steps another was unlocked. According to Vincent, 'They appeared stiff, absolutely bewildered and completely terrified. They ran in a blind panic in the only way open to them.' Three of them fell heavily on their way up the steps.

As the unloading went on, said PO Vincent, there was a permanent banter from the police: 'They seemed to be trying to frighten or intimidate the men.' When Walker appeared, someone shouted, 'This one's the brigadier.' Hunter was referred to as a captain. Vincent lost sight of the prisoners as they disappeared through the door at the top of the steps, each accompanied by two policemen, but he could hear the muffled sounds of a struggle taking place in the small ante-room at the top of the steps. His view of the prisoners as they went up the steps was also obscured by the line of detectives in front of him, but, as one prisoner went up, Mr Vincent remembers hearing 'a noise which I immediately recognised as being similar to a head hitting a wall very hard indeed'.

Prison officer Derek Warner had a better view of the unloading. He was standing at the top of the steps and immediately recognised the first prisoner, Paddy Hill, as a former inmate. A plain clothes detective had Hill in a half-Nelson and Hill appeared to be struggling. 'This bastard's being awkward,' the detective said as he propelled Hill up the steps.

Hill stumbled and fell to his knees. The detective grabbed him again and pushed him through the door. 'Put him against the wall,' Warner shouted to the detective as he passed. Warner heard Hill hitting the wall. The officer then emerged alone from the ante-room. The next two prisoners were each escorted by two police officers. Warner stepped back to let them pass. 'As they came up the stairs,' he said, 'I heard considerable scuffling noises together with bumps and shouts'. One of the prisoners, later identified by Warner as McIlkenny, fell heavily and struck his face on the wall at the top of the steps. McIlkenny was then picked up and pushed inside with the others. At least two of the prisoners, says Warner, were pushed against the wall with sufficient force to cause them to strike their heads. By now the ante-room of the reception area was jam-packed with prison warders, prisoners and armed detectives. In the confusion Warner received a sharp kick on his left ankle. Whether it came from a prisoner or a police officer he could not tell. Someone shouted that a prisoner was missing. It was Hughie Callaghan, who had apparently taken refuge from the mêlée under the finger-print table just inside the door. He was soon found and thrust against the wall with the others.

At this point P O Vincent appeared and, alarmed to find the entrance to the reception area swarming with armed detectives, herded them out of the door and back down the steps. As he did so, he caught sight of Chunky Payne at the foot of the steps trying to make his way back up. When he saw the detectives leaving, Payne turned about and went back to the prison van, his body receipts unsigned. The detectives went back to their cars and the convoy drove out through the gate. It was clocked out at 11.15. The police had been inside the prison for just eight minutes.

Later there would be an inquiry into the manner of the Irishmens' reception at Winson Green. One by one, nineteen police officers who had been involved in the escort would testify that they had seen nothing untoward. Most of them also said they had seen no one fall on the steps. Only one officer recalled going into the reception and he said he left immediately. He did not recall seeing any other policemen there. D C Rex Langford, who escorted McIlkenny up the steps, said he had seen one of the men slip, but it was not McIlkenny. The evidence of Inspector Moore, who had been standing next to prison officer Vincent throughout the unloading, was typical. He said, 'Each prisoner left the van in a normal manner. None of them fell and I heard no shouts or abuse.'

The prisoners have a vivid recollection of their arrival at Winson Green. This was Johnny Walker: 'As I put my foot on the step from the van, I suddenly found myself in mid-air. I don't know if I was thrown out or kicked out. I next remember standing facing a wall with Hunter next to me. Someone was banging my head against the wall.'

Hunter said, 'I was facing a wall and some of the other five were there. I felt a kick which buckled my knees. I fell to the ground and when I got up someone grabbed my hair and banged my face against the wall, cutting my left eyebrow. Blood was running down my face. I was then called into reception.'

David Parling and Peter Bourne were the officers responsible for receiving new prisoners. They were seated at desks just inside the glass doors which separated the ante-room from the main reception area. It was their job to receive the committal warrants from Chunky Payne and to transfer the details onto each man's prison record, known as a form 1150. This was a cumbersome process, since each form was twenty-four pages long and had to be stamped several times with a rubber stamp bearing the legend 'Birmingham Prison'. The last page of the form is headed, 'Information of special importance including bodily injuries'.

As soon as he saw Chunky Payne appear with the committal warrants, Peter Bourne unlocked the glass door and let him in. Payne appeared to be in a hurry. He rushed up to Parling's desk, dropped the committal warrants and called out, 'Six bodies, no property, no cash'. And with that he was gone. Normally the police officer with the warrants would remain in reception to identify each prisoner and to obtain signatures in the Body Receipt Book. It was, Parling said later, the first time he had ever known prisoners to be handed over without a body receipt.

After five minutes, most of the preliminary paperwork was completed. Bourne and Parling were ready to receive the first prisoner. It was at this point that they noticed that Chunky Payne had not returned. Bourne ran to a telephone in the reception office and called the prison gate, but it was too late. He was told the police escort had already left and Payne had gone with them.

What followed was, according to prison officer James Bluett, 'an explosion of physical and verbal assault'. Bluett went on, 'I saw officers that I knew to be decent men lose control of themselves.' By now there was more than a dozen officers in reception. Some had no business to be there, but had come for a glimpse of the men who were to become Winson Green's most notorious prisoners.

The prisoners were called in one by one. Two of them, prison officer Parling recollected, stood stiffly to attention. They gave their names but could not or would not answer any other questions until shouted at and abused by Derek Warner, the officer who had been standing at the top of the steps during the unloading. The others, said Parling, were noticeably terrified. Some were actually shaking with fear. One was dripping blood from his face. Blood dripped onto the sleeve of Parling's white jacket.

When the first stage of the bureaucracy was complete, each prisoner was taken to a set of scales to be weighed and measured. Martin Bubb was the prison officer in charge of this. He later recalled bringing the measuring bar down hard on the head of one of the prisoners. After being measured each of the men were manhandled into the reception office where another officer, Pat Murtagh, was waiting to take their clothes. The trusty prisoner, James Murphy, was with him.

Walker was first. 'He ran blindly across in front of the desk and straight into the wall', Murtagh recalled. 'He even kept running after he had run into the wall, as though trying to run up it.' As Walker stripped, Murtagh noticed a number of marks on his body. A long yellowing bruise extended from his waist up across the front of his ribs. Murtagh had the impression that the injury was two or three days old.

According to Murtagh, at least two of the six men ended up on the floor of his office 'One man appeared to fling himself onto the floor in panic, terror and desperation.' Murtagh believes he heard the man mutter something to the effect that he had not meant to injure anybody. After seeing three of the men, Murtagh went outside and asked another officer, Brian Sharp, to phone for a hospital officer in view of their injuries. Murtagh said that none of the men were assaulted during their brief sojourn in his office. 'For my part,' he said, 'I contented myself with verbally abusing them'.

Brian Sharp was also in the reception office when Walker stripped off. Sharp said later, 'I saw bruises on many parts of his body. His torso was more or less covered. They were all colours. Black, blue, yellow, purple and most of them looked oldish.'

Paul Burton was a prison officer whose duties should not have taken him to reception that day but, hearing the commotion he went down to see what was going on. He arrived just in time to see one of the prisoners on cleaning duty (who had somehow avoided being locked up) punch

Johnny Walker in the face. Burton's statement says, 'I saw Walker spitting out some teeth'. It then goes on to say that he went and stationed himself across the corridor to prevent other prisoners attacking the new arrivals. A moment later he saw two prison officers, whom he refused to name, set about two of the Irishmen.

'Let's get these men away before someone gets killed,' said Brian Sharp to Pat Murtagh.

Gerry Hunter remembers being punched in the face as he was struggling to put on his prison clothes in the corridor outside Murtagh's office. Hunter said later, 'I got up, put my clothes on and one of the prison officers threw me against the wall.' Out of the corner of his eye he could see one of the others, either McIlkenny or Hill, picking himself up off the floor. Hunter also heard Callaghan screaming, 'Let me die, please let me die.'

Billy Power remembers being naked when he was called back to the table in reception to sign for his property. He was kneed in the leg for not calling the officer behind the desk 'Sir'.

Hill remembers a prisoner trying to strike him as he was getting dressed, but a prison officer intervened. By now more prisoners had appeared. According to Hill, 'The cons and prison officers were shouting, saying we ought to be hung. They said we were animals and dirt.' He was told to stand facing a low door leading to a bathroom. While he stood there he was punched and kicked by prison officers. 'One officer had hold of the back of my neck and slammed my face against the top of the door. My nose bled like a water tap. The officer told me to keep my head up because my blood was making a mess on the floor. When I held my head up the blood ran onto my shirt.'

Callaghan had collapsed on the floor next to Hill. The prison officers were shouting at him to get up. Hill recalled, 'They said he was lucky to have two legs to stand on. There were people in hospital with no fucking legs.'

Reception formalities over, the six men were taken upstairs and locked for fifteen minutes in a large cell while cells were prepared for them. By now Walker's face was covered in blood, some of it coming from his mouth. McIlkenny had blood running down his face and the front of his neck. Hill's shirt was red with blood. 'If this keeps up, I'll kill myself,' said Gerry Hunter.

As they sat there, abuse was shouted at them through the peephole in the door. Someone said, 'It's only just started, you bastards. You've got a lot more coming yet.'

After about fifteen minutes, the men were unlocked, given a chamber-pot and a bedroll each, and ordered upstairs to cells on the third landing which had now been cleared. They had to run the gauntlet of officers and prisoners. Paul O'Neill was one of several prisoners locked in cell D17 on D3 landing. He and fellow prisoner Dave Gleeson watched through the spyhole as the men were brought up. 'Gleeson said, "Good God, Jesus, look at this man coming up, he's covered in blood." I looked through the spyhole and saw a prisoner being put in cell 2. He was being roughly handled by two officers. A third officer opened the door and he was flung in. I saw that he had blood on his face. Later I saw the name Richard McIlkenny on the card outside his cell.' O'Neill saw another prisoner, probably Paddy Hill, being thrown into cell 6. 'As he was being run along by two officers he was kicked in the testicles by a third officer.' The next prisoner was brought along the landing by two officers and, said O'Neill, a third officer behind beating the back of his head.

Later, a number of prisoners were detailed to clean up the reception area. One of them was James Murphy, the trusty who had been helping officer Murtagh in the reception office. As he was mopping up, Murphy saw something on the floor. He bent down and picked it up. 'Here,' he said to Murtagh, 'a souvenir for you'. On the palm of his hand was one of Walker's teeth.

21

Gerry Hunter had been in his cell for about an hour when the screaming started again. He heard footsteps on the landing and the sound of a cell door being unlocked. Then more screaming. Someone was shouting 'Run, run, run you murdering bastard.' Another voice said, 'Get that fucking bastard down to us'. There was the sound of a person falling and then a voice saying in a tone of mock sympathy, 'Oh did you fall?' And then in a harsher tone, 'Get up you bastard'. From further away came the sound of splashing water. More obscenities. More cries of, 'Move, you bastard'. A door was locked. A voice from below called out, 'Next one, Mr Powell'. Another door was unlocked and the whole process was repeated. It was bathtime at Winson Green.

When his turn came, Hunter ran along the landing and down the first flight of stairs. At the bottom were two prison officers. One of them took a swing at him but he ducked and stumbled down the next flight of stairs. Five or six officers in short white coats were waiting for him at the bottom of the second flight. 'This way, you bastard,' they shouted and Hunter dodged past them as they flailed at him with feet and fists. At the end of the second landing he found himself in a bathroom. There was a bath two-thirds full of bloody brown water. An officer in a white coat screamed at him to get in the bath. He was about to undress when another officer came at him from behind and pushed him, fully clothed, into the water. It was ice cold. The officer who had pushed Hunter just stopped himself from falling in too. Hunter scrambled out again and undressed. All the time they were screaming at him. One of them sounded almost hysterical. While Hunter was in the bath, a third officer appeared 'It's just as well I didn't lose no relations in that bombing,' he shouted as he pushed Hunter's head and held it under the water.

He held Hunter down for three or four seconds and then let go. Hunter got out of the bath, grabbed his clothes and ran naked up the two flights of stairs back to his cell, prison officers kicking and punching as he passed.

Everyone got the same treatment. McIlkenny was picked up by his hair and tossed into the bath. He remembers seeing a handful of his hair floating in the bloody water. Hill had his head held under three or four times until he was fighting for breath. He left the bathroom so quickly that he forgot to take his clothes. Later someone came round with fresh clothes.

Geoff Abbott was the officer in charge of the bathing detail. He first ordered the other prisoners to be locked up in their cells. Abbott said later that he was anxious not to inflame an already delicate situation. He, therefore, chose with care the officers who were to supervise the bathing operation. He put Gordon Willingham and Paul Manders in charge of the bathroom. Willingham was chosen because, according to Abbott, he lacked natural aggression, Manders, a big man, 'because, despite his size, his disposition was mild and diffident'. Arthur Powell was the officer who unlocked the cells. Bill Green was stationed at the top of the stairs on the D3 landing and was responsible for escorting each man down to D2. That, according to Mr Abbott was the line-up. 'At no stage did I see any officer actually touch the prisoners as they went down the stairs.' Abbott said later. The only piece of aggravation that Abbott recalled seeing was what he described as an eyeball to eyeball confrontation between a laundry officer called Dolan and one of the prisoners. Dolan, said Abbott, pushed the man fairly hard with the flat on his hand. That was the only physical contact between officers and prisoners that Abbott witnessed. Other officers were more observant, however.

Arthur Powell said that, after unlocking the cells, he sent each prisoner along to Bill Green who escorted him down the stairs to D2 landing. 'As Green went down with each prisoner I saw him give them a couple of thumps on the body, in the stomach I think'.

Bill Green said he saw the first man down 'slapped about by various people'. Green said he merely gave this man a shove. His statement goes on, 'The next one came down and as he reached the bottom of the stairs, I landed him one in the stomach with my fist. It was a fairly hard blow.' There was a lot of noise coming from the bathroom. 'All I want to do is die,' the second prisoner screamed, 'Let me die. Just let me alone.'

Green said he didn't hit the third man. He just ran him down the stairs and along the landing, all the way to the bathroom, and threw him through the doorway. The laundry officer, Dolan, picked the prisoner up and dumped him fully clothed into the bath. Then, said Green, Dolan grabbed the prisoner's shirt front and thrust him up and down under the water. Green said that he and Abbott then hustled the officer out of the bathroom. 'Willingham,' said Green, 'was getting a bit carried away screaming and shouting.'

134

According to Willingham, 'When each of the men reached the foot of the D1 steps they were seized by Mr Abbott and Mr Hughes who punched, kicked and flung them along to us.' He went on, 'When they reached us, some of them at least got a thump in the stomach by Mr Manders [the officer with the mild disposition] and were then flung into the bathhouse by me.'

Mr Willingham was frank about his own role: 'I recall grabbing them by the scruff of the neck and threatening them. When they had their clothes off I kicked them into the bath. They were very roughly bathed and I continually harangued them. The very sight of them confirmed my opinion that they were fucking animals.'

The first visitor was the prison doctor, Kenneth Harwood. He was accompanied by Principal Officer Geoff Abbott who brought with him a batch of 213 forms on which he recorded details of the men's injuries together with their own explanation of the cause.

Dr Harwood's inspection would provide the first official record of the injuries inflicted on the men during their first four days in custody. For Harwood this would prove to be the unhappiest case of his career.

He found that Walker had a left black eye, cuts on his nose and right eyebrow. Four of Walker's upper teeth were missing and the sockets were still bleeding. On his body he had bruises on his right side, under the ribs and at the base of his spine. Walker also had an old scar on his stomach from an operation on an ulcer. The bruises and the black eye were, in Dr Harwood's view, between three hours and four days old. Asked how he came by his injuries, Walker replied that he had fallen down stairs. Harwood asked no more questions. He said later, 'Walker's injuries were consistent with what he was saying in the absence of anything to the contrary.'

Gerry Hunter was found to have cuts on his nose and left eyebrow, bruising on the left side of his chest and a grazed loin. The cut above the eye required two stitches. Asked how he came by his injuries, Hunter said he had fallen on the steps of the police van. 'These injuries,' Harwood noted, 'were consistent with what Hunter was saying in the absence of any other evidence'.

Richard McIlkenny had two black eyes, cuts on his nose and under his chin. The cut on his chin required two stitches. According to McIlkenny, Harwood said to him, 'I should be cutting your throat, not stitching you.' Harwood also noted bruises on McIlkenny's chest and left shoulder.

McIlkenny said he had slipped on the stairs on the way back from being bathed.

Hughie Callaghan had bruises on his right temple, left eyebrow and on his back, on his right ribs. He also had cuts on his back. Like Walker, he had an old scar from the repair of a perforated ulcer. Asked how he came by his injuries, Callaghan, too, said he had fallen down stairs. Again Harwood noted. 'These injuries were consistent with what Callaghan said in the absence of any evidence to the contrary.'

Paddy Hill had bruising on both arms, chest and left ear. Harwood noted that Hill also had a scar from an operation on ulcers. Like Hunter, Hill said that his injuries had been caused by a fall getting out of the prison van. Again Harwood accepted the explanation without question. It was to be another ten days before his attention was drawn to the injuries to Hill's right leg caused, as Hill was later to allege, by cigarette burns. By the time Harwood saw them, these had turned septic.

Billy Power had a black eye, bruising on his right upper arm, right hip and lumbar region. Billy Power was the only one of the six men to tell Dr Harwood that his injuries had been caused in police custody.

By any standards Harwood's examination could only have been cursory. He failed to note the dimensions of the bruising. He saw no sign of scratching on Hunter's chest. Photographs taken two days later showed two distinct circles about the size of ten pence pieces on Johnny Walker's forehead. Dr Harwood saw no sign of these. Photographs taken later also showed black eyes on both Hill and Callaghan which did not feature on Harwood's records. In due course Dr Harwood would have cause to regret that he had not taken more interest in the injuries inflicted on the six Irishmen.

There was another visitor that afternoon: Principal Officer Vincent who had been in charge of security when the men arrived. Mr Vincent was also responsible for liaison with the police. In contrast to everyone else whom the Irishmen had met in the previous four days, Vincent's manner bordered on the friendly. Make a clean breast of it, he advised each man in turn. If anyone wanted a quiet chat with a senior police officer, he could arrange it. None of the others need know.

It was an offer which everyone declined. Except Johnny Walker.

22

The six men in Winson Green were by no means the only Irishmen to be arrested in connection with the pub bombings. On the day after the bombings fifteen people travelling with McDade's coffin were arrested soon after crossing the border into Northern Ireland from the Republic. Among them was George Lynch, the Birmingham organiser of Sinn Fein who had accompanied McDade's remains on the plane to Dublin the previous evening. Lynch and his colleagues were taken to the notorious Castlereagh interrogation centre where they were questioned for seventy-two hours before being released. He was later made the subject of an exclusion order and never returned to Birmingham.

In Birmingham, police mounted a series of raids on the homes of known Republican sympathisers, some of whom had been under surveillance for several weeks.

The following Monday, police officers went to Garrington's Forging and Pressworks to question the workmates of Walker and McIlkenny. The mood at Garrington's was ugly. At a union branch meeting on the Sunday morning there had been talk of reprisals against Irish employees at the factory. There was even talk of calling on management to dismiss all Irishmen working at the plant. Several of Walker's workmates made statements which would later be used against him in court.

The police took particular interest in one workmate of Walker and McIlkenny – Michael Murray, a crane-driver, known to his mates as 'Big Mick'. According to the police, Murray first entered their sights on Sunday morning when Paddy Hill had mentioned his name to DS Roy Bunn as being one of a number of Irishmen who frequented Sinn Fein gatherings at The White Horse pub in Nechells. Hill later denied that he ever mentioned Murray.

Whether or not he did, it was unlikely to be the first time the police had heard of Murray. In June he had been among the party of Sinn Fein supporters who had travelled to Bodenstown near Dublin for the annual commemoration of the Republican hero, Wolfe Tone. Many of those who went regarded it simply as an excuse for a cheap weekend in Dublin, but the police had kept a careful watch on the Birmingham contingent and their vigilance had been rewarded. Among those who went from Birmingham were Jimmy Ashe, Gerry Young, Paddy Hill, Gerry Hunter and Johnny Walker. Ashe and Young had been arrested six weeks later and charged with the earlier series of explosions in Birmingham.

Mick Murray had also been on the Bodenstown trip. He was from Dublin and a staunch Republican. In his younger days he had been sentenced to six months in Mountjoy prison for selling Easter lilies without a licence. Easter lilies are the Irish Republican equivalent to the poppies sold in Britain on flag day, except that in this case the proceeds go to the IRA. One of Murray's friends later testified that he had seen Murray's children spit at the television set when the Queen appeared.

Murray lived with his wife and children in Watt Road, Erdington. He made no secret of his Republican sympathies. Along with Walker and McIlkenny, he organised raffles and the occasional dance in aid of the families of internees. His wife purchased the raffle prizes at the Soho Pool discount warehouse. It was to Murray that Walker passed the proceeds of his raffles.

Mick Murray was taken into custody at 2.45 on Monday, November 25. He was taken to Queen's Road police station where he was photographed, finger-printed and had his hands swabbed. The swabs proved negative for nitroglycerine but showed faint positive traces of amonium and nitrate. He was then taken to his home in Watt Road which was searched from top to bottom. The detectives who conducted the search and the subsequent interviews with Murray were DS Roy Bunn and DC Paul Matthews, the officers who had briefly interviewed Paddy Hill on Sunday morning.

At Murray's house the police found several items of interest. A receipt for £41 from Her Majesty's Prison, Birmingham, made out to a Mrs Sheehan of 92 Parkeston Crescent, Kingstanding. Apparently Murray had loaned her the money to pay a fine on behalf of her husband, Mick Sheehan. Bunn and Matthews also found a collecting sheet for *An Cumman Cabhrach*, the Irish Prisoners' Dependents' Fund. Walker's wife, Theresa and four of their children were listed as having contributed a total of fifty pence. Most interesting of all, a postcard was discovered, addressed to Murray in Mountjoy Prison, Dublin, where he had served his sentence for selling Easter lilies. The card was postmarked Westminster and said, 'Congratulations on your fine stand ... Irish race pledge our full support to you in your fight against the new Black and Tan terror which the Free State Hitlers are hell bent on bringing about.'

Mick Murray was soon to admit that he was a member of the IRA, but that was all he ever owned up to.

Kate McIlkenny, Sandra Hunter and Theresa Walker spent the Monday morning frantically searching for their husbands. They were afraid to go into the court because of the mob outside. Instead they went to Steel-house Lane police station where they were told that the men had been remanded to Winson Green. The women then phoned the prison and were told they could visit in the afternoon at 2.30. They were waiting outside the prison as their husbands were receiving their final beating on the way to the bathhouse. Nora Power and her brother, Eddie, were there, too. They waited, but were not allowed in. Eventually, they were told to come back next day.

Solicitors Ian Gold and Anthony Curtis had some difficulty trying to find doctors willing to examine their clients. It seemed that the Hypocratic Oath did not extend to suspected IRA bombers.

By now Gold and Curtis had more reason than ever to be concerned for the safety of their clients. At midday on Monday, in the corridors of the courthouse, Curtis had met Charles Royle, the solicitor acting for some of the IRA men arrested a few months earlier. Royle told Curtis that, as the men were being taken out, he overheard a woman prison officer say to one of the warders from Winson Green, 'We're counting on you to see they get what's coming to them'. The following morning he rang the prison and expressed concern for the safety of his clients. He was told that his concern would be noted. Five minutes later PO Vincent rang back. Mr Vincent made no mention of the serious beatings that had already been administered. Instead he asked if Curtis was making an of-ficial complaint. If so, an inquiry would have to be organised. Curtis said he was not. He merely wished to express his concern. He then went on to discuss with Vincent arrangements for bringing a doctor to the prison that afternoon. Still Mr Vincent gave not so much as a hint that anything was wrong.

On Tuesday morning at 10.15 a curious episode took place. Chief Superintendent Harry Robinson and Superintendent Andy Crawford later testified that they had visited Winson Green and were met at the gate by PO Vincent. Mr Vincent showed them into a room in D Wing and a few minutes later Johnny Walker was brought in. Walker said he could take them to a house where ammunition and detonators were stored. He did not know the address or the name of the man who lived there, but he could show them where it was. Robinson and Crawford then left, saying they would make arrangements.

Johnny Walker testified that this meeting never took place.

Sandra Hunter and the other wives finally got into Winson Green on Tuesday afternoon. They were allowed about fifteen minutes each, separated from their husbands by a glass screen. The warders did their best to make the visit as unpleasant as possible. 'Visitors for the bombers,' they called out in front of the other visitors. It would be like that for as long as the men remained at Winson Green.

Gerry Hunter was in a bad state. His face was cut and swollen. Sandra was crying. 'Who did that to you?' she asked. Gerry insisted he was all right. 'I fell out of a car,' he said.

Nora Power went in with Billy's brother, Tony. Billy had a black eye and his neck was bruised. His shirt was buttoned up to the collar. He didn't normally wear his shirts like that. Nora told him to open it. 'Shh,' said Billy looking at the warder standing beside him. 'He fell,' said the warder.

Kate McIlkenny went in with Richard's mother and brother who had come over from Belfast. Old Mrs McIlkenny nearly fainted when she saw the state Richard was in. 'Who did that to you?' she shouted. 'I fell getting out of the bath,' said Richard. After a few minutes, they were hustled out.

Johnny Walker was in a dreadful state when Theresa saw him. His front teeth were missing, his face was black and blue. He walked with a limp and stooped as though in agony. He told Theresa, 'It's not safe for you in Birmingham. Get yourself and the kids over to Ireland.'

Hughie Callaghan was in a daze when Eileen and Geraldine saw him. He had two black eyes and his mouth was swollen. He seemed very weak and had lost weight. He was wearing a prison jacket with a torn shoulder. He put his hands up to the glass screen that separated them and tried to speak. When the time came to go, Geraldine threw herself on the floor screaming, 'Oh, my dad.' On the way home they bought an *Evening Mail*. It was full of demands that the bombers should be hanged.

An hour after Sandra had gone, a prison warder came to see Gerry Hunter. 'Your solicitor's here and he's brought a doctor.' It would not be in Hunter's interests to see a doctor, the warder warned.

Hunter went downstairs. Curtis and the doctor were waiting in a medical room on the first floor. 'I don't want to see a doctor,' Hunter told Curtis. Two prison warders were by the door listening to every word. It was for Hunter's own good, said Curtis. The doctor would not ask questions about the origin of the injuries. Hunter still refused.

Curtis had rung half a dozen doctors before he found one willing to examine his clients. Eventually he called a medical agency who came up with Dr Alan Cohen. Curtis did not tell Cohen who his patients were to be until he arrived at the gates of the prison.

Johnny Walker and Richard McIlkenny did agree to be examined. According to Dr Cohen they seemed frightened and neither of them said much. A prison hospital orderly was present throughout the examination. On Walker, Dr Cohen found a three inch bruise under his left eye and a larger, paler bruise five or six inches in diameter over the base of his chest. Dr Cohen was no forensic expert, but he estimated that the bruise under the eye was one or two days old and the one on Walker's chest three or four days old. On Walker's forehead he noticed the two circular ring marks that Dr Harwood had failed to notice. He found other abrasions on the bridge of Walker's nose, over his right eyebrow, on the corner of his mouth and in the centre of his spine. He also found abrasions on Walker's right calf and on the base of his right big toe, where Walker later alleged that DS Kelly had stubbed his cigarette. These injuries, he said, were one or two days old.

Richard McIlkenny had a cut about one and a half inches long under his chin (which had been stitched by Dr Harwood). There was a dark bruise in the centre of his chest, about four inches in diameter. A dark, oval shaped bruise on his left shoulder, about five inches by three. Dr Cohen estimated that the bruises were aged up to two days old. The cut, he thought, was no more than a day old. He also found a number of superficial abrasions on McIlkenny's head, neck, right arm and hands. He guessed that these, also, were up to two days old.

Mick Murray was held at Queen's Road for thirty-six hours. For much of that time he was questioned by DS Roy Bunn and DC Paul Matthews. According to their note of the interview, Murray admitted being a member of the IRA and said that the money from the raffles and dances he helped organise went to dependents of internees and some went to the widow of a colleague at work. He was asked about Mick Sheehan, the man whose fine he had paid. Murray at first denied knowing where

Sheehan lived until Bunn showed him the receipt found at his home. Murray denied ever handling explosives and said he had been drinking and playing pool at the Church Tavern in Aston between about seven and nine o'clock on the evening of the pub bombings. Told that forensic tests had found traces of an explosive substance on his hands he is alleged to have said, 'Oh my God what am I going to do?' He declined, however, to make a statement. 'Just charge me and get it over with.'

On Wednesday morning, solicitor John Bradley received a telephone call from Assistant Chief Constable Maurice Buck who asked if he would be prepared to represent Murray. Why an Assistant Chief Constable should put himself out to find a lawyer for a man accused of being involved in bombings is unclear. When Bradley saw Murray in Winson Green later that day, the marks of beatings he had received were quite obvious. According to Bradley, 'He was like a punch bag. His cheek and eye were badly puffed up. As soon as I saw the state Murray was in I asked if he wanted to make a complaint. I told him to complain immediately or to never mention the subject again, and he never did.'

At 8.30 on Thursday morning the six Irishmen were brought back to the Victoria Law Courts for their second remand. Security was as tight as ever. Police motorcyclists preceded the prison van and it was accompanied by six carloads of armed detectives. Officers with shotguns rode inside. The corridors of the Central Lock-up were swarming with young detectives armed to the teeth. It would be like this each time the men appeared on remand. The security arrangements did not impress everyone. Inspector Rawsthorne said later, 'I think the CID chappies went a bit over the top.' The solicitor John Bradley, went further: 'Whoever was in charge of that escort must have been a lunatic.'

What happened next is disputed. According to Superintendent Andy Crawford, then head of the West Midlands Special Branch, Johnny Walker was quietly taken out of the cells and loaded into a police car. A blanket was put over his head and he was driven north towards Sutton Coldfield. The driver was PC George Cole. DC Rex Langford was in the front passenger seat. Superintendent Crawford sat in the back next to Walker.

When they reached the Chester Road the blanket was removed from Walker's head. Walker directed them to a cul-de-sac called Lime Grove, where he pointed to Number 22. 'That's the house,' he said.

'Are you sure,' asked Crawford.

'Certain'.

Walker was then returned to the Lock-up. He had been away about forty minutes and none of the others knew he was missing.

That is Superintendent Crawford's account of the incident. PC Cole and DC Langford tell the same story.

Walker testified that the incident never took place.

When the men appeared in court for the second time it was obvious to everyone that they had been beaten. Michael Posner, the journalist who had failed to see Walker's black eye on the first remand, noticed their injuries. So did George Clark, the court usher. Chief Inspector Rawsthorne ordered his deputy, Inspector Raymond Cartwright, to make a note of the men's injuries. In due course, the Assistant Chief Constable of Lincolnshire, Davis Owen, would be asked to inquire into the cause of the men's injuries. His report would absolve the police and place the blame squarely on the prison officers at Winson Green. It is a matter which, to this day, is the cause of bitterness between the prison service and the West Midlands police.

23

It was not until Thursday afternoon, over three days after he had first seen Callaghan, Hill and Power in the cells at Steelhouse Lane that the solicitor, Ian Gold, managed to find a doctor willing to examine his clients. Dr Dharm Adlakha was a general practitioner from Kings Heath. Like Dr Cohen, who had examined Walker and McIlkenny two days earlier, Dr Adlakha was not a forensic expert. His speciality was eyes.

Dr Adlakha saw Paddy Hill first. Hill refused to be examined. 'I'm all right, sir,' was all he would say. Hughie Callaghan also refused. Adlakha noticed only that he had bruises under both eyes.

Only Billy Power agreed to be examined. Before seeing the doctor, Power has said, he was asked several times by prison officers whether he really wanted to. When he insisted, he was told to make no complaints. A prison officer was present throughout the examination.

Dr Adlakha found that Power was extensively bruised. He testified that Power had bruising round his left eye, a two by three inch bruise on his upper right arm, two bruises on his left nipple, three over his epigastrium (lower abdomen) and a large area of bruising on the back of his right hand where, Power said, he had been hit with handcuffs. There were two large bruises on his left hip, one over his right calf, a cut on his left shin and another on his elbow. Dr Adlakha estimated that the injuries were about forty-eight hours old. This was not a lot of use since no one has alleged, before or since, that they were assaulted within the preceding seventy hours.

At the request of Anthony Curtis, who was in the prison seeing his clients, Dr Adlakha also agreed to examine Hunter. Curtis saw Hunter first and eventually persuaded him to be examined. Hunter was brought down with an escort of two prison officers. On the way, they passed a cell containing a coloured prisoner. 'See that spade?' asked one of the officers. 'He lost a half brother in one of those pubs. It would be terrible if he was let loose on you'. By the time they arrived at the medical room, Hunter had changed his mind.

There then ensued a tug of war between Curtis and the prison officers. 'He's seeing the doctor,' shouted Curtis. 'He doesn't want to,' said a prison officer. Hunter was taken away without being examined.

Gold later wrote to the Regional Director of Prisons expressing concern for the safety of his clients. He also asked to see the governor of Winson Green, but had to make do with an assistant governor, whose name he did not record. Gold told the assistant governor that his clients were refusing medical examinations, apparently because they were frightened of reprisals by prison staff. The assistant governor was non-committal. He said only that prisoners were not obliged to have medical examinations. They had a free choice.

Mick Sheehan's home was raided at 6.50 on Friday morning, one week after the bombings. The police had his address from the receipt found at Murray's house.

Sheehan is a tall, thin, gaunt man. He was born in County Kilkenny, but had come to Birmingham in search of work at the age of fifteen. At the time of his arrest he had lived in Birmingham for twenty-three years. He had a steady job operating a rolling machine in the IMI sheet-metal mill at Witton. Like Walker and McIlkenny, he was a regular at The College Arms and Crossways pubs. On a couple of occasions he had helped McIlkenny organise dances at the Crossways. One had been scheduled for that very night. Ostensibly it was in aid of two local men who had been off work through illness. There were those, however, who believed that the proceeds were destined for the family of James McDade.

Sheehan's role in the dances had been to arrange for the hire of a band and to sell tickets. He had sold twenty-five tickets for the dance due to be held that night and had had the bad luck to be seen calling at McIlkenny's house in search of more tickets on the day of the bombing. McIlkenny had been in bed, having just come off night-shift and so Sheehan had left empty handed. Following McIlkenny's arrest, the dance had been cancelled.

Sheehan was taken to Queen's Road police station where he was interviewed by Detective Inspector John Frazier and DS William MacDonald. 'How many of the men charged with the bombings do you know?' they asked. He told them he knew McIlkenny, Walker and Hunter. They asked where he had been on the night of the bombing. At work, he said. He had clocked in at 9.30. Before that he had been at home. He might have stopped off for a pint at the College Arms, on his way to work. He couldn't remember.

'Are you in the IRA?' asked Frazier.

'No, sir.'

'A lot of your friends are.'

Sheehan's alibi was checked out. He then made a short statement detailing his association with the arrested men. At 3.30 he was released.

Twenty-two Lime Grove, the house Walker was alleged to have pointed out, was raided at nine o'clock on Friday morning. The raiding party included DCs Rex Langford and Brian Morton. There was no one at home so they let themselves in. In a cupboard off the hallway they found a booklet published by Her Majesty's Stationery Office. It was entitled, *The Use of Explosives in Quarries.* On the cover was the name 'Mr Kelly.' The book contained detailed descriptions of detonators, fuses and blasting explosives together with advice on how to use them safely. At 9.30 the owner, Mrs Dolores Kelly, returned home and was surprised to find police officers searching her house. They showed her the explosives booklet and said they were taking it with them. They also took papers showing that her husband, James Kelly, had several years earlier changed his surname by deed poll to Woods.

That afternoon Morton and Langford returned to Lime Grove and arrested James Kelly, alias Woods.

Kelly had an unlikely background for an IRA man. He was thirty-two years old and came from a Protestant family in Portadown, Armagh. His father and brothers were members of the Orange order. He had come to England in 1963 to join the British army. A year later, while serving in Germany with the Royal Signals Regiment he had deserted and returned to England, changing his name to avoid detection. Between May and October he, too, had worked as a machine operator in the IMI sheet metal mill. The man who had taught him his job was Mick Sheehan.

Kelly was not surprised to see the police. 'I thought you blokes might be here,' he told Langford. On the way to Queen's Road he said, 'I want to see your Assistant Chief Constable. It's urgent. I think his name is Buck.'

'What makes you think Mr Buck will want to see you?' asked Langford.

'All I'm saying is that it is in his interests. I've infiltrated the IRA. I can give him the names of some of the men who did the bombings.'

Kelly did not get to see Assistant Chief Constable Buck. Instead he had to make do with Superintendent Crawford. Kelly told Crawford that soon after starting work at IMI, Mick Sheehan had been assigned to teach him his job in the sheet metal mill. After a while they got chatting about the situation in Ireland. Kelly had given no hint of his Protestant origins and eventually Sheehan had told Kelly that he had been a member of the IRA for sixteen years. Gradually Sheehan began to hint that he was mixed up in the bombings which were now taking place all over Birmingham. One day Sheehan confided to him 'We done the Rotunda,' which had been bombed several times that year. At first Kelly did not know whether or not to believe Sheehan, but he went out of his way to be agreeable because, he claimed, he wanted to worm his way into Sheehan's confidence. By now they were working opposite shifts on the same machine, only meeting briefly when the shift changed. One morning, as Kelly was going home, Sheehan asked if he would mind looking after 'a bit of hardware'. 'It's for the lads,' he said. Kelly agreed. A few nights later Sheehan handed Kelly a package wrapped in brown paper. Kelly opened it when he got home. Inside was an automatic pistol and eight rounds of ammunition. The pistol was oiled and ready for use.

Kelly kept the package for about a week. He told no one. Dolores would have gone spare if she had known. When Sheehan asked for the package, Kelly took it to work and handed it over as they swapped shifts. Two days later Sheehan brought the pistol back. This time Kelly held it for only a few days before Sheehan asked for it back. The pistol changed hands regularly for about two weeks. Kelly guesses he looked after it four times in all. He had the impression he was being tested.

On the last occasion that Kelly handed back the pistol Sheehan gave him a brown paper bag containing a revolver. 'Put that away,' he said. 'It's got a broken trigger.' One day Sheehan suggested they have a drink together at the College Arms. They met at about 8.15 on a Friday evening. When Kelly got there, Sheehan was with a man he recognised as Richard McIlkenny and a woman he took to be Kate McIlkenny. Sheehan suggested they go to the Emerald Club at Small Heath. He had already ordered a taxi. The McIlkennys went with them.

At the Emerald, Sheehan introduced Kelly to a man identified only as 'Big Mick' whom he later came to know as Mick Murray. It was a social evening. Nobody mentioned the IRA. Kelly and Murray chatted on and off about nothing in particular. When the time came to go home Sheehan said he could arrange a lift. 'We've got a bit of Army transport,' he said. Outside there was an old dormobile van with sliding doors at the side and two doors at the rear. Kelly climbed in the back with Sheehan, Murray and the McIlkennys. Kelly didn't recognise the driver or the woman in the passenger seat. 'Meet me in the Church Tavern, tomorrow lunch-time,' Sheehan said to Kelly as they dropped him off near his home.

Next day Kelly met Sheehan and Murray at the Church Tavern. Still there was no talk about the IRA. Murray just said that, if he had nothing better to do next Tuesday, he might like to come over a game of pool. In fact it was another week before Kelly went back to the Church Tavern. It was a Saturday evening in August. Murray was collecting money for the families of internees. He recorded contributions on a collection pad. Someone gave twenty pence. Someone else just laughed and said 'I'm not giving anything to your bloody IRA.' Murray laughed too. 'Better keep quiet about it,' he said with a smile, 'Or you'll get me arrested.'

Kelly, anxious as ever to ingratiate himself, chipped in fifty pence. Later that evening Murray asked if he would be willing to take a trip home to Ireland.

'What for?'

'To pick up a car. Bring it over on the ferry. You'll be told where to leave it.'

Kelly said he would be glad to assist but the subject was never mentioned again.

One Sunday evening in mid-September, Kelly was alone at home. Dolores was out and the children had gone to their grandparents. At about nine o'clock there was a knock on the door. It was Mick Sheehan. A grey J4 van with two men in it was parked outside.

'Is anyone else at home?' asked Sheehan.

'No.'

'Can you hold something for us?'

'Yes.'

Sheehan turned and called, 'All right, John.'

At this Johnny Walker appeared holding a blue canvas shopping bag and a white plastic bag. Sheehan took the bags from Walker and set them down in Kelly's hall.

At first Kelly told police that Walker had not spoken when he brought the bags out of the van. Later he claimed that Walker had said, 'Mick, tell him to put those away now.'

Sheehan pointed to the plastic bag and said, 'They're dets. Put them in a cool, dry place.'

As soon as they had gone, Kelly took the bags upstairs to the bathroom.

148

He opened the blue bag and on top there was an automatic pistol, clean and well oiled. Kelly's brief army career had taught him something about pistols. He removed the magazine from the butt of the revolver to check if it was loaded. It was not. There were two tins in the bag. The biggest had 'Weedkiller' hand-painted on the outside. The other was not labelled. Underneath there were five cardboard boxes. Each contained bullets. Three were full. The bag also contained a bandolier with eighteen shot-gun cartridges, a fuseboard with six circuits and a coil of wire. Lying loose in the bottom were several thousand rounds of rifle ammunition. Kelly glanced in the plastic bag. It contained about a hundred detonators, each individually wrapped in tissue paper. He recognised them from his HMSO explosives manual. Hastily Kelly repacked the two bags with everything save two bullets which he stored behind a ventilation block as evidence which, he claimed, he intended to show the police. He then put the two bags in the loft.

After about a week, Kelly began to worry that the loft would be too warm for the detonators. He went to his shed at the back of the house and took an empty one-gallon can of paint thinner. He cut round three sides of the can and opened the top. Then he went to the loft and removed the bag of detonators, placing it inside the can which he resealed with masking tape. He then hid the can in an old box in the shed and covered it with pieces of card. The blue canvas bag, however remained in the loft where, several weeks later, it was discovered by Dolores.

For some time before she made her discovery, Dolores Kelly had noticed a change come over Jim. He seemed to have become moody and agitated. They started having rows. At first she couldn't put her finger on the cause. Later she guessed it might have something to do with Micky Shee-han whom Jim had been seeing a lot of lately. It was not until the evening of Friday, October 18, that she found the cause.

Jim had gone to collect his cards from IMI. There had been a strike and he had decided to look for work elsewhere. While he was out Dolores searched for some personal papers which she had mislaid. Not finding them in the house, she decided to try the loft. She dragged a chest of drawers from her daughter's bedroom onto the landing, beneath the trap-door leading the loft. Standing on the chest, she eased open the trap door with one hand and groped inside with the other. It was then she came upon the blue canvas bag.

The zip on the bag was open. She put her hand inside and pulled out a small cardboard box labelled 'Kynoch', an IMI brand name. She opened the box. Inside were bullets, each about an inch long with a snub nose. She took another box. This one was full of smaller bullets. The third box contained bullets about two-and-a-half inches long. Next, she found the tin with 'Weedkiller' written on the front. It was heavy for its size. She shook the tin, but did not open it. She removed a small plastic bottle with 'Nasal spray', written on it. Then a couple of yards of black flex. By now she realised that Jim was in deep trouble.

Dolores didn't say anything to Jim. Not at first anyway. She put the boxes and the wire back in the bag, closed the trap-door and dragged the chest of drawers back to her daughter's bedroom.

Next evening, there was another row. Dolores had gone out leaving her baby daughter in the care of her son, Stuart. But there was a misunderstanding and Stuart had gone out leaving the baby unattended. Jim was furious when he found out. When Dolores came home he threatened to pack a suitcase and leave. Dolores told him not to be so silly, but Jim insisted. 'In that case,' said Dolores, 'You had better pack everything. Including what's in the loft.'

Jim Kelly didn't leave. He had already made up his mind to give the bag back to Sheehan. At lunchtime on the Saturday before Dolores announced her discovery, Kelly had searched out Sheehan in the Crossways and told him the bags would have to go. He was having rows with Dolores, he said, and might have to leave. Sheehan didn't argue. He just said, 'You'll have to see the big man.'

Kelly did not see Murray until the following week, Saturday, 19 October, the day of the row with Dolores. They met in The Yenton, a pub about ten minutes' walk from Kelly's house. Kelly told Murray the same story he had told Sheehan. Murray listened. 'You'll have to make arrangements,' was all he said. A week later Sheehan told Kelly to meet him in the car park of a pub called The Golden Cross at 8.00 in the evening and to bring the bags with him.

By now Kelly was storing the bags in his car, an old Hillman Imp parked outside his house. The car wasn't working and he had to take a bus to the Golden Cross. Kelly had put the bag of detonators inside the blue canvas bag with the zipper. Sheehan and Murray were waiting in the carpark. Kelly put the bag down beside them, Murray picked it up. 'Get yourself a drink,' said Sheehan, indicating the pub.

As he was walking towards the pub, Kelly saw an old white Jaguar move forward. Murray walked towards it carrying the bag. Kelly never saw Murray again. A minute later Sheehan came in and bought himself a drink. They drank in silence. Then Sheehan said he had to see someone. As he was leaving, he said to Kelly, 'Keep your mouth shut.'

That was the story Kelly outlined to Superintendent Andy Crawford on the evening of his arrest. He filled in the details later. Dolores corroborated his story.

Three hours after Kelly's arrest, Detective Inspector John Frazier went in search of Mick Sheehan. He found him in the social club at IMI. 'Hello Michael, remember me?' he said. 'It seems you didn't tell me the truth this morning.'

24

Theresa Walker and her family never went back to live in their house in Enderby Road. At the beginning of December she took six of her children to Johnny's relatives in Londonderry. Only the oldest daughter, Bernadette, remained in Birmingham, staying with her fiancé's family. Several days after her father's arrest she went back to Enderby Road to collect a letter. The house had been wrecked. Windows were smashed, the television had gone, and the gas meter had been broken into. The Christmas presents had been stolen, including two large teddy bears which Johnny and Theresa had bought for their two youngest children. A dustbin had been thrown through the front window and was lying on the living-room floor.

Nora Power's neighbours stuck by her. One sat all night with her after Billy's arrest became known. She later went to live with relatives in London. Eileen Callaghan and Kathleen McIlkenny had no problems with neighbours. Sandra Hunter and her family stayed on at first in their house at Wyrley Way, Erdington. Eventually, however, they were driven out. Paint was thrown at the house. Beer glasses would come flying over from a nearby pub. There was banging on the door in the middle of the night. Nooses were left hanging on the front gate. Slogans appeared on the walls, one saying, HANG IRA BASTARDS. Sandra and the children stuck it out until the following June. Then she took the children to Gerry's family in Ireland. When she came back the house had been looted.

Not until December 3, eight days after his clients had been admitted to Winson Green, was solicitor Ian Gold able to persuade Paddy Hill and Hughie Callaghan to submit to an independent medical examination. Once again Dharm Adlakha was the doctor. By now most of the bruises were beginning to fade.

Dr Adlakha reported that Hill had bruises under both eyes. He had three bruises on his upper left arm. The largest was three inches by two and a half. There were another three bruises on his right shoulder and two large areas of bruising on his upper right arm which was tatooed with his wife's name, Pat.

There was a bruise, three and a half inches by two and a half, on the left side of Hill's chest, and several bruises on his loins. Just below the knee, on his right calf, there was a septic wound about half an inch in diameter and a similar one above his right ankle. Dr Adlakha drew these to the attention of the prison doctor, Kenneth Harwood, who had so far failed to notice them. A course of antibiotics was prescribed.

Hughie Callaghan still had a black right eye and bruising around the left eye. There was a three inch bruise and five smaller bruises on the upper part of his right arm. On his upper left arm there was a three inch by two inch bruise. On the back of the same arm there was an injury that appeared to have been inflicted by a sharp instrument with nine teeth. A scab had formed. There were scratches on his left shoulder blade which were also scabbed. Other injuries included a five inch bruise on the lower part of his back and scratching on the left of his chest. There were also two large bruises and multiple smaller ones on his left buttock. Most of the bruises were superficial. The exceptions were those to Callaghan's eyes which, said Dr Adlakha, 'were worse than what I would classify as minor'.

Ten days after the bombings, David O'Connell, a senior member of the IRA, gave an interview in an Irish newspaper, the *Sunday Press*. O'Connell said it had not yet been established whether the bombings had been the work of a provisional IRA unit. It had, however, been established that the six men charged with the bombings were not members of any branch of the Irish Republican movement. The IRA would be holding its own inquiry to establish responsibility. O'Connell added: 'If we find that, as a result of our inquiries, there is a definite conclusion, we shall state so, irrespective of how unpalatable the truth may be.'

Murray, Sheehan and Kelly were charged with conspiracy to cause explosions. No specific explosions were referred to in the charges although it would later be alleged that Murray's finger-print had been found burned into the clock-face on a bomb that had exploded on July 26 at the offices of Harris and Sheldon, a firm of shopfitters in Aston Hall Road. This would be the subject of a separate trial.

The three men were remanded to D Wing in Winson Green, along with the six Irishmen already charged with the pub bombings. At first they appeared together on remand and they also took exercise together.

One day, several weeks after the arrests, Johnny Walker and Paddy Hill were walking together in the exercise yard when Mick Murray sidled up to them. 'Sorry to see you lads in here,' he is alleged to have said. 'Nothing went right that night. The first telephone box was out of order.'

Later, according to Walker, Murray said, 'Keep your mouth shut or I'll have you shot.'

25

The trial opened at Lancaster on June 9, 1975. Mr Justice Bridge presided. The son of a Royal Navy commander, he had been educated at Marlborough and was a former junior counsel to the Treasury. Later he would chair the Security Commission, the official body charged with overseeing the intelligence services. Mr Justice Bridge liked to involve himself in cross-examination and did not suffer fools gladly, as a number of defence witnesses were soon to discover.

Harry Skinner QC, led for the prosecution. He was forty-eight years old, eight years a Queen's Counsel and destined shortly to become a judge. It was not is first IRA trial. Two years earlier he had successfully prosecuted a Catholic priest, Father Patrick Fell, and five other Irishmen for running an IRA cell in Coventry.

Ian Gold had engaged John Field Evans QC to act for his clients – Callaghan, Hill and Power. Mr Field Evans had a reputation as a brilliant cross-examiner, but did not endear himself to his clients when he told them a few days before the start of the trial that, in view of their confessions, they hadn't a hope in hell. Billy Power was livid. He wanted to dismiss Field Evans on the spot but was eventually talked out of doing so.

Solicitor Anthony Curtis had engaged Michael Underhill QC to act for Hunter, McIlkenny and Walker. Within a year of the trial all three of the leading counsel – Skinner, Field Evans and Underhill – were appointed judges and Mr Justice Bridge had been made a Lord Justice of Appeal.

Defence lawyers are, of course, obliged to present the defence that their clients instruct, but they would be less than human if they did not form their own view of their clients' guilt or innocence. In this case there is no doubt that some of the defence lawyers shared the general belief in the guilt of their clients. One defence barrister says today of his erstwhile clients, 'If they had said they had placed the bombs but had no intention of causing such horrific casualties, then our defence would have been that they were not guilty of murder.' Instead, however, the six men stubbornly insisted on their innocence.

Despite Mr Field Evans' pessimism, the six Irishmen were in a buoyant mood when the trial started.

The move to Lancaster was a boost to their morale. Their treatment in Lancaster prison was in stark contrast to that in Winson Green. When the wives went to visit, they were met by an assistant governor who told them there would be no repeat of the treatment at Winson Green. As the trial progressed, according to the wives, some of the warders openly expressed doubts about the men's guilt.

Already, however, there was some dissatisfaction with their solicitors. The men and their wives felt that Gold and Curtis were not taking the case as seriously as the charges deserved. Power claims that it was only after three months, and after much pressing, that Gold was persuaded to take details of the alleged assaults at Morecambe. Power's suggestion that a newspaper advertisement be placed, appealing for witnesses who might have seen the men at New Street, was at first rejected by Gold. When one was placed, four months later, it was all but useless. Gold and Curtis had a difficult job. The climate in Birmingham after the pub bombings was such that no one wanted to be seen coming to the aid of the defence.

Curtis asked the *Birmingham Post* to publish an appeal for witnesses, but the editor refused. Eventually the solicitors hired a local private detective, Raymond Ketland of KK Investigations, to check out the men's alibis. Ketland interviewed barmaids and porters at New Street but, with one exception, was unsuccessful in finding anyone who remembered the men. He also interviewed workmates of Walker's and McIlkenny's and customers at the Crossways and College Arms in an effort to check out the men's alibis. He didn't have much luck. The assumption that the police had got the right men was widely held and no one wanted to get involved.

It was even harder to track down prison officers prepared to bear witness to the condition of the men on arrival at Winson Green. Curtis simply noted that 'attempts to obtain the cooperation of the prison staff appear to have come to nothing.'

The trial was held in the Shire Hall at Lancaster Castle, which also served as the prison. The court room was a cavernous, gothic chamber with high ceilings and masses of oak panelling. It was, in the words of someone who was there, 'one of those Majesty of the Law jobs'. The judge was a distant figure, seated high above everyone else beneath an array of baronial shields. Counsel were in a deep well at the centre of the court. The jury sat on one side, the prisoners on the other. The accoustics were abysmal and witnesses often had to be asked to speak up. A railway line ran nearby and occasionally counsel would pause to allow a train to pass. On the second day of the trial the court had to adjourn so that the new Sheriff of Lancaster's shield could be installed on the wall.

There was a flurry of public interest when the trial opened, but it soon died down. National newspaper journalists and television cameras attended the opening, but soon lost interest. Before long, coverage of the trial was left to a handful of agency journalists and local stringers. Many knew little about the background to the case and they were not very interested. They treated it as a straight reporting job. On most days it was worth no more than ten paragraphs.

Only two journalists took the view that there was anything more to this trial than met the eye – David Brazil of the *Irish Press* and Peter Chippindale of the *Guardian*. Even they had trouble persuading their news desks that the case was worth covering in detail. As early as December, Brazil had reported that the men had been seriously assaulted on admission to Winson Green and the story had been taken up by Chippendale and eventually by other national newspapers.

Brazil and Chippendale were the only journalists to make contact with the prisoners' wives and, as a result, their reporting benefited from a note of scepticism regarding the official version of events which was wholly absent from most other accounts of the trial.

Sandra Hunter, Kate McIlkenny and Nora Power spent the entire two months of the trial in Lancaster. They lodged with a friend of Nora's. By now they had abandoned their homes in Birmingham. Their children were all with relatives in Belfast.

The three women believed passionately in their husbands' innocence. For the six months before the trial they had lobbied every one who was prepared to listen. By a happy coincidence the Home Secretary, Roy Jenkins, was Kate's MP and the three women lobbied him in person. Their husbands had been framed, they told Jenkins. The police had beaten the confessions out of them. Mr Jenkins was courteous, but unhelpful. 'I sympathise with you,' he said. 'I really do, but my hands are tied. It's up to the courts.'

The wives also did their own detective work. With the aid of Sinn Fein friends in Birmingham, they put together a list of names of those rumoured to be responsible for the bombings. Gerry Hunter's brother,

Billy, who lived in Ardoyne, and Johnny Walker's brother-in-law, Brian Kelly, who lived in Londonderry, went to see Martin McGuinness, who was said to be a leading member of the IRA. McGuinness said he would see what could be done, but nothing came of this. Eventually, in desperation, Johnny Walker spoke out on his own – an initiative which backfired badly.

Walker was by now an isolated figure. With the exception of his eldest daughter, his family were in Londonderry. He rarely received visits. His wife, Theresa, was hardly seen during the trial and her absence was much talked about. Some said that maybe she believed her husband was guilty or, if not guilty, at least involved in some way. Pat Hill did not attend. Eileen Callaghan attended only the judge's summing up, but she visited Hughie regularly during the trial as she has done ever since.

Kate McIlkenny and Nora Power attended every day of the trial. So did Billy Power's sister, Patsy. Sandra Hunter was not allowed into most of the trial because she would later be called as a witness. Every day, after the court adjourned, the women would visit their husbands in the prison. To begin with they talked about the trial and how it was going. As the trial progressed, it was clearly going badly and the wives concentrated instead on cheering the men up.

'Nothing went our way at that trial,' said Sandra Hunter. 'Not one single thing.'

had several suitcases with them. Ms Vines put the time of this conversation at around 7.45, ten minutes before the Heysham train departed. It seemed a little late to be buying another round of drinks.

There was no sign of a statement from Pearl. Nor was there any sign of Ms Vines. Her statement, however, was read to the court, but, unknown to the court, she also gave a statement to Ray Ketland, the private investigator hired by the defence solicitors. In her statement to Ketland she put the time that she had seen the men at around 7.30. The difference in time was crucial since, if the men were in the Taurus Bar at 7.30, the time when they could have been away planting bombs had narrowed considerably.

Defence solicitors noted the discrepancy, but concluded merely that Ms Vines was an unreliable witness. They did not ask for her to be called. Nor did they track down her friend, Pearl. Charles Tremayne and I traced Julia Vines ten years later. She told us she had refused to testify because she was not certain of the time or even that she had seen the men. In spite of this, the prosecution still used her statement.

Day four was the turn of the forensic scientists, Donald Lidstone and Douglas Higgs, from the Royal Armament Research and Development Establishment at Woolwich Arsenal.

Mr Lidstone, who had thirty-six years' experience with explosives, had sifted through the ruins of The Tavern in the Town. He had also examined the remains of the bomb recovered from outside Barclays Bank on the Hagley Road on the night of the pub bombings.

Lidstone told the court that the damage to the Tavern was consistent with the use of about thirty pounds of explosives. He had recovered the remains of two General Time alarm clocks which indicated either a single bomb wired to two clocks or two separate bombs placed very close together. Other ingredients of the bomb or bombs included a four and a half volt Ever Ready battery and a Phillips-head screw. Similar items had been recovered from seven other explosive or incendiary devices placed in and around the Birmingham area in the sixteen days preceding the pub bombings. These included the bomb at Coventry telephone exchange which had killed James McDade. Lidstone concluded that all seven were the work of the same team.

The most significant part of Lidstone's evidence concerned the two sets of steel D-shackles he had recovered from the debris. They were, he said, 'of a type used in the handle arrangements of a carrying case'. In his view, 'Such a case could have been used to contain a high explosive bomb. The presence of two sets of shackles suggests the involvement of two separate, but similar cases.'

Douglas Higgs, who had sixteen years' experience with explosives, had made a similar discovery in the wreckage of the Mulberry Bush. He had recovered fragments of two alarm clocks, a tiny piece of battery, a piece of D-shackle and the remains of a small lock of the sort found on a briefcase or attaché case. He also recovered two pieces of perforated plastic, one of which appeared to be the remains of a Co-op carrier bag. In his view the plastic had not been used to contain the explosive. Had it been, he said, the plastic would have been totally consumed in the explosion. Mr Higgs concluded that there had probably been two separate bombs amounting in total to between twenty-five and thirty pounds of explosive and that these had been contained in 'a form of briefcase or attaché case'.

He was questioned closely on this by John Field Evans. 'You have no doubt, have you, that the device or devices were contained in some sort of suitcase, briefcase or hold-all'?

'That is my opinion.'

'A confidently held opinion?'

'Yes.'

Mr Higgs tossed one other spanner into the works. The Mulberry Bush explosion had, he said, occurred by the wall of the liquor storeroom just inside the rear entrance. There was not much room for doubt since there was a hole more than three feet wide in the ten-inch thick concrete floor. Billy Power, however, had confessed to placing it by the juke box at the foot of a staircase, well away from the site of the crater.

The evidence of Lidstone and Higgs presented the prosecution with a serious difficulty. Each of the four confessions before the court referred to the bombs having been in plastic bags and yet here were two experienced forensic scientists saying that this was not so.

27

Higgs and Lidstone were followed into the witness box by Frank Skuse. He was the most important witness of the trial. Were his tests to be discredited, the prosecution would have nothing but the deeply flawed confessions and circumstantial evidence upon which to fall back.

If, on the other hand, Skuse were not discredited, then the defence was in trouble. Confessions could be explained away by allegations of police violence. Association with known IRA men was not in itself proof of guilt. There was, however, no innocent explanation for being found on a train to Ireland with nitroglycerine on your hands three hours after a bombing.

Skuse, according to Peter Chippindale, was a good witness. 'He didn't go over the top. He certainly gave the impression that the tests were more conclusive than they really were, but he was not silly. He conceded quite a bit, but not the central premise.'

Dr Skuse began by describing the procedure he had followed: First cleaning his own hands with distilled water and ether; then swabbing his hands to ensure that he was not contaminated. He described the Greiss test and how he had applied it to each of the five men in turn. First he had swabbed their hands and then behind the fingernails. When he obtained a positive reading for nitroglycerine, he would then carry out a water swab for traces of ammonium or nitrate ions.

Skuse then went on to describe his findings:

Negative Greiss tests on Richard McIlkenny and Gerry Hunter.

A positive Greiss on Billy Power's right hand followed by positives for ammonium and nitrate on the same hand.

A strong positive Greiss from Paddy Hill's right hand. Positives for ammonium and nitrate from Hill's left hand.

On Walker, negative Greiss, but faint positives for nitrate on both hands and a further faint positive for ammonium and nitrate from the water swabs.

Back at his laboratory, Skuse carried out a further test, Thin Layer Chromatography (TLC), on the samples taken from Power, Hill and Walker. He also went to Aldermaston and had the samples put through a process known as Gas Chromotography/Mass Spectrometry (GCMS).

For a layman it is only necessary to know that TLC is regarded as being at least as sensitive as Greiss. GCMS is said to be at least one hundred times more sensitive than Greiss. These tests ought, therefore, to have confirmed Dr Skuse's findings at Morecambe. The results, however, were surprising.

The sample taken from Billy Power's right hand, which had proved positive on Greiss, proved negative for both TLC and GCMS.

The sample taken from Paddy Hill's right hand, which had produced a 'strong positive' Greiss, now showed no trace of nitroglycerine under either TLC or the one hundred times more sensitive GCMS. Skuse had then tested the sample from Hill's left hand, which he had not subjected to the Greiss test at Morecambe. This time, he said, the GCMS test proved positive though he offered no documentary evidence to this effect.

Both TLC and GCMS tests on the sample taken from Walker proved negative, as had the earlier Greiss test. Before testing Walker, Skuse had also swabbed his own hands and found that this proved positive for nitrate. In other words, the positive nitrate tests on Walker could have been the result of contamination.

None of this confusion dented the confidence of Dr Skuse. He told the court that, on the basis of the Greiss tests alone, he was 'quite happy' that Power and Hill had been in contact with commercial explosives.

'What do you mean by "quite happy",' he was asked.

'Ninety-nine per cent certain,' was his reply.

He was asked to explain why a sample which gave a positive reading on Greiss should have given a negative reading on tests that were supposed to be up to a hundred times more sensitive. Evaporation was one possibility, said Skuse.

Surely, it was put to him, you are preserving your sample with the greatest of care? 'As well as I can, yes.'

Were there any other substances which might produce a positive Greiss test?

'Yes, ethylene dinitrite. That, too, is an additive of commercial explosives.'

Apart from that? 'No'.

What about nitrocellulose of the sort found in varnished railway carriages and bars? 'No. It doesn't give the result in the cold. You have to heat it up.'

If nitrocellulose is heated to sixty degrees centigrade? 'The test was controlled. It never got anywhere near sixty degrees centigrade.' Room temperature, said Skuse, was around fifteen degrees.

Skuse was asked about the GCMS test on Hill's left hand, the only laboratory test which had proved positive. It involved taking readings from an oscilloscope, a television-like instrument on which a small blip appears indicating the atomic mass of the substance being examined.

Was there any documentary evidence that the oscilloscope readings were consistent with the presence of nitroglycerine? 'No.'

'I take it there is a possibility of human error,' suggested Mr Field Evans.

'I would not agree with you there.'

'Not even the possibility?'

'No.'

The questioning then turned to ammonium and nitrate ions, traces of which were said to have been found on the hands of Power, Hill and Walker. Wasn't it true that they could arise from a number of wholly innocent substances? 'Yes.'

First, nitrate ions. They could be produced by, for example, burning fuel? 'Yes.'

Car exhausts? 'Yes.'

Thunderstorms? 'Yes.'

Garden bonfires? 'Yes.'

Next, amonium ions. Could they not come from biological decomposition? 'Yes.'

From urine? 'My tests on a hand with a drop of urine proved negative.'

Dr Skuse accepted that ammonium and nitrate ions could come from innocent sources. He accepted, too, the possibility that he might have contaminated Walker's hands with nitrate. Even so, he would not be shaken from his conclusion: 'The result of my examination is consistent with the opinion that contact between the hands of Mr J. Walker with an ingredient of commercial explosives could have occurred.'

The arguments were complex. Judge and counsel alike expressed themselves ignorant on matters chemical. For hours the cross-examiners meandered back and forth between Greiss tests, mass spectrometry and thin layer chromatography, ammonium and nitrate ions, nitrates and nitrites. In the confusion, Dr Skuse was never asked to account for simpler matters such as the one and a half hour gap between his finishing with Paddy

Hill at around 7.30 and seeing Johnny Walker at 8.55. Nor was he asked if he had heard any of the sounds of violence which, it is alleged, was taking place well before he left the premises. Or if he had seen any of the West Midlands policemen in the corridor outside the matron's room where he was conducting his tests. He had, after all, been the only civilian to see the men in the space of three days.

There was no possibility that the jury could have absorbed the complex arguments surrounding Dr Skuse's evidence. At best, all they could hope to come away with was an impression. And the main impression was inescapable. Dr Skuse was an expert surrounded by self-confessed amateurs. He was experienced in the conduct of forensic tests and absolute in his confidence that there could be only one explanation for the positive Greiss tests: Billy Power and Paddy Hill had recently handled explosives.

Because most forensic scientists are in the employ of the Government, it has always been difficult to find scientists of sufficient stature and practical experience to stand up to Crown experts like Dr Skuse. This case was no exception.

To rebut Skuse's evidence the defence called Dr Hugh Black, who had retired four years earlier as Chief Inspector of Explosives at the Home Office. On paper he seemed a formidable witness. Much of his career had been spent advising government departments on explosives. In practice, however, Dr Black was a disappointment.

Greiss, said Dr Black, was not by itself adequate to detect the presence of nitroglycerine. There were, he said a wide range of other substances which would give a positive Greiss test. Among them nitrocellulose of the sort commonly found in lacquers, varnishes and paints on furniture in hotels and bars. Certain types of motor fuel, although not those available in petrol stations, might also give a positive Greiss test. So, too, might drugs prescribed for increasing blood pressure and certain types of fungicides.

It was put to Dr Black that Skuse had tested nitrocellulose and obtained a negative Greiss test. This would depend what type of nitrocellulose he had tested, replied Black. Old nitrocellulose would, in his view, give a positive result.

He was then asked about GCMS. Dr Black said that if he had obtained, as Dr Skuse had, a positive Greiss and a negative GCMS on a portion of the same sample, he would reach the opposite conclusion.

Namely that nitroglycerine was not present. Black was asked about Dr Skuse's explanation that the sample may have evaporated in storage. Not if it had been properly stored, he said.

He was asked about Skuse's one positive GCMS test, from the sample on Paddy Hill's left hand. Dr Skuse's finding was, said Black, inadequate. He had taken only one reading from the oscilloscope. He should in fact have taken three.

Dr Black was asked about the three negative TLC tests. TLC was, he said, at least as sensitive as Greiss. What would be his conclusion, he was asked, if faced with a sample that gave a positive Greiss test and a negative TLC? 'That there was no nitroglycerine present,' he replied.

In his statement, prepared before the trial, Dr Black had also referred to tests carried out on the clothing worn by the men at the time of their arrest. These tests had proved negative. Black commented: 'Had the men had contact with commercial explosives, then it would seem probable that traces of explosives would be transferred to their clothing and a positive test would have been obtained from any traces found.'

Dr Black had also referred, in his statement, to the pack of playing cards that the men had used on the train. These had been tested and found negative. He had commented: 'In my opinion explosive ingredients would be transferred to the cards from contaminated hands and a positive test would have been obtained from those cards.'

These seemed important points. They were touched on by the defence, but no one made much of them. As for the playing cards, they were exhibited in court and much later they would assume a vital importance. By then, however, they had disappeared without trace.

From an early stage in Dr Black's evidence, it was apparent that the judge did not find him a satisfactory witness. Gradually Mr Justice Bridge began to intervene in the cross-examination. At first he exhibited only impatience. As it became clear, however, that Dr Black had conducted no tests of his own and had virtually no practical experience, Mr Justice Bridge's attitude changed from impatience to outright hostility.

The following was a typical exchange when Dr Black was under pressure from one of the prosecuting counsel, Thomas Russell QC.

Mr Russell: 'Would you answer that specific question?'

Dr Black: 'I am trying to answer it specifically.'

Mr Field Evans: 'May I ask that the witness should be allowed to answer the question in his own way?'

Mr Justice Bridge: 'He is apt to introduce a great deal of irrelevancy and I do not blame Mr Russell for trying to keep him to the point, but if he wants to wander off and put his answer in a lengthy and elaborate way, I suppose he will have to.'

There were times when Mr Justice Bridge took over cross-examination on behalf of the prosecution: 'Your conclusions are not based either on practical experience or upon any text book, but upon your own theorising?'

Dr Black: 'No, because the tests have not been carried out to my knowledge'.

Mr Justice Bridge: 'Do you quarrel with the words, "Your own theorising"?'

'That has an unfortunate connotation which, I think, is not quite fair.'

During one of the judge's lengthy interventions, the unfortunate Dr Black was unwise enough to commence his reply before the learned judge had finished speaking.

Dr Black: 'I am sorry.'

Mr Justice Bridge: 'You go on and give your evidence in your own way. Do not accept any help from me.'

Dr Black: 'I am sorry. I thought you had finished.'

Mr Justice Bridge: 'I do not generally finish in mid-sentence.'

For all his tetchiness, the judge had a point. It seems incredible that the defence should attempt to rebut Dr Skuse's evidence with a scientist who had conducted no tests of his own, who had absolutely no experience of a forensic laboratory and who could quote no authority for his views. It seems incredible, too, that a scientist as distinguished as Dr Black should submit himself to cross-examination on a matter of such importance without on his own initiative attempting the very simple tests involved. Yet that is exactly what happened. Poor Dr Black was slaughtered:

'You have never swabbed anyone's hands?'

'No.'

'Have you ever carried out a GCMS test?'

'No.'

'You have never used that equipment?'

'No.'

'Ever?'

'No.'

'What is the extent of your practical experience in the sphere of forensic science?'

'I have never been in a forensic science laboratory at all.'

It would be another ten years before anyone bothered to put Dr Black's opinions to the test. And, as we shall see, the results would prove that, for all his ineptitude, Dr Black had been right all along.

28

After Dr Skuse, the trial was dominated by the confessions. The accused men had high hopes that their confessions would be ruled inadmissible. 'They simply did not believe what was happening to them,' said journalist David Brazil who was in touch with the accused through their wives. 'The men thought, "Surely they can't go through with this. As soon as the court accepts these confessions aren't the real thing, we can all go home". They were keyed up for the beginning of the trial.'

Several days after the trial opened, counsel for the defence applied for the confessions to be struck out on the grounds that they had been extracted under duress. This entailed a trial within a trial – an eight day hearing by the judge in the absence of the jury. It was a course that John Field Evans had advised his clients against, on the grounds that it gave police witnesses the opportunity for a dress rehearsal before they put their evidence to the jury. Mr Field Evans' advice was rejected, however, and the trial within a trial went ahead.

It was to be an uneven contest. Apart from the accused men, the defence had no strong witnesses to call upon. A handful of civilians had glimpsed them in the court on the Monday, but no one had more than glanced and no one had seen any more than the faces of the accused. There were, of course, the photographs taken on the Saturday or Sunday in Queen's road – shadowy polaroids on which even Walker's black eye hardly showed: to the untutored eye they were not much use. The issue was confused by the beatings at the prison. No one denied that the men had been seriously assaulted at Winson Green. Much depended on how far it was possible to distinguish between injuries inflicted on admission to the prison and any that may have been inflicted before. Here the evidence of the doctors was important. The prison doctor, Kenneth Harwood, had seen the men only three hours after admission. If anyone was qualified to assess the age of the injuries, it was he. The defence case would depend heavily upon him.

There was also Alan Cohen, the doctor who had examined Walker and McIlkenny the day after their admission to Winson Green.

Finally there was Dharm Adlakha, the doctor who had examined

Power three days after admission to Winson Green, and Hill and Callaghan a week later. He had expressed the view that Power's injuries had been about forty-eight hours old which made him quite useless as a witness since, by any reckoning, Power's injuries must have been at least seventy hours old by the time he was examined on Thursday 28 November. The defence did not bother to call Dr Adlakha.

In the end it came down to a straight choice. Either the police were lying or the accused were. It was for Mr Justice Bridge to decide where the truth lay.

The West Midlands police officers, who had travelled to Morecambe in the early hours of November 22, were called first. They all told a similar story. That they had arrive around 3.15. That none of them had gone near any of the accused until after forensic tests were complete. That the interviews had commenced at 9.30 and continued on and off until just before five when the accused were driven to Queen's Road in Birmingham. That no one had laid a finger on any of the accused, apart from a tussle with Gerry Hunter who had kicked out at Superintendent Reade and had to be restrained. That Johnny Walker's black eye had been caused by his bumping his head as he got into the car which was to take him to Birmingham. That each officer had made up his notebook either during or immediately after each interview.

Try as they might, barristers John Field Evans and Michael Underhill did not succeed in introducing so much as a chink of light between the stories told by the West Midlands officers. They were experienced witnesses. Their answers were confident and clear. They relied heavily on their notebooks. One or two had difficulty reading their notes, but that was nothing very remarkable. They were after all, describing events that had occurred seven months previously.

The allegations made by the prisoners were put one by one to the officers. They replied with short, crisp denials, rarely elaborating unless pressed. Peter Chippindale describes the scene: 'The police did quite well. They were not noticeably nervous. No one let the side down, but on the other hand no one said anything very convincing either. There was a definite undercurrent of resentment. They were short and uncooperative. They didn't volunteer anything. It was very much, 'Yes, we understand these allegations have been made about us', and then silence. Is it true that you hit people? 'No', and then another silence. It was really getting nobody anywhere.'

An extract from John Field Evans' cross-examination of Detective Inspector Moore is typical of the exchanges. Moore was being asked about his journey down the motorway with Paddy Hill.

'You sat in the front, did you not?'

'Yes, sir.'

'You had a gun with you?'

'I had.'

'You never spoke to him at all?'

'Never spoke to him on instructions.'

'That may have been your instructions, but you had plenty to say to him, I suggest.'

'No, sir.'

'And plenty to do as well, Mr Moore.'

'No, sir.'

'You hit him with the gun, did you not?'

'No, sir.'

'You twice put the muzzle of the gun in his mouth and pulled the trigger, did you not?'

'Completely untrue, sir.'

'You put it in his eye and did the same.'

'No, sir.'

And so it went on. Hour after hour. Day after day. As Peter Chippindale says, it was getting no one anywhere.

Superintendent George Reade was called. He was asked if it were true, as Hunter had alleged, that he had been drinking before the trip down the motorway? 'That is not true.' Had he gone to sleep during the journey with his head on DS Millichamp's coat? 'I did not sleep on the way back.'

Several Lancashire officers were called, including Sergeant Buckley, the officer in charge of the cells at Morecambe. He had heard nothing and seen nothing unusual, except the scuffle when Hunter was said to have kicked Superintendent Reade. His account of the incident precisely matched that of Reade and Inspector Moore.

Superintendent Ibison testified that the Birmingham police had not taken over the inquiry until 9.30. He had personally seen Power being taken up for interview in the CID rooms on the first floor. At no time had he seen any violence against any of the prisoners. He was asked to speculate about the identity of the tall, older officer with the greying sideboards who, it was alleged, had dragged Power into the small, dark room where he claimed to have been beaten by five or six unidentified officers. There were, of course, a number of older, senior officers on the premises at the time. Chief Superintendent Alf Collins, Superintendent Roy Lenton, Superintendent Frank Taylor, head of the Lancashire Special Branch. There was no suggestion that any of them had anything to do with an attack on Power, but Mr Ibison did not even refer to their existence and none were called to give evidence.

Constable Brian Pinder was called. He was the Lancashire officer responsible for collecting the prisoners' clothes and possessions. He had been in the matron's room and the prisoners had been brought to him one by one. He had started at nine o'clock and finished at 10.35. Walker had been first. Power followed at about 9.20. He had noticed that Power's underpants were fouled.

Then came the uniformed officers who had been in charge of the cells at Queen's Road police station where the men had been held from Friday evening to Sunday afternoon. Sergeant Eric Holland had been on duty, from 5.30 in the morning until 2.00 in the afternoon. He was followed by Sergeant John Wilkinson who remained on duty until 9.30 in the evening. The night sergeant had been Dennis Holt. Each testified that they had made periodic visits to the cells during the time that the men were in their custody. They had seen no signs of injury on any of the prisoners except for Walker's black eye. They had asked each man whether he had any complaints and each had either not replied or said, 'No.' No one had asked for more than a cup of water.

Chief Inspector Norman Gamble was called. He was in charge of the armoury at West Midlands police headquarters. His records showed that on the night of the bombings he had issued thirty .38 Special Smith and Wesson revolvers. Twenty-four had been returned by eight o'clock next morning. Five had been issued to the officers who had gone to More-cambe with Superintendent Reade and they had remained out until the Sunday. Another five were issued to the second batch of officers who had gone to Morecambe later on Friday morning.

During cross-examination of Chief Inspector Gamble, it became clear that the procedure for issuing guns to West Midlands policemen left a certain amount to be desired. In theory the issue of guns is strictly regu-lated. Each must be signed for in a register which also records the date and time of issue. The practice, however, was different. The first twenty-four revolvers had been signed out under the name of a single officer who had signed for them on a sheet of paper because the register was locked up and Inspector Gamble had inadvertently left the keys at home. Where guns had been signed for, the signatures were in most cases illegible and the times had not been noted. Nor was there any record of shotguns being issued, even though it was not disputed that officers on guard duty at Queen's Road and Steelhouse Lane had been armed with shotguns. So had several of the officers who formed the escort to Winson Green.

Chief Inspector Gamble was asked about blank ammunition. The subject was of interest in view of McIlkenny's claim that blank shots had been fired at him during the alleged mock execution at Queen's Road. Mr Gamble said that all ammunition issued from the armoury, live and blank, had to be accounted for. According to his records, none had been fired during the four days the men were in police custody.

McIlkenny had alleged that DC Woodwiss had fired the gun twice. Shreds of black material had been emitted from the barrel and floated down the floor. Chief Inspector Gamble was asked whether wax ammunition was issued for training purposes. It was, he said. It was prepared by removing primer from existing bullets and then dipping them in a tray of molten wax. Was this done at a factory, he was asked. No, it was done by the firearms instructor, Detective Constable Jennings. DC Jennings had been one of the armed officers on night security duty at Queen's Road.

Inspector Gamble went on to say, however, that wax bullets could only be fired by a .38 standard Smith and Wesson revolver. According to his somewhat limited records, all the revolvers issued over the period in question were .38 Specials which were not capable of firing wax bullets. What's more, said Inspector Gamble, his armoury stocked no blank ammunition capable of being fired from a .38 Special.

Even so, it was not without interest that Richard McIlkenny was able to describe symptoms consistent with the firing of a wax bullet, if such a thing had never happened. A small point. It was not pressed, but it should have sowed the seeds of a tiny doubt.

Sergeant David Prince, DC Fred Jennings and PC William Coffey were called. They were the armed officers on security duty and Queen's Road and Steelhouse Lane. Prince had been on duty on Friday night. Coffey and Jennings had been on duty on each of the three nights the men had remained in police custody. Both had been armed with revolvers and Jennings had a shotgun. They all denied threatening or abusing the prisoners. Each said he had heard no one else threaten or abuse the prisoners.

When it was put to P C Coffey that he had hung a noose on the door of Hunter's cell, he replied, 'That is untrue.'

Chief Inspector Rawsthorne, the officer in charge of Steelhouse Lane Lock-up, testified that he had seen all the men stripped. He had noticed no obvious signs of injury, apart from Walker's black eye. He declined to say that they were not injured. Only that he had seen no sign of injuries.

Ian Gold and Anthony Curtis were called. Their evidence was potentially vital since they were the only witnesses to have close contact with the men in police custody. Curtis said he had seen scratches and marks on Gerry Hunter's chest. 'They were parallel and they appeared to cover the whole area of his chest from the neck to about the level of his trousers.' They were, said Curtis, like scratches one would get from a briar bush after a day or two. He could offer no information about injuries to McIlkenny and on Walker he noticed only a black eye. He had asked about the black eye and Walker had replied, 'I fell down.'

Gold could not even recall the order in which he had seen his clients. Each had complained of being beaten by the police. Power and Hill had unbuttoned their shirts. 'I glanced momentarily at their chests,' said Gold, 'and saw some discoloration. I can put it no more strongly than that.' It was put to him that his recollection was 'pretty vague'.

'It is indeed,' he replied.

Dennis Hinton and David Little, prison officers from Winson Green, were called by the defence. Just why they had been called is unclear since their evidence was useless. They had been on duty in the Lock-up and had seen the men being taken up to court for their first remand. Mr Little had seen no injury other than Walker's black eye, which no one disputed. Mr Hinton claimed to have seen a plaster over an injury to McIlkenny's chin – a claim which not even McIlkenny supported.

Kenneth Harwood, the prison doctor, should have been the star defence witness. He had examined each of the men three hours after their admission to Winson Green. If anyone was in a position to offer an informed opinion as to the age of the injuries it was he. Dr Harwood, however, was a disaster as a witness.

He described the extensive bruising he had found on all the men. In every case he estimated the injuries to be between twelve hours and three to four days old. Black eyes, he said, took twelve hours to develop (Dr Cohen had earlier destified that they can develop within half an hour). Dr Harwood said he had not noticed the septic wounds on Paddy Hill's legs until they were drawn to his attention by Dr Adlakha nine days after the men were admitted. As for the cuts on the faces of McIlkenny and Hunter, both of which had required stitching, he was unable to estimate when they had been caused.

Dr Harwood's evidence was riddled with inconsistencies. Before long Mr Justice Bridge had taken over the cross-examination from the prosecution.

'Did you know,' asked the judge, 'that these men had appeared in court that morning?'

'Yes, sir.'

'If men had appeared in court that morning with faces such as you saw it would have caused some remark, would it not?'

'I would think so, my Lord.'

'Was it obvious to you that, at least the facial injuries you saw, had been caused in prison?'

'No, my Lord.'

'As the prison doctor, have you any responsibility for seeing men do not get injured in prison, or do you not care?'

'I care, my Lord.'

'Were you anxious to find out how these men sustained the injuries to their faces?'

No response.

Harwood was asked about McIlkenny's explanation for his injuries – that he had fallen on the way back from the bath twenty minutes earlier. Harwood had reported, 'These injuries were consistent with what he told me in the absence of any evidence to the contrary.' How, Harwood was asked, did he reconcile his acceptance of McIlkenny's explanation with his view that most of McIlkenny's injuries were at least twelve hours old? 'It was an acceptable explanation at the time without enquiring further into it.'

'How could it possibly be acceptable, having regard to what you say is your medical opinion?'

178

No response.

The question was repeated.

'It was an explanation which I recorded at the time. I did not necessarily have to agree with it.'

'Do you generally accept explanations which you believe to be medically impossible?'

'Not generally, my Lord.'

'Did you realise the explanation was hiding the truth?'

'Yes, my Lord.'

'You did?'

No response.

With the destruction of Dr Harwood's credibility, the men's only hope of being believed rested with their own evidence.

29

Billy Power was the first defendant to enter the witness box in the trial
within a trial. He came across as a shy, nervous man. He was, as his counsel pointed out, on tranquillisers. Repeatedly he had to be asked to speak
up. Peter Chippindale says, 'You couldn't help feeling that if Billy Power
had anything to do with the bombings, it wasn't very much.'

In a low voice, prompted by John Field Evans, Power recounted his
version of the interrogation at Morecambe which had resulted in his confession. He was asked to indentify the police officers whom he alleged
had beaten him. DS Watson and DC French were no problem since
their names were at the bottom of his statement. He was unable, however,
to identify the older officer with greying sideboards who he said had
dragged him into the darkened room and he could only guess at the identity of the half dozen officers who had beaten him there. One, he thought,
might have been DS Millichamp, but he could not be certain. (In fact
Millichamp had not arrived at Morecambe until midday on Friday and
could not, therefore, have taken part in Power's interrogation.)

Identification was a problem which dogged the defence. Some officers
could be identified from their signatures at the bottom of statements, but
others could not be recognised until they appeared in the witness box.
The men were being asked to identify officers, some of whom they had
only seen fleetingly, seven months after the event. Mistakes were inevitable. At one point, the judge ordered that the defence be provided
with details of all the officers on duty at Morecambe police station while
the men were in custody. It is unclear whether this was done. Certainly
many officers on duty in both Morecambe and Queen's Road police
stations were neither identified nor produced in court.

Power was asked about the statement at the bottom of his alleged confession: *'I have read the above statement and I have been told that I can correct,
alter or add anything I wish.'* The handwriting seemed firm considering the
beating he was supposed just to have received.

'That is in your handwriting, is it not?' asked Prosecution counsel,
Harry Skinner.

'Yes, sir.'

'It is a fairly firm hand that you wrote it in, is it not?'

'Yes, sir.'

'A firmer hand than Mr Watson's, who wrote the statement?'

'Yes, sir.'

'Do you remember initialling various alterations in the statement.'

'I can't remember, sir.'

'That is your initial, is it not?'

'I think it is.'

'In your handwriting?'

'I think it is, yes.'

Callaghan was next. His confession took the most explaining given that, even by his own account, he had received only one punch and several kicks and slaps in police custody. Apparently without much prompting he had volunteered that he and Hunter had planted the bomb in the Mulberry Bush, that Walker was an IRA brigadier, that McIlkenny was a captain and that the others were lieutenants. Thomas Russell QC questioned him:

'No actual violence was done to you at the time you were making the written statement?'

'No, my nerves just went. It was shock. I was shocked by what they were accusing me of.'

'At the moment of your arrest you were shaking with fear?'

'I don't deny that, sir. I am a nervous type of person and when people are shouting at me and bawling, I shake.'

'You involved Hunter?'

'Yes, sir.'

'Why?'

'Because it was just one of those things that came out of my head. It could have been any one of the five.'

'Why implicate an innocent man?'

'Because they were prodding me all the time.'

'They were not asking you to confess it was Hunter?'

'If you had four officers behind you, prompting you, you would say things you didn't mean.'

'Was any further violence shown to you between Saturday afternoon and Sunday morning?'

'No, sir.'

'And yet on Sunday morning you disclosed to the police the various ranks of the people you knew?'

'There again I was saying things I didn't mean.'

Paddy Hill was, by contrast, a good witness. Ian Gold says Hill was one of the best witnesses he has ever seen. Under cross-examination his answers were clear, concise, confident. 'The trouble was,' says Peter Chippindale, 'Hill gave the impression that he might have been capable of doing it. He looked the part. Rough, roly-poly, very Irish. The sort of guy who was always in bundles and chaos.'

Hill was asked what he thought of McDade.

'He was all right as a person.'

'What did you think when you realised he was planting bombs?'

'I was shocked.'

'In what way were you shocked?'

'I didn't think he would have anything to do with things like that.'

'You were a friend of his?'

'No, sir.'

'You knew his wife and family?'

'No, sir, I did not.'

'You were going to his funeral to pay your last respects?'

'No, sir. I was going to see my aunt and, as I have admitted, I would have gone to the funeral while I was in Ireland.'

'That is absolute nonsense'

'It is absolutely true.'

'He was a fellow soldier of yours?'

'No, sir, I am a soldier of nothing.'

Gerry Hunter was asked about his allegation that he had repeatedly been punched in the face by officers of all ranks, including Superintendent Reade. 'If you were punched repeatedly in the face, can you tell my Lord why your face was not reduced to a pulp by Sunday lunchtime?'

'No, I can't answer that.'

He was shown the polaroid photograph which the police say they had taken on Sunday morning. Hunter said it was taken on the Saturday. He was asked to point out his injuries. The photo was far from clear, but Hunter pointed to his eye and his lip.

'That is a fair representation of the state of your face after many hours of beatings with clenched fists in the face by different officers?'

'It is marked, isn't it?'

Hunter was asked why he had not complained about his treatment to

Chief Superintendent Robinson, the officer in charge of the inquiry.

'If I had, I would have got punished.'

'You have no reason to think Robinson would countenance this conduct from his officers?'

'He seen the state of us.'

'He has told us what he has seen.'

'His story and mine is different.'

Richard McIlkenny was the most impressive witness, according to Peter Chippindale. 'He was older than most of the others. He was straightforward, he had a stable background and he came across as a good, solid Birmingham resident.'

Johnny Walker was the last of the six to give evidence. He was not a good witness. His recollection was often vague and it grew more vague as the trial wore on. He said he had been unconscious for long periods during his interrogation. He said he had signed his statement with D C Sutcliffe guiding his hand. It was signed in many places. Was the signature his, he was asked.

'I don't know, my Lord.'

'Do you have any recollection?'

'No my Lord, not very much. I am very sorry.'

'How have you been able to say Mr Sutcliffe held your hand, if you have no recollection of signing the document at all?'

The trial within a trial lasted eight days. When it ended, Mr Justice Bridge had no difficulty in making up his mind. 'Many of the allegations made against the police are,' he said, 'of the most bizarre and grotesque character.'

If the defendants were telling the truth, he went on, 'I would have to suppose that a team of some fifteen officers ... had conspired among themselves to use violence on the prisoners and to fabricate evidence.'

The Lancashire policemen were complete strangers to the Birmingham officers. The Birmingham officers would, therefore, be taking the risk that if a single Lancashire officer was straightforward and honest, he would report them and put their careers in jeopardy. 'That,' said Mr Justice Bridge, 'seems to me a most extraordinary state of affairs.'

His Lordship then cited what he described as two dramatic instances which in his view 'proved beyond peradventure' that the defendants were willing to fabricate evidence. The first was Billy Power's suggestion that DS Millichamp had been one of the officers who had assaulted him in the darkened room when in fact Millichamp had not reached Morecambe. This, Mr Justice Bridge chose to regard as conclusive evidence of Billy Power's duplicity. In doing so he overlooked Power's clear statement that he could not be certain of Millichamp's identity. Nor was it clear why someone being beaten in a darkened room should be expected to identify his assailants seven months later.

Mr Justice Bridge's second illustration of fabrication on the part of the defendants, concerned Richard McIlkenny's allegation that a gun with blanks in had been fired at him in Queen's Road police station. The learned judge disposed of this in a single sentence: 'Having heard the evidence of Chief Inspector Gamble of the nature and character of the weapons which are available within the Birmingham police force, I am wholly satisfied that the story is a complete invention.' This, of course, was no proof that McIlkenny was lying. All it proved was that, faced with a conflict of evidence between a defendant and a police officer, Mr Justice Bridge could be expected to side with a policeman. Indeed he went on to say as much: 'All the police officers who gave their evidence of the circumstances in which the statements were taken impressed me as being straightforward and honest witnesses.'

Dr Harwood was easily disposed of: 'The substance of his evidence in the witness box is that in his medical opinion not one of the bruises he observed could have been caused after the prisoners arrived in prison. Not only do I not accept that opinion, I do not for one moment believe that Dr Harwood honestly holds it.' Harwood, said the judge, was a most unsatisfactory witness. 'I place no reliance on his evidence whatever.'

Dr Cohen, who had examined Walker and McIlkenny the day after their admission to Winson Green, presented only slightly more difficulty. The judge accepted that he was an honest witness. He had testified that almost all the bruises he had seen were up to two days old. He apparently included among these Walker's black eye which, everyone accepted, was four days old by the time Dr Cohen examined Walker. The only exception to Dr Cohen's belief that the injuries were no more than two days old was a large pale bruise over the base of Walker's chest which, Dr Cohen estimated, was at least three or four days old.

Dr Cohen's belief that Walker's black eye had been inflicted within the two previous days ought, if nothing else, to have alerted Mr Justice Bridge to the difficulties of estimating the age of injuries. Instead, however, he

184

chose to accept Dr Cohen's evidence which was, he said, entirely consistent with the injuries having been inflicted the previous day.

The only remaining problem was the large bruise on Walker's chest, diagnosed by Dr Cohen as being three or four days old. Here the judge engaged in some deft footwork. Having accepted Dr Cohen's evidence where it was consistent with the prosecution case, he simply declined to accept it where it disagreed. 'That is his opinion,' said the judge. 'I am sure he honestly entertains it, but such opinions must in the nature of the case be approximate and not precise. It does not seem to me that the opinion of Dr Cohen is such in relation to the age of that single bruise as to raise a doubt in my mind about the voluntary character of Walker's statements.' As for Walker's black eye, he would return to that later.

The only other problem was the evidence of the two solicitors, Ian Gold and Anthony Curtis. Vague and woefully inadequate though their observations may have been, there was no doubt that they had seen something. Unlike Dr Harwood and the six defendants, the two solicitors could not easily be dismissed as liars. The evidence of Gold and Curtis had, confessed the judge, troubled him the most. They were, he said, transparently honest, fair and careful witnesses. 'I accept their evidence without any hesitation.' With one leap, however, the learned judge extricated himself from the implications. Such injuries as Gold and Curtis had seen could, he said, have been self-inflicted. It was by no means unheard of for men who have confessed to serious crimes later to allege that their confessions had been beaten out of them. There was nothing inherently improbable, said Mr Justice Bridge, that by Monday morning the men had taken a decision to allege that they had been beaten. 'If by that time they had decided to allege that they had been beaten up, it would not be wholly surprising if, to give some colour to that allegation, they were anxious to have something to show their solicitors in support of it. It is quite apparent that some scratching type of discoloration upon the chest is a very easy mark for man to produce on his own body.'

Quite so, but why should four out of six men, who had no opportunity to communicate with one another, more or less simultaneously allege that they had been beaten? Particularly when two of them – Hunter and Hill – had no confessions to discredit. These were matters that Mr Justice Bridge did not address. He simply pronounced himself wholly satisfied that the confessions were genuine and adjourned for lunch.

When he returned, he was reminded that he had forgotten to explain Walker's black eye, which nobody alleged was self-inflicted and which everyone agreed had occurred on the Friday. The police witnesses said Walker had hit his head while getting into a car that was to take him from Morecambe to Birmingham. Walker said it had been caused by a blow inflicted by DC Sutcliffe during the journey from Morecambe.

Surprisingly, Mr Justice Bridge did not take the easy option of simply accepting the police evidence and rejecting Walker's. Instead he recalled Walker's brief interview with Curtis in the cells at Steelhouse Lane. Curtis, in the presence of DC Jennings, had asked Walker how he came by his black eye and Walker had replied, 'I fell.' 'That,' concluded Mr Justice Bridge, 'seems to me to have been a truthful reply and it removes any doubt that I might otherwise entertain as to how that injury was sustained.'

It was the only moment in the entire forty-five days of the trial when anything said by Johnny Walker was taken at face value.

30

After the confessions were ruled admissible, the men's demeanour became defeatist. They knew now that the odds against them had lengthened and they began to seek other ways proving their innocence. Johnny Walker announced he was going on hunger strike. It lasted only a few days and, if anything, only tended to confirm suspicions that he was an IRA man.

Walker also took another exceptional step. He wrote two letters to the Home Secretary, Roy Jenkins. The first was dated 2 July, 1975, three weeks into the trial. He dictated the letter to a prison officer. In it he described how one Saturday afternoon the previous year he had run into James McDade in the Kingstanding Ex-Servicemen's Club. McDade had a cloth bag with him which, he said, contained radios and table lighters for raffling. He asked Walker to look after it for him and said he would call for it later that night. Walker took the bag home and put it in the wardrobe in his bedroom.

McDade did not come for the bag that night. Next day, Sunday, Walker went to work. He was on the early shift and when he got home at about half past two the bag was still uncollected. At about eight o'clock that evening, as Walker was setting out for the Crossways, Mick Sheehan called for the bag. He had a van outside and Walker asked for a lift to the Crossways. There was another man driving the van whom Walker recognised as Jimmy Gavin, a regular at the Emerald Club in Small Heath. They set off in the van, but did not go directly to the Crossways. Instead they went towards the Chester Road. Sheehan said he had a call to make at a mate's house. They pulled up outside a council house in a cul de sac called Lime Grove. Sheehan got out and knocked on the door and then called to Walker to bring the bag over. Walker got out of the van and handed over the bag. Sheehan introduced him to the man whose house they were visiting. His name was James Kelly.

Two weeks later, said Walker in his letter to the Home Secretary, Sheehan had approached him in the Crossways and asked, 'Do you know what was in that bag?'

'Radios and lighters,' said Walker.

'You are in for a surprise because Kelly told me it was guns and ammunition'.

That was Walker's account of the James Kelly incident.

Walker's first letter to the Home Secretary also recounted the conversation he claimed to have had with Mick Murray in the prison exercise yard at Winson Green in which, he said, Murray had admitted being involved in the pub bombings. Murray had warned him to say nothing or he would be shot. Walker's letter went on, 'The next day he approached me again and said, "Remember the conversation we had yesterday? Well, not only will you get it, but your wife and family will go to bed one night and the house will go up."' That, said Walker, was why he had kept quiet for so long. His letter concluded, 'Will you please have these facts investigated so that justice in this trial may be done?'

Later, during the trial, Walker dictated a second, undated, letter to the Home Secretary. It began, 'Since I submitted my last petition I have received more information. I can now say for sure that Michael Murray was the ring-leader of the group of men who planted the bombs in the Birmingham pubs.' The letter went on to name three other men who were said to have been involved in the bombings:

Jimmy Gavin, the man who had driven the van on the visit to Kelly's house. Gavin was said to be aged about forty, to be about five feet seven inches tall, with dark wavy hair and glasses. He had five children and was now living in Shannon in Ireland.

'Belfast Jimmy', a nickname for a man said to be only five feet tall, in his early twenties. Said to be a close friend of Gavin's and also now living in the Irish Republic.

Dave Doyle, aged about thirty, blue eyes, fair hair, formerly living at Selly Oak and now in Dublin. According to Walker, Doyle had admitted planting the Hagley Road bomb.

Walker's letter offers no clue as to the source of his information. Nor did it help his case. Instead it only added to the list of questions he would have to answer on his next appearance in the witness box.

The trial went on throughout July and into August. The outside world lost interest. Few spectators braved the awesome security arrangements for a seat in the public gallery. When, at the end of each day, the cast of lawyers, jury and relatives, emerged blinking into the sunlight, they were not greeted by screaming newspaper headlines or waiting crowds. The people of Lancaster were not much interested. Bombings in Birmingham were no affair of theirs.

With the return of the jury, all the evidence that had been heard in their absence had to be repeated. One by one the West Midlands detectives trooped through the witness box, sullenly repeating answers to questions they had already answered. Altogether thirty West Midlands policemen and half a dozen Lancashire officers gave evidence. They ranged in rank from constables, sergeants, inspectors, superintendents to Assistant Chief Constable Harry Robinson (he had been promoted shortly after the arrests). All were rigorously cross-examined and not one admitted to any knowledge of any violence used against any of the accused during the three days they had been in police custody.

Only Sergeant Ronald Buckley slipped up. He had been the officer in charge of the cells at Morecambe. He had come on duty at seven in the morning and he was being asked by Mr Field Evans whether the prisoners in his custody would have had access to the lavatory. The question was of interest since if, as the police suggested, Billy Power had fouled his trousers before being interviewed, why he had not cleaned himself up before the interview. 'Suppose,' said Mr Field Evans, 'one of the suspects wanted to use the lavatory. There would have been nothing to prevent him, would there?'
    'No, sir.'
    'Indeed your duty would be to see that he was able to use the lavatory facilities, would it not?'
    'Not necessarily, because of the Birmingham City officers that were with the prisoners.'
    The Birmingham officers had all testified that they had been nowhere near the prisoners until 9.30 in the morning. This had been corroborated by Superintendent Ibison of the Lancashire police. If Sergeant Buckley was correct, they were all lying. Perhaps he had made a slip of the tongue. Mr Field Evans pressed the point.
    'Please let me understand. From the time you arrived at seven o'clock in the morning we should understand, should we, that there were Birmingham city officers with these people from time to time?'
    'Yes, sir.'
    'Was that the situation when you arrived on duty?'

'Yes, sir.'

'Were those Birmingham officers in and out of this corridor area where the cells are from seven o'clock onwards?'

'Yes, sir.'

'You would not know the names of any of the officers?'

'No, sir.'

'But there were a number of them?'

'Yes.'

'You understood them to be plain clothes officers from Birmingham?'

'Yes, sir.'

It must have been an embarrassing moment for the prosecution. Harry Skinner was soon on his feet trying to repair the damage. 'You said in answer to Mr Field Evans that Birmingham officers were with the prisoners from the time you came on duty?'

'Yes, sir.'

'How did you know they were Birmingham officers?'

'I was informed by Superintendent Ibison that they were being looked after by officers of the Birmingham force and that I was to have nothing whatsoever to do with the prisoners.'

In the end, it was Mr Justice Bridge who came to the rescue. 'Sergeant Buckley, it may be of importance to fix as accurately as you can the time when the Birmingham officers started interviewing any of these prisoners. If you are able to tell us accurately and with precision from your knowledge when that time was, that will be very important evidence. But if you do not really know one way or the other and cannot fix that time with accuracy, then again it is important that we should know that you are uncertain. Do you understand?'

'Yes.'

'Are you able to fix with accuracy the time when Birmingham officers, as opposed to Lancashire officers, were first engaged in interviewing prisoners at Morecambe police station?'

'No, sir.'

And that was that. It was the nearest the defence ever came to undermining the police evidence.

One other small inconsistency emerged during the cross-examination of the police. D S Watson and D C French had testified that they had collected Billy Power from the matron's room at Morecambe at 9.30 and taken him upstairs for interview. They were definite about the time. 9.30 and not a moment before.

The matron's room was also where PC Brian Pinder had collected the men's clothes and possessions. He testified that he had arrived there just before 9.00. The room was empty when he arrived and he had started collecting the clothes at 9.00.

It was hard to see how Watson and French could have collected Power from the matron's room at 9.30, if it was occupied by PC Pinder. The point was not pressed. There may have been a perfectly simple explanation for the discrepancy. If so, however, the court was not told.

After the police, it was the turn of the defendants. This time round the questions were not confined to the manner in which the confessions had been obtained. Each man was in the witness box for between one and two days. Each was asked to give a precise account of his movements on the day of the bombing. Each was asked for his views, on Ireland, on the IRA, on James McDade. Each was asked about his relationship with the others and with men already convicted of earlier bombings in Birmingham. And for the first time, too, the names of the other three defendants charged only with conspiracy 'Murray, Sheehan and Kelly' began to creep into the proceedings.

Billy Power was first. He was less nervous this time round, but still answered questions in a low voice. Several times he had to be asked to speak up.

'Would you regard a man in the IRA as a wicked man?' asked Harry Skinner.

'Not them all, sir.'

'What about a man who was in the IRA who you knew was planting bombs?'

'Yes, sir.'

'And a man to be kept away from at all costs?'

'Yes, as much as possible, sir.'

The next question was inevitable. Billy Power's reply was less than frank. 'When did you first know that your friend Mr James McDade was a member of the IRA?'

'When he was killed, sir.'

'Why was it that James McDade stayed in your house towards the end of 1973?'

'His wife came round and asked if I could put him up.'

'But this was at the height of the IRA bombing campaign.'

'Was it, sir?'

The questions followed one another inexorably.

'When McDade was killed, you certainly knew that he was a man who planted bombs.'

'Yes, it was obvious, by that time.'

'Well why was it that you were taking the trouble to borrow money to go to his funeral?'

Whatever Power knew or did not know, it did not look good.

Callaghan spent a full day in the witness box. He was asked again why he had signed his statement in no less than ten places, if it was a fabrication, given that he was alleging relatively little violence on the part of the police. 'The explanation is, sir, that with the strain I was under, I would have done anything they asked me.' It could not have sounded very convincing to the jury. On the other hand, the speed of Callaghan's confession hardly squared with the prosecution picture of a hard IRA man.

At one point the prosecution sprang a surprise. Thomas Russell QC tried to put Callaghan down for the Hagley Road bomb. The others, after all, could not possibly have planted it. Callaghan, on the other hand, had been in Yates' Wine Lodge, a mile from Hagley Road. What's more, the number 5 bus, which Callaghan had later caught to Lozell's Working Men's Club passed near the Hagley Road. It would, Mr Russell suggested, have been an easy matter for Callaghan to have nipped up to Hagley Road, planted his bomb and have caught the bus to Lozell's.

While he was about it, Mr Russell also tried to put Callaghan down for the warning telephone call at 8.11. The others were on the train by this time so none of them could have phoned through the warning. Anyone who saw Callaghan in the witness box will have realised his was far from being the calm, clear voice described by the telephonist who had taken the warning call. Nevertheless, it seemed a convenient way of tying up a couple of loose ends.

This line of questioning drew an objection from John Field Evans. The prosecution had given no notice that they intended to suggest Callaghan had been responsible for the Hagley Road bomb. In any case, Callaghan had an alibi. John Fannon, the friend he had come across in the wine bar. Mr Fannon was eventually called, after which the prosecution did not pursue the matter.

Paddy Hill was asked about the trip to the Wolfe Tone commemoration at Bodenstown in June, 1974. It was the only time he had visited Ireland in his fourteen years in Britain. The trip had been organised by the Birmingham Sinn Fein. Fifteen or sixteen regulars at the Crossways had gone. The Birmingham contingent had included Johnny Walker, Gerry Hunter, Mick Murray, Mick Sheehan and someone called Jimmy Ashe.

'Where is Jimmy Ashe now?' asked Harry Skinner casually.

'In prison.'

'Is he the man who pleaded guilty to conspiring to cause explosions?'

'He did, sir, yes.'

'And conspiring to cause arson?'

'I believe he did.'

'Do you remember, when Mr Ashe pleaded guilty, he admitted that he had put cigarette burns on his own arms at the time of his arrest.'

'No, sir.'

'And initially he tried to suggest that the police had caused those burns.'

Only half an hour before, Paddy Hill had been showing the jury the cigarette burns on his own legs.

It was with the appearance of Paddy Hill in the witness box that the names of Micky Sheehan, Jimmy Kelly and Mick Murray began to feature. The trial was now in its second month and the members of the jury, not to mention most of the press, must have been wondering what the other three defendants were doing there, sitting apart from the others in the dock. Murray, in particular, was the mystery man. Unlike all the other defendants, he took little interest in the proceedings. His counsel, Mr Taylor, was instructed not to involve himself in the cross-examination and sat in silence for most of the trial.

Hill was asked about the conversation he had overheard between Murray and Walker as they were leaving an exercise yard at Winson Green the previous December. He had not heard all of it. Only the bit about a telephone not working and having to look for another one. The next day, said Hill, Murray had approached him and said, 'You had better keep your fucking mouth shut.'

Several months later, Hunter, Power, Hill and Sheehan had been taking a shower one Sunday. Sheehan, apparently referring to Murray, had said, 'If that big bastard opens his mouth you blokes could be free in a few days.'

All eyes were on Murray, but he just sat in silence. 'There was a great drama about whether Murray was going to give evidence,' recalls Peter Clippendale, There was a brief flurry of excitement when Murray's counsel announced in one of his rare interventions that his client was proposing to make an unsworn statement from the dock. Later, however, Murray changed his mind. He was to remain silent to the end.

Dr Harwood made another appearance in the witness box and earned himself another going over from the judge. He continued to insist that most of the injuries he had seen on his clients were more than twelve hours old.

Then it was Gerry Hunter's turn. He, too, recounted the conversation in the shower with Sheehan. Like the others, he was invited to dissociate himself from the IRA and all its works. He was not impressive.

'You would be prepared here and now to condemn as wicked what James McDade was doing when he met his death?'

'Yes, sir.'

'Why were you prepared to borrow money in order to go to the funeral of somebody whose activities, at the moment of his death, were wicked?'

'Because I knew him, sir. I liked him.'

'Did not your feelings change when you realised what he had been doing?'

'I did not think of it at that moment.'

'When did you first think of it, that he was putting people's lives at risk?'

'When you mentioned it, sir.'

Richard McIlkenny was asked about the dance at the Emerald Club which he and his wife had attended with Mick Sheehan and Jimmy Kelly. He remembered the occasion. It had been purely social. He had never set eyes on Jimmy Kelly in his life before. Afterwards they had been given a lift home in a van. The driver had been aged between thirty-five and forty and he wore glasses. McIlkenny did not know his name.

He was asked about the half dozen or so copies of *Republican News* which he had distributed at work and in the Crossways. Copies were produced. Extracts were read. McIlkenny was asked to say whether or not he agreed with the sentiments expressed. It had nothing to do with the bombings, but must have made an impression on the jury.

Johnny Walker was the last of the six to give evidence. He was also the one with the most questions to answer. What was in the heavy duty sacks that his neighbour, Mrs Wickett, and her son said they had seen being delivered late at night? What was the truth about the cloth bag which he agreed had been left at his house by McDade, collected by Sheehan and taken to Jimmy Kelly's house? How did he explain the receipts for clocks and Sheehan's driving licence found at his house? What was his account of the meeting which Superintendent Crawford and Assistant Chief Constable Robinson said they had had with him the day after he was admitted to Winson Green? Had he gone with Crawford and two other policemen to point out Kelly's house? These questions cried out for straight answers. This was Walker's one chance to come clean about what he knew. Everyone was waiting to see what he had to say. But Walker simply did not rise to the occasion.

The clocks were easily explained. They were for raffling. In any case, they weren't the sort of clocks bombs were made of. Mostly they were ornamental clocks. It was not only clocks that were raffled. There were sets of cutlery, cigarette lighters, radios, Teddy bears. Mick Murray used to buy the prizes from a discount warehouse. Walker would raffle them and pass the proceeds back to Murray for the Prisoners' Dependents' Fund. As for Mick Sheehan's driving licence, that was left at Walker's house as security for a £2 loan.

That was plausible enough but Mrs Wickett and her son were the main stumbling block. Walker agreed that he had been on the best of terms with the Wicketts. So far as he knew, they bore him no grudge. Yet all he could say in answer to their allegation was that it never happened. 'It just did not make sense,' says Peter Chippindale. 'The whole court was saying to Walker, "Why would Mrs Wickett make up these stories?" All he could say was, "It never happened." People just looked at each other and shook their heads.'

Walker was asked about the trip to Kelly's house to deliver the bag left by McDade. He was not very clear about the date, but he guessed it was May or June. Kelly said it was in October. So did his wife. Walker said he did not know the contents of the bag until Mick Sheehan had described them to him two weeks later.

Walker was asked about the driver of the van. In his letter to the Home Secretary he had identified the man as Jimmy Gavin, but in court he could only remember the man's first name.

He was asked about the meeting at the prison with Crawford and Robinson. It did not take place, he said. What about Crawford's account of the journey from the Lock-up to point out Kelly's house? That had not taken place either. He had told the police about Kelly during his interrogation five days earlier (the police denied this). Could he think of any earthly reason why the Assistant Chief Constable of Birmingham would want to fabricate this story? No, he could not. If he had told the police five days earlier, why hadn't they picked up Kelly then? He had no idea.

The court did not appear to be aware of the letters which Walker had sent three weeks earlier to the Home Secretary giving the names of three men and the nickname of a fourth said to be responsible for the bombings. Had they been, the lawyers would no doubt have wanted to know from where Walker had obtained this information. If he had some startling new facts to reveal, now was the time to do so. He confined himself instead to recounting the conversation he was said to have had with Murray in the exercise yard at Winson Green and the alleged threats which followed. 'After what I have told this court today,' said Walker, 'my life is not worth a plugged nickel.'

31

Mr Justice Bridge's summing up was, in many ways, a masterpiece. It took more than three days to deliver and the transcript covers two hundred and eighty-nine typed pages. On the second day he had to adjourn early because he was losing his voice. The summing up brought together, with beautiful clarity, the mass of detailed evidence through which the jury had sat for most of the preceding nine weeks. It was, said the judge, 'the gravest and most important case I have ever tried'. His job, he made clear, was simply to set out the facts. The duty of the jury was to interpret. They should not, he said, allow emotional considerations to cloud their judgement. Nor should they be swayed by any interpretation of the facts that he might offer. The decision was theirs and theirs alone.

Mr Justice Bridge, however, made no secret of his own views. 'I am of the opinion,' he told the jury, 'not shared by all my brothers on the bench, that if a judge has formed a clear view, it is much better to let the jury see that and say so and not pretend to be a kind of Olympian detached observer.'

Mr Justice Bridge organised the evidence into half a dozen 'chapters'. These were the forensic evidence of Donald Lidstone and Douglas Higgs as to the construction and location of the bombs; the background of the defendants and their association with each other and with James McDade; their movements between seven and eight on the evening of the explosions; evidence against Walker and Callaghan from friends and workmates; the evidence of Dr Skuse and Dr Black on the forensic tests; and, finally, the sharp conflict of evidence between the defendants and the police as to how the confessions were obtained. These last two 'chapters' were, said the judge, undoubtedly the most important.

Five of the six defendants, said Mr Justice Bridge, had unstained characters and no weight should be attached to the criminal record of the sixth, Paddy Hill. He reviewed the circumstantial evidence. The links with McDade, the fund-raising for Republican causes, the trip to Bodenstown. 'If you put upon those matters of background the sinister construction which the Crown invite you to, they do not go beyond raising suspicion, strong suspicion perhaps, but these matters . . . still fall a long way short of anything that anyone could possibly regard as proof.'

When he came to the evidence of the defence forensic scientist, Dr Hugh Black, Mr Justice Bridge left the jury in no doubt where he stood. Dr Black had testified that a Greiss test on old nitrocellulose could give the same result as a test on nitroglycerine. 'That opinion,' said the judge, 'cannot be based on his practical experience because he has none.' The judge went on, 'Is it based on any textbook authority or is it based on practical experience? He was asked over and over again whether he could cite any textbook in support of his theory. It was on that topic that we had a long irrelevant digression about dyestuffs but, reluctant as he was to admit it, Dr Black could refer to no textbook authority which refuted Dr Skuse and validated his own theory.'

Dr Black, said the judge, had known for weeks before he gave evidence what Dr Skuse's evidence would be. He had had plenty of time to carry out his own tests. 'He could, to his heart's content, have gone round all the public houses in the country rubbing his hands on bar counters. Did he do any such test? No, ladies and gentlemen, he did not.'

'Please do not think,' Mr Justice Bridge added disingenuously, 'that I am seeking to pre-empt your decision on this important issue. You may see it differently from me.' But in case anyone had not got the message he added that, if Dr Black was right, the Greiss test was of no value and Dr Skuse had spent most of his professional life wasting his time. 'Do you think that Dr Skuse has been wasting most of his professional time? It is entirely a matter for you.'

There was, of course, another possibility. Namely that, whatever view one took of Dr Black's evidence, Dr Skuse's tests stopped far short of proof that two and possibly three defendants had been in contact with nitroglycerine; that not one of his confirmatory tests had proved positive and that he had offered no adequate explanation for this. This possibility does not seem to have occurred to the learned judge. Or, if it did, he did not see fit to put it to the jury.

Mr Justice Bridge then embarked upon a lengthy review of the sharply different accounts of the interviews at Morecambe and Birmingham which had resulted in four confessions. He had, of course, many weeks earlier made up his mind about the validity of the confessions – in his judgement following the eight day trial within a trial. He had accepted without reservation the evidence offered by the police and rejected as entirely false the account given by the defendants. It was now for the jury to make up their minds and for Mr Justice Bridge to guide them. Characteristically, he did not attempt to hide his own view whilst emphasising at regular intervals that the decision was a matter for the jury.

As he reviewed the allegations made by the accused, Mr Justice Bridge many times drew attention to what he regarded as inconsistencies or shortcomings in the defendants' version of events. Why, he asked, referring to Billy Power's allegation that he had been hit on the back of his hand with handcuffs, was the hand not fractured? Some might say, said the judge, that Paddy Hill was a little arrogant in the manner in which he gave evidence. 'That (members of the jury) is entirely a matter for you.'

Mr Justice Bridge referred to the incident in which Hill said Chief Superintendent Harry Robinson had visited him in the cells at Queen's Road on the Sunday and asked if he was going to recognise the court. According to Hill, Robinson had shaken his hand when Hill had said he would recognise the court. 'Members of the jury, it is entirely a matter for you. Do you believe that the most senior officer of the Birmingham CID would go round asking if they were going to behave in court? Does this have the ring of truth about it?'

Mr Justice Bridge's review of the police evidence is peppered with signals to the jury of his own view. After reviewing Gerry Hunter's evidence, he said, 'You may think it odd – it is entirely a matter for you – that, if the police are inventing all the incriminating parts of the evidence which they put forward, they should have the subtle artistry, in Hunter's case, to mingle two different reactions, at one moment arrogant defiance, at another remorse . . .'

McIlkenny's account of the mock execution is described, for what reason is not clear, as 'one of the most important pieces of evidence of the whole case'. To the learned judge this was the clinching proof that McIlkenny was lying and he made no attempt to hide his view. Had not the firearms officers testified that all the ammunition issued from the armoury at Lloyd House was returned unused? Had he not also testified that there was no blank ammunition available at the time which would have fitted the .38 Special Smith and Wesson revolver, the only type issued from Lloyd House? 'Members of the jury, if that evidence is true, it is conclusive, is it not, that McIlkenny's story of a mock execution is false?' Conclusive though it may have seemed to Mr Justice Bridge there was, as we shall see, a perfectly reasonable alternative which somehow escaped the notice of both judge and defence.

No less than eight pages of Mr Justice Bridge's summing up are devoted to administering the *coup de grâce* to the wretched Kenneth Harwood, the prison doctor. There was a reference to his 'so-called medical opinion'. 'There are,' said the judge, 'inescapably many perjurers who have given evidence from that witness box. If Dr Harwood is one of them, is he not one of the worst?'

Mr Justice Bridge was in no doubt about the significance of the prison beatings. 'If the defendants' complaints of serious assaults upon them by the police are true, then the attack in Winson Green Prison came as a godsend to the police.' He was unable to leave it at that, however. The men, he went on, had been attacked in the prison in a way which must produce substantial injuries and yet they were saying that the bulk of their injuries came not from the attack by prison warders, but from previous attacks by the police. It was, said Mr Justice Bridge, 'a strange coincidence'.

The discrepancies in the confessions ought to have posed a serious problem for the prosecution case. Mr Justice Bridge, however, managed to turn them to the Crown's advantage. 'Of course,' he said, 'it is inescapable that these statements are not accurate in detail. But do they necessarily show that the statements are not genuine?' It was, after all, fairly common for criminals to seek relief from inner tensions by confessing. Experience also taught that men who make confessions often seek to minimise their role. 'They are often anxious to show that somebody else has really induced them against their better judgement to do what they have done, to shift the main responsibility on to someone else's shoulders. Read through, if you will, the statements of Power and Walker in particular to see whether you cannot detect that psychological process at work.'

For good measure Mr Justice Bridge wondered aloud whether the same explanation might apply to Callaghan's confession that he had placed the bomb outside the pub when in fact it had been placed inside. 'When he realised the enormity of what had happened . . . would it not be a way of seeking to minimise the extent of his own responsibility, even while making a partial confession?'

Just how admitting to planting bombs in plastic bags – as opposed to the hold-alls or briefcases they were actually in – helps to minimise responsibility, Mr Justice Bridge did not explain. Nor did he explain how four men, none of whom had contact with any of the others, should each make the same error in the course of their confessions.

Mr Justice Bridge concluded by outlining the implications for the police if the defendants had given an accurate account of their interrogation. His every sentence reeked of incredulity. If the six Irishmen were telling the truth, he said, the police had been involved in a conspiracy 'unprecedented in the annals of British criminal history'. It involved innumerable assaults and the fabrication of false evidence. 'It involved giving perjured evidence in which the police must have spent many hours ... trying to ensure to that their various lies would accord with each other.'

'Secondly, consider the scale of the conspiracy in terms of those involved. It ranges, does it not, from detective constables and police constables right up through the police hierarchy to Chief Superintendent Robinson, in charge of the whole CID of the West Midlands, who has now been promoted to Assistant Chief Constable. It involved, what is more, if you believe what Superintendent Reade has told you, close collaboration in a criminal enterprise between officers who did not know each other ... What is more, it seems to be inescapable that this conspiracy at Morecambe involved collaboration in the criminal enterprise between the Birmingham police and the Lancashire police, who were of course total strangers to each other. If there had been one officer (out of) the whole lot who had said to himself, "I cannot stomach this." If he had reported the matter to some very senior officer, or even to some independent force. If he had even gone to the press and said, "This is what is happening," the gaffe would have been blown, would it not?

'Consider, lastly, the artistry that has gone into the preparation of these statements, if indeed they are works of fiction. If the evidence of the defendants is true, it shows the police not only to be masters of the vile techniques of cruelty and brutality to suspects. It shows them to have a very lively and inventive imagination.'

A study of the statements shows the opposite to be true. The passages that are rich in circumstantial detail are based on what the defendants might plausibly have said during their many hours of interrogation. Much of this was not disputed. The passages describing the planting of the bombs are, on the other hand, remarkably thin. One would expect someone who had planted bombs in crowded pubs to remember every step of that walk from the Taurus Bar to the target. They would surely recall precisely where they placed the bomb, precisely what it was contained in and precisely which pub it was they had bombed. Yet Billy Power's confession devotes only one hundred and forty words to describing the planting. Richard McIlkenny and Johnny Walker dispose of the planting in less than one hundred words apiece. Callaghan blows up the Mulberry Bush in only seventy words. Not one of them mentions priming the bomb once he had reached the target.

In contrast to their rather thin confessions, each of the defendants provided their solicitors with detailed accounts of their alleged treatment at the hands of the police and prison warders. Hill's statement ran to nineteen typed pages. They had each been cross-questioned in the witness box for between one and two days by some of the most expensive barristers in the land. Minor inconsistencies had been revealed, it was true. By and large, however, they had stuck to their story. Mr Justice Bridge might have commented on the subtle artistry on the part of the defendants if, as the prosecution alleged, they were making all this up. How was it possible, he might have asked, for six ill-educated Irishmen to have fabricated so detailed an account of their treatment at the hands of the police?

Of course, many of the points made by Mr Justice Bridge were reasonable. Dr Black, the defence forensic scientist *was* a hopeless witness. Dr Harwood *was* covering up for his cronies in the prison service. There *were* inconsistencies in the stories told by the defendants. What seems extraordinary, however, is that Mr Justice Bridge did not use his undoubtedly considerable intellect to analyse the prosecution case with a fraction of the same rigour as he applied to the defence. Quite apart from the holes in the confessions, the prosecution had failed to explain where the bombs came from; failed to explain why a search of the men's homes had revealed nothing more incriminating than a few copies of *Republican News* and receipts for ornamental clocks; failed to explain why none of the men alleged to have gelignite on their hands, had any trace on their clothes; and failed to find a single witness from either the Taurus Bar on New Street station or from either of the devastated pubs who recalled seeing any of the six men with plastic bags. They were all points to which Mr Justice Bridge might have drawn the attention of the jury. Yet he chose not to.

Having dealt with the case against the six men charged with the bombings, Mr Justice Bridge went on to deal with the conspiracy charges against Jimmy Kelly, Mick Sheehan and Mick Murray. These he disposed of briefly. The cases against Sheehan and Kelly amounted mainly to the different versions of the incident in which a bag or bags containing detonators, guns and ammunition had been delivered at Kelly's house by Sheehan and Walker in a van driven by a man whose identity was not disclosed to the court but whom Walker, in his letter to the Home Secretary, had identified as Jimmy Gavin.* No one disputed that the delivery had been made but Walker and Sheehan both said they had not known what the bag or bags contained at the time of delivery. Kelly, who discovered at once what the bags contained, claimed that he had been infiltrating the IRA and had intended to report what he knew to the police. The weakness of his story was that he had not done so not even after the pub bombings. Mr Justice Bridge contented himself merely with reminding the jury of the different versions between which they had to choose.

The case against Mick Murray was thinner. Indeed, said the judge, it was so thin that he had seriously considered whether there was sufficient evidence to allow it to proceed. On balance he decided that there was, but there was little to go on. Murray was the only one of the nine defendants who had admitted he was a member of the IRA. Membership of the IRA had, however, not been made illegal until after Murray's arrest. He collected money which he said went to the families of internees and no one had proved that it did not. The only witness to speak against him was Kelly who had said that Murray had been present in the carpark of the Golden Cross when the bag had been returned. Kelly's evidence, said Mr Justice Bridge, should be treated with scepticism.

Then there was Murray's alleged conversation with Walker in the prison exercise yard. 'One wonders,' said Mr Justice Bridge, 'how Walker, not having found the courage to disclose this all-important conversation immediately after the event, found the courage to disclose it in evidence.'

As for Sheehan's alleged remark in the showers at Winson Green – 'If that big bastard opens his mouth you blokes could be free in a few days' – which Hunter had recounted to the court, Sheehan had denied saying anything of the sort. This was hearsay and, said Mr Justice Bridge, should be disregarded.

There was only one other piece of evidence against Murray. Tests on his hands had resulted in faint positives for ammonium and nitrate but these, Mr Justice Bridge reminded the jury, could arise from sources which were entirely innocent.

* Jimmy Gavin left Birmingham in January 1975. He is now serving a life sentence in the Irish Republic for a murder committed in 1977.

As he concluded his summing up, it became apparent that Mr Justice Bridge had developed a soft spot for Mick Murray. 'You may think,' he told the jury, 'that Murray's conduct in this trial has shown a certain measure of dignity which is totally absent from the conduct of some of his co-defendants. You may find yourself in difficulty in withholding a certain grudging measure of respect.' Murray, said the judge, had behaved like a captured soldier and given only his name rank and number. He had remained silent throughout. He had instructed his counsel not to cross-examine any co-defendants except in the case of Walker, 'And that presumably was because the evidence of Walker was too much even for Murray to stomach.' Perhaps even Mr Justice Bridge realised he had gone too far for he immediately added, 'Members of the jury, if that is an unfair comment, disregard it.'

By now, no one in the jury could be in any doubt as to the verdict expected of them by Mr Justice Bridge. He left them with one parting shot. 'One possibility which you may want to bear in mind is that the others, knowing that Murray has all along admitted that he is a member of the IRA, may have known or guessed that he is the one man in the dock who would honour and stand by the IRA's code.

'What better whipping boy could they have found upon whom to shuffle the blame?'

Not even the prosecution had thought of that one.

The jury retired at 3.33 on the afternoon of August 14, 1975. Their verdict was a foregone conclusion.

32

On the last night of the trial, the police organised a party. It was held at the Elms Hotel in Morecambe. Although, as Mr Justice Bridge had said, the Lancashire and Morecambe police were total strangers to each other at the start of the inquiry, they were by now on good terms. Many of the Birmingham officers who had given evidence during the trial were there. They had returned to Lancaster for the verdict. The party went on until the early hours. Dennis Holt, one of the sergeants in charge of the cells at Queen's Road, remembers that it was five in the morning before he got to bed. Throughout the trial the police had kept very much to themselves. The West Midlands detectives were accommodated at a small hotel in Lancaster and generally steered clear of the press. Peter Chippindale, who had covered several previous IRA trials for the *Guardian* says, 'We got much less cooperation from the police than we would normally expect. They were paranoid about saying anything that would upset the court.' The police did, however, meet with certain favoured reporters on an off-the-record basis. One of them was Bob Satchwell, the chief reporter on the *Lancashire Evening Post*. Satchwell spent several evenings drinking with them. He says of the West Midlands detectives, 'They were hard bastards, hard drinkers, they drove their cars fast. The Sweeney bit before the Sweeney were fashionable.'

There seems to be general agreement that the West Midlands detectives were a different breed from their Lancashire brethren. One Lancashire detective, who was on duty in Morecambe police station the night Superintendent Reade and his men arrived, describes them as 'a right rough bunch'.

'A heavy looking lot,' says Peter Chippindale who observed the West Midland detectives in court. 'Mostly they were quite big men. One or two looked as if they were going to seed through beer drinking. They wore good suits that didn't quite fit in the middle. There was even a tie-pin or two. They were the sort of people the public imagines the Sweeney to be.'

Chippindale describes the scene in court on the morning after the party at the Elms. 'The jury were still out but there was a generally festive atmosphere. When the judge was out, the West Midland detectives behaved like schoolboys when the master is out of the room. They were lounging about, telling jokes. By this time it was obvious that the police had got their verdict and they were feeling pleased with themselves. A lot of them knew their careers were going to be changed as a result of this case.'

'There was one extraordinary moment,' says Chippindale, 'when the jury were still out. About twenty detectives went and sat where the jury should have been. We looked at them and said, "If those were the defendants, we would have found them guilty on the spot.' It was purely irrational. There was no basis for it, but they were not a nice-looking bunch of people.'

The jury returned at 12.28 on the afternoon of August 15. It had taken them six and a half hours to reach unanimous verdicts on the one hundred and thirty-two charges. There was standing room only in the court room. Many prosecution witnesses had returned for the verdict. The nine defendants stood silently in the dock. Mick Murray was as calm as ever. The others appeared subdued and bewildered. Billy Power was wearing a bright green shirt. Mr Justice Bridge looked down impassively from his high place beneath the shields of the Sheriffs of Lancashire.

On the twenty-one charges of murder against each of the first six defendants, the foreman of the jury pronounced the 'Guilty' verdict one hundred and twenty-six times. The clerk of the court then turned to the charges against the other three defendants. 'In respect of the twenty-second count, charging James Kelly, Michael Bernard Sheehan and Michael Joseph Murray with conspiring to cause explosions, do you find the defendant James Kelly guilty or not guilty?'

'Not guilty.' It was the only not guilty verdict of the trial. It meant the jury had believed Kelly's story about infiltrating the IRA.

Sheehan and Murray were found guilty of conspiring to cause explosions. They were also found guilty of possessing explosives. So was Kelly.

Mr Justice Bridge now pronounced sentence. 'William Power, Hugh Callaghan, Patrick Joseph Hill, Robert Gerald Hunter, Noel Richard McIlkenny and John Walker, you stand convicted on each of twenty-one counts, on the clearest and most overwhelming evidence I have ever heard, of the crime of murder. The sentence for that crime is not determined by me. It is determined by the law of England. Accordingly, in

206

respect of each count each one of you is now sentenced to imprisonment for life. Let them be taken down.'

To the surprise of many, Mr Justice Bridge made no recommendation that they should serve a minimum number of years.

IRA men convicted by British courts often, at the moment of sentence, make some parting gesture of defiance. Gerry Hunter recalls that, as they stood there, some of the West Midlands detectives, who were seated directly opposite the dock, appeared to be mouthing abuse, perhaps in the hope that the prisoners could at last be provoked into admitting membership of the IRA. The provocation, if that is what it was, was not successful. The six men were taken down in silence to serve their twenty-one life sentences.

There were now three men left in the dock, Kelly, Sheehan and Murray. Kelly's counsel, Edwin Jowitt said that his client had already served the equivalent of a one-year sentence. If Kelly was now to be released, Mr Jowitt asked that he be kept in custody for a further week while arrangements were made for him to disappear since he was plainly at risk from IRA reprisals. Mr Justice Bridge accepted this request and ordered that Kelly be released eight days hence.

Sheehan's counsel, Patrick Bennett made a clumsy attempt to enter a plea in mitigation. Mr Justice Bridge cut him short. 'If it helps you, Mr Bennett, I will say frankly that I suspect he may be much more deeply involved than the evidence here discloses, but I shall sentence him on the basis of what the evidence does disclose.' Sheehan received nine years.

That left only Mick Murray who, true to form, had instructed counsel that no plea in mitigation was to be entered on his behalf. Mr Justice Bridge now revealed to the court what he had known all along. That Murray was already serving a twelve-year sentence imposed three months earlier for conspiracy to cause explosions. For Murray the outcome was academic which, no doubt, helped explain his general lack of interest in the proceedings. He received nine years to run concurrently with his existing sentence, which made no practical difference to the number of years he would spend in prison.

When the last of the defendants had been taken down, Mr Justice Bridge, then turned his attention to those who had made the whole affair possible. He praised the sharp-eyed ticket collector at Heysham who had noticed that four of the five men passing the barrier had consecutively number tickets. He praised the British Transport police whose swift action had resulted in the arrests. He praised defence counsel, John Field Evans and Michael Underhill. Never once, said Mr Justice Bridge, had they overstepped the bounds of propriety while subjecting the police witnesses to searching cross-examination on the allegations of brutality.

He praised the police officers responsible for the security of the court. 'I am,' he said, 'lost in admiration for the way these officers have done their job.'

Finally, Mr Justice Bridge summoned the Chief Constable of Lancashire, Stanley Parr, and Assistant Chief Constable of the West Midlands, Harry Robinson. On them he bestowed 'the highest commendation' for the work of both forces. 'I am entirely satisfied,' he said, 'and the jury by their verdicts have shown, that these investigations both at Morecambe and Birmingham were carried out with scrupulous propriety by all your officers.'

33

The day after the trial ended, *The Times* published an editorial headed 'Justice for the Birmingham Bombers'. 'One of the disturbing features of this case', said the paper, 'has been the evidence that (the bombers) were at some stage beaten up.' *The Times* said that while men convicted of such outrages deserve no sympathy they had the right enjoyed by all accused persons, whether innocent or guilty, to fair and proper treatment. 'One of the most critical tests of any judicial system is that standards are upheld to the full for those least deserving of sympathy... The final judgement on this whole affair ought to be that justice was done to and for these men.'

In December, 1974, soon after the allegations of the beatings had become public, the Assistant Chief Constable of Lincolnshire, Mr Davis Owen, had been asked by the Chief Constable of the West Midlands, Sir Derick Capper, to investigate allegations that the men had been beaten in police custody. Mr Owen had taken a series of statements from all the police officers involved and satisfied himself that the police were blameless. He had then spent several months investigating the events surrounding the men's admission to the prison. At Winson Green Mr Owen was met with a wall of silence. He said later, 'I did not get from the prison authorities the standard of cooperation that I would have liked.' He had persevered, however, and in February, 1975, commenced a series of rigorous interviews with every prison officer who had been on duty in the vicinity of the reception area at the time of the men's arrival. He also interviewed the prison doctor, Kenneth Harwood, and the Assistant Governor, Donald Vuller. Only one prison officer, Derek Warner, conceded that he had witnessed any violence. There had, he told Mr Owen, been a general mêlée as the prisoners had been roughly manhandled into reception by their police escorts. He had, however, seen no prison officer strike any of the prisoners.

Mr Owen left no stone unturned in his efforts to establish what had happened at the prison. As well as prison officers, he had interviewed the six victims of the assaults who were at the time awaiting trial. Each insisted he had been beaten in police custody as well as on arrival at the prison. Mr Owen also interviewed many of the prisoners who had been in

D Wing at the time of the men's arrival. They gave detailed accounts of the scenes they had witnessed.

The Owen inquiry had lasted nearly five months. His report had been submitted to the Director of Public Prosecutions in May 1975 after which an eerie silence had descended. The trial came and went. Still nothing happened. Parliamentary questions to the Attorney General elicited only the reply that the matter was *sub judice*.

The first anniversary of the beatings passed and still there was no sign of anybody being charged. Then, out of the blue, on New Year's Eve, 1975, the Director of Public Prosecutions announced that fourteen Winson Green prison warders were to go on trial charged with the assaults.

By now the men convicted of the bombings had served notice of appeal. The main grounds were, firstly that, by giving his own views so forcibly, Mr Justice Bridge had pre-empted the views of the jury. Secondly, 'That in his summing up the Learned Judge overstepped the bounds of his judicial function in his denigration of defence witnesses', particularly Dr Harwood. The defence also complained, 'That the Learned Judge omitted to remind the jury sufficiently or at all of certain essential ingredients of the defence case.' These included, said the notice of appeal, 'The impossibility of packing into two cases containing clothing and other personal effects some sixty pounds of gelignite, electric batteries, switches and wiring, and bags with D-shackles.' The defence also claimed that Mr Justice Bridge had not given sufficient weight to the discrepancies in the alleged confessions.

The appeal was heard on March 30, 1976, before the Lord Chief Justice, Lord Widgery, together with Lord Justice Lawton and Mr Justice Thompson. Judgement was delivered by Lord Widgery. In his review of the evidence Lord Widgery took a fairly casual attitude towards the allegations of beatings in police custody. When the defendants had made their first appearance in court, he said, their faces seemed undamaged, apart from Walker's black eye 'the origin of which I have forgotten, but I do not think it matters very much anyway'. There was, said Lord Widgery, no evidence to suggest they had at this stage experienced damage or knocking about 'beyond the ordinary'. As to what constituted ordinary knocking about, Widgery did not say.

He was also surprisingly dismissive of the forensic evidence. 'This is not a point, as we see it, of great importance in this case because there was no trace of explosives found on other hands and even in the case of Hill and Power a subsequent and more precise and accurate test failed to confirm the original one.' That was a direct contradiction of Mr Justice Bridge's description of the forensic tests being one of the two 'absolutely critical' chapters in the case against the men. It also challenged Dr Skuse's ninety-nine per cent certainty that Power and Hill had been in recent contact with explosives. Unhappily, however, the forensic tests were not part of the grounds of appeal.

The Appeal Court ruled that Mr Justice Bridge had not erred in making his own views known to the jury. He had made clear at the outset that members of the jury were free to differ from him, if they wished, and he had not strayed beyond what the Court of Appeal regarded as reasonable limits.

As regards Mr Justice Bridge's assaults on defence witnesses, the appeal judges dealt only with his treatment of Dr Harwood. Although they felt that Mr Justice Bridge 'unhappily went somewhat far' in some of the language he used about Dr Harwood, they did not feel that this undermined the basis of the convictions.

The suggestion that Mr Justice Bridge should have invited the jury to consider the difficulty of putting sixty pounds of explosives and other material into the cases the men were carrying was dismissed in a single sentence: 'This is such an isolated matter and so unimportant when compared with the main body of the evidence that we do not find it necessary to go into detail.'

The appeal was, therefore, dismissed.

The trial of the prison warders opened at Birmingham Crown Court on June 10, 1976. Mr Justice Swanwick presided. Although the state of public opinion in Birmingham had earlier been judged unsuitable to guarantee the men charged with the bombings a fair trial, no one suggested a Birmingham jury might not be able fairly to assess the case against the men charged with beating up the alleged bombers. As the trial proceeded, some of the prison officers were embarrassed to receive letters from members of the public congratulating and wishing them good luck.

The defendants were divided into two groups. Prison officers Peter Bourne, David Parling, James Bluett, Derek Warner, Patrick Murtagh and Principal Officers Brian Sharp and Ivor Vincent were charged with the assaults in the reception. Officers Arthur Powell, William Green, George Hughes, John Gowenlock, Gordon Willingham, Paul Manders and Hospital Principal Officer Geoffrey Abbott were charged with the assaults while the prisoners were being bathed.

In the absence of any serious cooperation from the prison officers, the charges were drawn up largely on the basis of who happened to be on duty when the assaults had taken place. Witnesses for the prosecution consisted mainly of prisoners who had been in D Wing at the time, many of whom gave evidence anonymously, and doctors Dharm Adlakha and Alan Cohen, who had examined the men in the three days after their admission to prison. Nineteen police officers who had taken part in the interrogations and the escort to the prison were called and all testified that they had delivered their charges to Winson Green unblemished save for Walker's black eye. The other main prosecution witnesses were, of course, the six victims of the beatings.

The Director of Public Prosecutions had not at first intended calling them and it was only after news of this leaked that he was persuaded to do so. There was speculation that the reason for the DPP's reluctance to call the men was fear that they would use their appearance in the witness box to assert their innocence and repeat their embarrassing allegations against the police – which is, of course, exactly what they did.

The fact that the DPP had waited more than a year before charging the prison officers was helpful to the officer's defence. It meant that the six victims could be referred to throughout as 'bombers'. This afforded great sport to the defence barristers. 'For what it is worth', Brian Escott Cox QC, asked Billy Power, 'you say you were knee-ed in some way?' Almost every question from Mr Escott Cox was prefaced by the phrase, 'For what it is worth'. Eventually prosecution counsel Douglas Draycott intervened, 'This is comment which has been repeated now about six times . . . It is an interpolation which ought not to happen.'

Mr Justice Swanwick upheld the objection. There was obviously a limit to the amount of derision that could be heaped upon the evidence of the six. After all, they had been savagely beaten. This was not disputed. Someone must have been responsible. If not the prison officers, who? The alternative was too awful to contemplate.

Each of the six men took the opportunity to assert his innocence and to say that not all his injuries had been caused at the prison. Billy Power and Hughie Callaghan, far from being the timid witnesses they had been at their own trial, stood up squarely to the continuous baiting from the defence barristers. At the end of his evidence Billy Power again attempted to give his version of how his confession was obtained.

'My Lord, if I may add . . .'

'Is it an additional answer to the question that you have been asked?'

'Yes . . . If I may be blunt, the shit was kicked out of me, and evidence was produced at Lancaster to this effect. The police had mentioned . . .'

'Well, I think that is enough.'

'My Lord, if I may say . . .'

'No, you may not. Take him away.'

Not one of the prison warders was prepared to give evidence on oath. They did, however, make unsworn statements – which defendants have the right to do – from the dock, in which they explained their reluctance to testify on the grounds that they would be forced to implicate other officers, not present in court. Unknown to the court, however, each of these officers had provided their defence solicitors with statements (see chapter 20) in which many of them admitted taking part in the assaults. In their brief to counsel, defence solicitors frankly admitted that, if the truth came out, their clients would be convicted. 'That evidence,' wrote one of the defence solicitors, 'would in my opinion be sufficient to convict Bluett, Sharp, Abbott, Gowenlock, Green, Hughes, Manders and Willingham of assaults upon the murder prisoners and thus to make it likely that all the defendants would be convicted of assaults occasioning actual bodily harm.'

The prison officers' secret statements are of interest for another reason. They describe in some detail the condition in which the men were received and the manner of the arrival at the prison. And, as we shall see, their evidence sharply contradicts that of the police. The statements have remained unpublished to this day.

The prison officers had another embarrassment in store for the police. They called in their defence Dr David Paul, a consultant in clinical forensic medicine. Dr Paul was a formidable witness. A former police surgeon and a coroner, he lectured in clinical forensic medicine at no less than five London teaching hospitals. During the course of his career he had been asked to examine and give opinions on many hundreds of wounds and other injuries. He specialised in the interpretation of injuries on photographs.

Dr Paul was asked by the defence to examine blow-ups of the polaroid photographs taken at Queen's Road police station to see if his expert eye could detect traces of the injuries which the men complained they had received in police custody. His findings contrast starkly with the police evidence.

On Johnny Walker, Dr Paul found, in addition to the undisputed left black eye, 'obvious bruising to the lower right jaw, below and lateral to the mouth... Obvious bruising and swelling of the right cheek below the eye.'

On Paddy Hill, Dr Paul detected a small dark mark on the left side of upper lip indicating a minor laceration and bruising below both eyes.

On Gerry Hunter, Dr Paul detected 'a slight swelling and darkening' under the right eye and a small split to the lower lip.

On Richard McIlkenny, there were marks on the top right of the forehead and on the tip of the nose.

On Billy Power, Dr Paul detected bruising below both eyes and a dark mark, 'presumably a bruise', on the left side of Billy Power's throat which corresponded to the injury Power said he received when he had been grabbed by the unidentified detective with greying sideboards.

On Callaghan, Dr Paul said he found the beginnings of two black eyes. These were injuries not even Callaghan had claimed.

All these injuries, Dr Paul concluded, were visible in the photographs taken on November 24 and must, therefore, have been sustained before admission to Winson Green. They would, he said, not necessarily have been visible to a casual glance by an untrained observer.

Mr Justice Swanwick's summing up was as friendly to the defence as Mr Justice Bridge's had been to the prosecution. He denounced each of the prosecution witnesses in turn. Throughout his summing up he made a point of referring to the six victims as 'the bombers'. They had, he said, committed a crime of cold-blooded barbarity and they had made 'lying accusations against the police at Lancaster in order to try and wriggle out of their true confessions'. The jury were not expected to take the accusations of such men at face value.

As to the twenty or so prisoners or former prisoners who had given evidence, Mr Justice Swanwick told the jury, 'What class of witness they are is a matter for you.' But he did not leave it there. 'You may think,' he added, 'that they are, some of them, second class and some third class or below as witnesses.'

Turning to the prison officers, Mr Justice Swanwick, reminded the jury that they were all men of exemplary character. He then ran through their records of service. Good character did not mean, he added, that they cannot be guilty of a crime for the first time in their lives, but it was something of which the prison officers were entitled to take advantage.

The trial lasted five weeks. The jury retired at 10.30 on the morning of July 15, 1976. By 7.30 that evening they had returned unanimous verdicts of 'Not Guilty' against each of the fourteen prison officers.

The next day the *Guardian* carried a leading article headed 'Who beat up the bombers?' It said: 'Unless the verdicts are to be regarded as perverse, it follows that the men who carried out the beatings have yet to be found and charged.'

There were those who hoped that the subject would now be quietly forgotten, but it would not lie down.

Armed with the evidence of Dr Paul, the six men took out a civil action against the Chief Constables of the West Midlands and Lancashire and the Home Office for the injuries they claimed to have received in police custody. They were also armed with statements from three prison officers, which had emerged during the course of their trial, suggesting that the men had injuries on arrival at Winson Green. By now the men had dispensed with the services of Messrs Gold and Curtis and were represented by solicitors with considerably more experience.

The action commenced in November, 1977. Legal aid to pursue the claim was granted. The Home Office admitted liability but the police applied to have the action struck out. They argued, firstly, that Dr Paul's evidence and that of the prison officers could have been available at the original trial and that the men were, therefore, estopped from calling it three years later. Secondly, the police argued that the action was an abuse of the legal process since the issue had already been resolved at the original trial. In November, 1978, Mr Justice Cantley dismissed the police application and ruled that the action could proceed. It was to be the only success the six men would enjoy in a legal battle which lasted seven years.

The police then appealed. The effect of their appeal was to impose another long delay. It was not until January, 1980 – more than five years after the alleged assaults – that a ruling was obtained from the Court of Appeal. It is tempting to speculate how quickly the matter would have been dealt with had it been the other way about and the men had been accused of assaulting police officers.

The appeal of the West Midlands police was heard by the Master of the Rolls, Lord Denning, together with Lord Justice Goff and Sir George Baker. The three judges were unanimous in upholding it. Dr Paul's evidence could, they said, 'with proper diligence' have been available at the time of the original trial. Sir George Baker went so far as to say that, in his view, Dr Paul's evidence was valueless since, in the case of Callaghan, for example, he was affecting to notice injuries that not even Callaghan complained of.

Lord Denning's was, by any standards, a remarkable judgement. At times he appeared more concerned with the consequences for the government and the police than with due process of law. 'Just consider the course of events if this action is allowed to proceed to trial,' said Denning. 'If the six men fail, it will mean that much time and money will have been expended by many people for no good purpose. If the six men win, it will mean that the police were guilty of perjury, that they were guilty of violence and threats, that the confessions were involuntary and were improperly admitted in evidence and that the convictions were erroneous. That would mean the Home Secretary would either have to recommend they be pardoned or he would have to remit the case to the Court of Appeal. This is such an appalling vista that every sensible person in the land would say: It cannot be right these actions should go any further.'

Lord Denning went on to rub salt into the wound. 'This case shows what a civilised country we are. Here are six men who have been proved guilty of the most wicked murder of twenty-one innocent people. They have no money. Yet the state has lavished large sums on their defence. They were convicted of murder and sentenced to imprisonment for life. In their evidence they were guilty of gross perjury. Yet the state continued to lavish large sums on them in actions against the police. It is high time it stopped. It is really an attempt to set aside the convictions on a side wind. It is a scandal that should not be allowed to continue.'

In November, 1981, almost seven years to the day since the alleged assaults, the House of Lords upheld Lord Denning's judgement.

The six men had now exhausted all the legal avenues through which they could hope to prove their innocence.

34

After the verdict, Sandra Hunter returned to her home in Wyrley Way, Erdington, to find that it had been looted. The council had boarded up the house, but looters had broken in. The windows were smashed. The house was wrecked and everything of any value had been stolen. Her three children had been staying with Gerry's relatives in Belfast during the trial and she went over to join them. She stayed in Belfast just two weeks. 'I didn't want the boys growing up in that environment,' she says. 'Word got round that their Dad was a hero of some kind. I didn't want that because their Dad was innocent and I didn't want to bury my sons when they were eighteen.'

Being English, Sandra Hunter had no roots in Ireland. She had been born and bred in Birmingham. She had met Gerry when she was fourteen, married him when she was sixteen and lost him when she was twenty-seven. After the trial she told a newspaper, 'I could easily make a new life for myself. All I have to do is get a divorce, but how could I when Gerry did nothing. I'll never give up. I'll carry on fighting for him even if he was six feet under.' And so she has.

She now lives in a part of Birmingham where no one knows who she is. 'The children have been brainwashed never to reveal who we are,' she says. 'Neighbours think I'm divorced or separated. We're on the run.'

Kate McIlkenny has never given up either. After the trial she and her children squatted in a run-down house in Belfast. After a few weeks she, too, returned to Birmingham to be nearer her husband. Through the efforts of the city's Irish Welfare Office she was rehoused in a council flat. She now lives in a house in the Alum Rock area of Birmingham surrounded by her children and grandchildren. She has made no attempt to conceal her identity and is on good terms with her neighbours, English and Irish. Of all the wives, Kate McIlkenny is probably the most resilient.

Johnny Walker's wife, Theresa, lives in Londonderry and has done since soon after the arrests. She still visits Johnny, but not often. Johnny Walker is philosophical about it. 'She always told me I'd get into trouble mixing with that crowd. And let's face it, she was right, wasn't she?'

Pat Hill divorced Paddy in 1983 and has since remarried. Nora Power remained at Walthamstow in the East End of London, near Billy's sisters, Patsy and Betsy. She involved herself for several years in the campaign to prove his innocence, but lately seems to have given up. She no longer visits Billy.

Eileen Callaghan and her daughter, Geraldine, still live in Birmingham. For several years they stayed in the house at Stanwell Grove, Erdington, and remained on good terms with their neighbours. Today they live in another part of Birmingham. Eileen visits Hughie every month or so.

As for the men, they are in remarkably good spirits. At the time of writing, they have served more than eleven years. They have been told that they will first be considered for parole in 1991, but none of them take that seriously. Hughie Callaghan says, 'We're hostages here, to keep the public quiet.'

Unlike most IRA prisoners, the six men are not moved frequently from jail to jail. At the time of writing, Billy Power and Richard McIlkenny are in Wormwood Scrubs. Power has been there for eight years, McIlkenny for five. Power is taking an Open University course in social sciences and has notched up three or four credits. McIlkenny has taught himself Spanish and jokes that he is going to join Ronnie Biggs in South America when he gets out.

Johnny Walker has been at Long Lartin near Evesham for six years. Gerry Hunter was with him until August, 1985, when he was moved to Frankland Prison near Durham. At Long Lartin both men received open visits in the main visiting hall. IRA men in the same prison for much lesser crimes are allowed only closed visits.

Paddy Hill is probably the one whose spirit is least dented by the disaster that has overtaken their lives. He and Hughie Callaghan are, at the time of writing, at Gartree in Leicestershire. Hill's life style is still as rumbustious as ever. He still gets involved in the occasional punch-up. His legs are still vividly scarred where he alleged Sergeant Bennett stubbed a lighted cigarette. From his prison cell he has continuously bombarded newspaper editors, MPs and other public figures with letters and articles protesting the innocence of himself and his co-defendants. The replies have not been encouraging. Tom Sargant, the secretary of Justice, the British section of the International Commission of Jurists, wrote: 'In a case like yours, so many reputations are at stake that in my view the obstacles to overcome are insuperable.'

In the outside world there was a small campaign for the case to be re-opened, but the cause did not prove popular, least of all in Birmingham. Two Irish Catholic priests, Fathers Denis Faul and Raymond Murray, published an eighty-page booklet entitled 'The Birmingham Framework' which set out the men's version of events. In Birmingham a group of people interested in the case set up an organisation called 'Rough Justice' which attempted to keep the issue alive. It did not achieve much, partly because it lacked resources and partly because some of its members became hopelessly bogged down in irrelevant conspiracy theories. Over the years there have been occasional articles in minority interest maga-zines such as *Time Out, Tribune* and *The Leveller*. By and large, however, the idea that the men might be innocent never penetrated popular con-sciousness. As late as January 1985 the news editor of the *Birmingham Post* was able to say that he had never heard it seriously suggested that there had been a miscarriage of justice.

Early in 1985 I was commissioned to investigate the case by the Granada television programme *World in Action*. Later I was joined by *World in Action* researcher Charles Tremayne. We divided the case into two main parts, the confessions and the forensic evidence. I also opened a third line of inquiry. Through contacts in Belfast I made known that I wished to meet the people who had carried out the bombings. It was six months before I received word that something was being arranged.

But first the confessions.

35

It is not unknown for persons in the custody of West Midlands detectives to confess to murders they did not commit. In December, 1984, twenty-three year old Derek Gordon was released after eight months in Winson Green awaiting trial on a charge of murdering a pub landlord. Mr Gordon was released because another man had been charged with the murder. But while in custody at Birmingham's Bridge Street police station Mr Gordon had signed a two-page confession describing how he had committed the murder.

By itself, of course, this proves nothing. Except that people in the custody of West Midlands detectives do sometimes confess to murders they have not committed.

In his summing up at Lancaster, Mr Justice Bridge had difficulty imagining that so many policemen would have kept quiet, if the confessions had been obtained in the way alleged. Officers of two police forces were involved, he said. They were of all ranks, ranging from Constable to Assistant Chief Constable. Surely, he said, someone would have blown the gaffe. It is in this context that the experience of P C Adrian Dart should be read.

Adrian Dart was a young probationary police constable based at Longbridge in Birmingham. On his second day on duty he arrested Junior Patrick Williams, a West Indian worker at the British Leyland car plant, on suspicion of stealing material from the plant. It was Adrian Dart's first arrest. He took Mr Williams back to Longbridge police station and handed him over to Detective Sergeant Brian Morton and two other detectives. They took Williams into an interview room from where, a few moments later, P C Dart heard sounds of disturbance. He could hear Williams crying and someone shouting, 'Admit you did it.' This was followed by sounds of banging and slapping and more sobbing. When the door opened, D S Morton emerged half carrying Williams whose face was covered in blood. Inside the room the other two detectives, D Cs Martin Lambert and Graham Stephen, were wiping blood off the floor. One of them shouted to Dart to get out of the station. When he came back on duty, PC Dart reported the incident to his sergeant. He was immediately transferred to another station, Belgrave Road three miles away. A few weeks later he was transferred again, this time to Smethwick. PC Dart persisted with his complaint, however, and the matter was eventually taken up by the Police Complaints Department at Lloyd House. According to PC Dart, there were three other policemen on duty at Longbridge who witnessed the incident but each of them returned what are known as negative statements. They had heard nothing and seen nothing. PC Dart was on his own.

As a result of PC Dart's action, DS Morton and the other detectives were suspended from duty and charged with assault. From that moment on, PC Dart was an outcast. Only two of the twenty or so officers on his shift at Smethwick would speak to him. When he went into the canteen, other officers would get up and walk away. On one occasion, in the toilet, one young officer apologised for not speaking to him. He was a Panda car driver and he did not want to be put back on the beat, he said.

As the trial got nearer, the harassment intensified. PC Dart's car, parked outside the station, was damaged. Inside the station his locker was broken open with a crowbar and his clothes stolen. He started receiving hate mail. Someone stuck his picture on a wall and drew a noose around his neck. Underneath was the caption, 'If all else fails . . .'

The harassment extended to his work. When out on patrol he would find himself being sent to incidents many miles away when there were obviously other officers nearer. When he radioed for help no one would come. On one occasion, he called for help at the scene of an incident where a man had gone berserk and was battering a young child. No help came. 'The child could have been killed,' says Dart.

The harassment was not confined to junior officers. Once, he says, when a colleague sat next to him in the canteen, Detective Chief Inspector Roger Ball, one of the senior officers at Smethwick, shouted, 'Don't sit next to that shit.' As a detective sergeant ten years earlier, Roger Ball was one of the officers who had been at Queen's Road while five of the six men were being interrogated. Johnny Walker alleged that Ball had assaulted him. Ball denied this. He was also one of the two officers who, on the Sunday morning, had questioned Callaghan about the men's IRA ranks. On the Monday he had taken part in the escort to the prison and, at the trial of the prison officers, he testified that the six men had walked unescorted up the steps to the reception. He has now retired from the police force and runs a greengrocer's shop at Leek in Staffordshire. In May,

1985, he was elected as a Conservative member of Staffordshire County Council.

In November, 1983, D S Morton and D Cs Lambert and Stephen were found guilty of assaulting Junior Patrick Williams. P C Dart gave evidence against them. Morton was sentenced to one year's imprisonment, half of it suspended. The others received six months each, half suspended.

As a detective constable, Brian Morton had also been at Queen's Road in November, 1974, while the men were interviewed. It was he who had taken the photograph of Paddy Hill on the Sunday and who later testified that Hill bore no sign of injury. Morton also took part in the escort from Steelhouse Lane to Winson Green. At the trial of the prison officers he was one of nineteen policemen who testified that the six men had been delivered to the prison without incident.

Three months after Morton was sentenced, P C Dart resigned from the police force. 'I couldn't stand the harassment any longer,' he says.

Mr Justice Bridge would no doubt argue that, far from undermining his case, P C Dart's experience proves his point. Despite all the pressures, there was one police officer, albeit with only two days' experience, prepared to speak out against his colleagues. There is, however, one obvious difference. The six Irishmen were not charged with stealing goods from work. They were charged with the biggest murder in British history. Their swift arrest was a triumph for the Lancashire and West Midlands police. The four confessions were a vital part of the case against the men. Any officer speaking up would have to take responsibility for undermining the case against men who had already been shown by forensic evidence to have been in recent contact with explosives. Whether or not those confessions were obtained under duress, one thing is clear. Every police officer involved in the case sincerely believed then, and still to this day believes, that they had caught the right men. If ever there was a reason for not speaking out, that is it.

Rex Bird witnessed an interesting incident on the night after the pub bombings. Mr Bird now works for Central TV. At the time he was a student. He recalls, 'I was passing Woodbridge Road police station on my way back from the launderette. It was about ten o'clock at night. Suddenly, four police cars, two of them unmarked, sped past me and drew up near the front of the station.' Mr Bird saw a number of men in civilian clothes, whom he took to be policemen, emerge from one of the unmarked cars. He was astonished to see that at least two of the men were carrying shotguns. 'They pulled a man from the back of one of the cars and threw him on the ground. The man wasn't wearing any trousers. I couldn't see whether he was handcuffed. Every time he tried to get up they kicked him and the armed men prodded him with their shotguns. They kicked him across the ten or twelve yards into the police station.'

Woodbridge Road is in the Moseley area of Birmingham. Ten o'clock on the Friday night was about the time Hughie Callaghan was arrested, although the man seen by Mr Bird could not have been Callaghan since he was taken first to Queen's Road police station and later to Sutton Coldfield. Nor is it suggested that any of the same policemen were involved. The incident, therefore, has no direct bearing on the fate of the six Irishmen. It does, however, offer a clue as to the kind of treatment anyone falling into the hands of West Midlands detectives on that night might have expected to receive.

Charles Tremayne and I began our investigation by seeking out as many as possible of the policemen who had been involved in the case to see if any would tell a different story today to the one they told ten years ago. We concentrated on officers who had since retired or left the force, reasoning that they would be more likely to speak to us than officers who were still serving. We began our search in Morecambe, in line with Mr Justice Bridge's reasoning that Lancashire policemen, against whom no violence was alleged, would be more likely to speak out.

Retired policemen are not always easy to find. Many are ex-directory. It was only by word of mouth and painstaking searches of the electoral register that we tracked many of them down. It soon became apparent to us that there were many more policemen in both Morecambe and Queen's Road police stations while the men were in custody than the defence ever managed to track down. At Morecambe there were also several civilian cleaners and clerical staff.

Former Chief Superintendent Alf Collins now lives in retirement at Windermere in the Lake District. He and Assistant Chief Constable Tommy Watkinson had arrived at Morecambe police station just after midnight. Mr Collins remained on the premises until after Billy Power had confessed at around ten o'clock on the morning of Friday, November 22. He was not called to testify. Nor was his presence referred to at the trial. Mr Collins said he had no contact with the suspects beyond checking them over in the early hours. He spent most of the night on the first floor, just across the corridor from where Billy Power was interviewed. He says he saw and heard no violence. 'The walls at Morecambe are very thin. Had there been violence, I would have heard it.'

Detective Superintendent Bernard Ibison has retired and lives at Broughton, near Preston. He spends much of his retirement running the Phoenix Club for supporters of Preston North End football team. Considering that the capture of the Birmingham pub bombers should be one of the greatest events of his career, Mr Ibison, seemed remarkably hazy on the details. He at first affected not to recall that there had been any allegations of violence at Morecambe until reminded that eight days of the trial, during the course of which he had twice testified, had been taken up solely with such allegations. He agreed that, had there been any violence at Morecambe, he would have known about it. He insisted that he had kept the West Midlands detectives away from the suspects until after the forensic tests had been completed at 9.30. He was extremely nervous that we might be secretly taping him (we were not) and switched on the television in order to frustrate attempts to tape our interview. Pressed to discuss the allegations of violence, he simply kept repeating, 'Take my word for it, the right people are inside.'

Superintendent Roy Lenton was in charge of Morecambe police station for the whole of the eighteen hours that the Irishmen were on the premises. He was not called as a witness and he was not involved in the interrogations. 'As far as I know, there was no violence. I had cleared civilians off the first floor so they would not get in the way, but there were civilians in the station. The Birmingham police would have been mad to carry out the type of beatings alleged.

'I admit there were often shouts and counter-shouts from the prisoners, but these could not be construed as violence. I was pleased that Bernard Ibison had the good sense to keep the West Midlands police away from the prisoners before the forensic tests were complete. They were very upset when they arrived from Birmingham to find they could not begin questioning immediately. After we managed to calm them down, however, I think they saw sense in Mr Ibison's decision.'

Ken Brown was the inspector on duty when the men were brought in. He remained on duty until 6.00 in the morning and returned again at 2.00 in the afternoon. He would, therefore, not be on the premises during the worst of the alleged violence. He says, 'my recollection is that Skuse did have a positive test by the time I went home, although I wouldn't swear to it.' Skuse testified that he saw Billy Power at 6.35 and Paddy Hill at 7.05. Assuming those times to be correct, the positives would not have been available until 7.00 and 7.30. According to Ken Brown, he was succeeded at 6.00 in the morning by Inspector Ken Teale. Mr Teale was not very helpful. 'It may have been my day off,' he says. He adds, however, 'I don't think I ever saw the prisoners but I did see the West Midlands police going in and out.' Obviously Mr Teale could not have seen the West Midlands police if it had been his day off.

Neither Ken Brown or Ken Teale were called to testify at Lancaster.

Detective Sergeant David Watson was the Special Branch officer at Heysham who escorted Paddy Hill to Morecambe. He has since left the police force and now lives at Hale on the outskirts of Manchester. Mr Watson remained on the premises until the men were taken to Birmingham at 5.30 the following evening. He interviewed one of the suspects in the cells and says he spent the rest of the day either in his office on the second floor or preparing his statement on the first floor. He flatly denies hearing or seeing any violence. Violence, he says, could not have taken place without his knowing. He adds, 'If I thought they had been assaulted, I would have spoken up. I got to know the Birmingham coppers quite well during the trial. They were not the violent types.'

Sergeant Ron Buckley, the officer in charge of the cells, has now retired and lives at Carnforth near Morecambe. He came on duty at seven o'clock in the morning and remained there throughout the day. It was he who, in the course of evidence at Lancaster, testified for several minutes that Birmingham officers were with the men from the time he came on duty. Later, following the intervention of Mr Justice Bridge, he had said he was unable to remember the times. If there had been any violence in Morecambe police station that day, Mr Buckley must know. We visited him on two occasions and he refused to discuss the matter.

Brian Pinder, the police constable who collected the clothes, is at the time of writing still based at Morecambe. He is now an inspector. We did not approach him directly but he agreed to be interviewed by a local journalist. The interview was later cancelled, however.

We found only one person who had been in Morecambe police station that day and who was prepared to concede, albeit in a round-about way, that violence had taken place. Let us call him Mr A.

Mr A is an honest, but cautious man. 'Only believe half of what you see and none of what you hear' is his motto. Mr A was on the premises from just after midnight until the early afternoon. Strictly speaking he should not have been there, since for most of the time he was off duty. 'I hung around because I was nosey,' he said. He spent time in the cell area and on the first floor while Billy Power was being questioned. He also watched Dr Skuse taking samples. Skuse, he remembers, was very confident of his results.

We interviewed Mr A three times and on no occasion did he offer us a frank account of what he saw or heard. He chose his words with care. For example:

> Q: Ibison would have been under a lot of pressure to let the Birmingham police interview them straight away, wouldn't he?
> A: 'Yep, and knowing him he wouldn't have stopped them, would he?'
> Q: 'I don't know. Did he stop them?'
> A: 'I don't think he could, do you?'

Mr A says he did not see violence but many of his remarks are ambiguous. 'If you're going to prove that there was violence,' he said on one occasion, 'which I think you are going to have to accept that there was . . .'

On another occasion he said that half the station had been sealed off. 'Why?'

'Because of the shouting.'

On another occasion Mr A said:

'I've got nothing but respect for those blokes from Birmingham. Ibison would not have done it, but to stick your neck out to get a confession about something . . . about something as serious as that . . .'

Out of the blue, on our first visit, Mr A said, 'One way of extracting a confession is to put a blanket over a suspect's head and hold it tight. If you are lying on the floor with a blanket over you and someone points a gun at you, you would sign. A blanket does not leave any marks.'

When pressed, Mr A refused to say whether he had witnessed such an incident. At one point he suggested that we had first raised the subject, which we had not. The matter is of more than academic interest since Johnny Walker alleged that this was exactly what happened to him early that morning in Morecambe police station.

36

Before starting to track down the West Midlands officers, I went to see Kenneth Littlejohn who is nowadays known as Kenneth Austen. Littlejohn is the man who earlier in 1974 had escaped from Mountjoy prison in Dublin where he and one of his brothers were serving long sentences for bank robbery. He caused a sensation by alleging that he had been recruited by MI6 to infiltrate the IRA. The Home Secretary of the day, Robert Carr, later admitted that Littlejohn did have connections with Intelligence.

By the time of the pub bombings, Littlejohn had been on the run for nine months and the police did not appear to be trying very hard to find him. While on the run, he had given several interviews to the press, including one to a Sunday newspaper in November, 1974, at the Albany Hotel in the centre of Birmingham. He had even enrolled on a course of touch-typing lessons to help him write his memoirs.

Littlejohn's name first crept into the pub bombings case when, at the trial in Lancaster, it emerged that on the night of the bombing he had been staying at the home of one of the main prosecution witnesses, Thomas Watt, Walker's workmate. Littlejohn had eventually been arrested at Watt's house three weeks after the bombings. Watt and his wife had also been arrested but later released. No charges had followed.

Littlejohn's name has haunted this case ever since. Watt's credibility as a witness was seriously impaired by his association with Littlejohn. Many of those who have since attempted to re-open the case have become obsessed with the Littlejohn connection. Some have even gone so far as to speculate – absurdly – that Littlejohn carried out the bombings in a bid to discredit the IRA. The truth is a little more down to earth.

When I went to see him, Kenneth Littlejohn was resident at Her Majesty's Prison, Nottingham, serving a six year sentence imposed in 1982 for his part in a bungled armed robbery at a house near Chesterfield. He is intelligent, good-looking, charming and plausible. His account of his colourful past is sprinkled with the names of the famous. Somewhere, buried deep, there is at least a germ of truth. It is difficult, however, to tell where fantasy takes over from fact. This is his story.

'On the night of the bombing, Tom Watt rang my elder brother, Robert, asking where he could contact me. When I spoke to Watt he told me that Johnny Walker had told him several times not to go into Birmingham that night. He gave me Walker's address in Kingstanding. I went down there. I was going to string him up from a lamp post, but when I got there I was told that Walker had gone to Belfast.'

Why should Watt want to confide in Littlejohn? 'The Littlejohn mythology. I suppose he thought I was British Intelligence or some such crap.'

Later that night, Littlejohn says he went to Watt's house. 'He told me that he had already informed the police. We kept in touch quite often after that. When I was on the run, I stayed at Watt's house. It was one of several safe houses. I stayed there only a couple of days. I was there on one occasion when the police called to interview Tom Watt about Walker.'

Littlejohn was arrested by armed detectives at Thomas Watt's house on December 11, 1974. That, no one disputes.

Tom Watt and his wife, Rose, are still to be found in the same house. It is in the Alum Rock district of Birmingham, a short walk from where Kate McIlkenny now lives. The Watts tell a slightly different story from Littlejohn's. Tom Watt had known Ken's elder brother, Robert, for some time. Robert Littlejohn was sales manager with a local company, R. J. Richardson's. 'At around 10.15 on the night of the bombing, Bob called round and said, "Will you put Ken up for a few days?" Ken came round later that evening.'

Mr Watt absolutely denies giving Walker's address to Littlejohn or that Littlejohn went round there. He says, 'On the night of the bombing he never moved out of this house.'

The Watts say that Littlejohn stayed for three weeks. He came and went quite openly. Once he went Christmas shopping in Birmingham with Rose. On another occasion there was an accident near the Watt's house. Littlejohn went out and chatted with the policeman who was called to the scene. Once, when detectives called to see Watt about Walker, Littlejohn made them coffee.

Kenneth Littlejohn's sojourn with the Watts came to an abrupt end on the morning of December 11. Tom Watt was at work. Rose was downstairs in the house. Littlejohn was upstairs in bed. Suddenly there was banging at the front door. Rose went to open the door and was brushed aside by armed men who bashed down an inside door and charged up-stairs. 'I thought they were the IRA,' she said.

In fact, they were West Midlands detectives. They bundled Littlejohn out of the house in his underpants, a quilt over his shoulders and a gun at his head. As Tom Watt arrived home that afternoon, at about 2.15, he was approached by three men. Two had revolvers. Tom, too, thought they were the IRA coming to exact vengeance for his informing on Walker. Watt was taken to Boardsley Green police station where, he says, Detective Superintendent Pat Cooney ordered him to be released. There was no deal with the police, says Watt. He could not be prosecuted for harbouring Littlejohn because Littlejohn was not wanted for a crime in the United Kingdom.

The Watts speak fondly of Ken Littlejohn. On the wall of their living-room there is a pastel sketch by Littlejohn of their daughter, Samantha. According to Tom Watt, 'Ken is a nice guy, but he's a bit of a Walter Mitty. He can't live down his reputation. His biggest problem is his name.'

As he closes the door on one mystery, Tom Watt unlocks the door to another. At the trial, Watt testified that he had first informed the police of his suspicions about Walker in June, 1974, a few days after Walker and several of his friends had been on the trip to the Bodenstown celebrations. Watt sticks by this claim. 'I estimate that the police called at my house two dozen times between June and November.' In court he said they called only three times before the bombings. Today he says, 'At one stage they were coming two or three times a week. They would say, "Next time Walker says he is going anywhere, give us a call."' Watt says he informed on Walker to stop him getting into any deeper water than Watt supposed he was already in. The inaction of the police angered him. 'I was getting really narked,' he says.

According to Watt, Special Branch and Bomb Squad officers who visited his home told him that Walker and his friends were being watched day and night. They even knew which shift he was on.

Whether or not the police were paying Walker quite the attention that Watt imagines, there is some evidence to suggest that Walker and possibly McIlkenny were on the books of the West Midlands police long before the bombing. Billy Power testified that Chief Superintendent Harry Robinson had told him that Walker was being followed on his way to New Street Station, on the night of the bombing, but that the police had lost him.

Andrew Crawford, head of the West Midlands Special Branch at the time, flatly denies that Walker was being watched. 'If Watt was informing,' he says, 'I don't know who he was informing to. Nobody could set up a surveillance team without my knowledge and I have no recollection. If someone from the Bomb Squad was going regularly to see Watt, I would have known. We had nothing definite on any of them.'

It is hard to know what to make of all this. Watt's wife corroborates his story and it seems unlikely they are lying, although they may be exaggerating. The most likely explanation is that the police checked Walker and McIlkenny out and found nothing against them, but that they strung Watt along, in case he came up with anything more concrete. Watt says they urged him to strike up conversations with Walker about the bombings and the IRA. He says, 'They told me to treat the subject light-heartedly, egg him on a bit.' That seems to be the origin of Walker's alleged diagram of a bomb. 'We were playing cards and the talk turned to the bombings. I said, "You couldn't even make faces, never mind bombs." Walker made a sketch on the back of a Park Drive cigarette packet and tossed it across.' It couldn't have seemed too incriminating at the time. Watt did not take the sketch to the police. He put it in his locker and forgot about it. It was only when the police raided the Forging and Pressworks on the day after the bombing that he handed it over.

Tracking down the West Midlands officers who were at Queen's Road during the interrogations proved far more difficult than finding those who were at Morecambe. Many of the West Midlands officers are still serving and, therefore, unlikely to talk frankly. Most have been promoted. Maurice Buck, Assistant Chief Constable at the time, is now Chief Constable of Northamptonshire. Detective Chief Superintendent Harry Robinson, who later became Assistant Chief Constable, is dead. George Reade, the Detective Superintendent from Walsall who led the squad that went to Morecambe, took early retirement after being passed over for promotion. He is now to be found in Rugeley, Staffordshire. He denies as strongly today as he did at the trial that violence was used to extract the confessions. 'All that hoo-ha about the confessions being knocked out of them is a load of nonsense,' he says. He is certain, too, that he caught the right people. 'I am satisfied that the six who were convicted planted the bombs. I have no shadow of doubt. One or two may have got away. I know we did the right thing and I know we got the right people. I sleep easy at night.'

Reade's second in command, Chief Inspector John Moore, has now retired and runs a property business. He is said to divide his time between his home in Shropshire and Miami. Alan Watson, the detective sergeant who interviewed Billy Power, is, at the time of writing, a detective chief inspector. James Kelly, the sergeant who interviewed Walker, is also now a DCI. So is Roy Bunn, who as a sergeant interviewed Hill on the Sunday morning at Queen's Road. Richard Bryant, the sergeant who was present when Callaghan alleges he was threatened with being dumped in the lake near Spaghetti junction, also became a DCI. And, by the strangest twist of fate, Alan Buxton, one of the officers who transported Callaghan from Queen's Road to Sutton Coldfield on the night of his arrest, is, at the time of writing, landlord of the Yard of Ale, in New Street, formerly known as the Tavern in the Town.

Brian Morton, the detective who was jailed in 1983 for assaulting a prisoner, now runs a large pub in the south of Birmingham. He was in Queen's Road while the interviews were in progress, but he refuses to discuss what happened. 'If there was violence, I wouldn't tell you.' Mr Morton reserves his indignation not for the suggestion that violence took place, but for the suggestion that any of his former colleagues could have admitted that violence occurred. 'I can't believe anyone told you that. That's totally out of order. Nobody's going to admit to any violence. As far as I'm concerned, it didn't happen. I'd like you to show me someone who says it did.'

Mr Morton did, however, offer a possible answer to one little mystery. There is a firing range at Queen's Road police station and, according to Mr Morton, both wax bullets and blanks for training purposes are likely to be stored on the premises. It would not, therefore, be necessary for anyone who was going to fire wax rounds at Richard McIlkenny to obtain them from the armoury at Lloyd House. So much for Mr Justice Bridge's conclusive proof that McIlkenny was lying.

The officer in charge of Queen's Road while the men were being questioned was Superintendent Joe Matthews. He was not directly involved in the investigation, but was on the premises day and night for the whole time the men were held there. His son, DC Paul Matthews, was also there and was involved in the interrogations. Joe Matthews says he saw the prisoners in their cells on the Saturday morning and recalls that some of them were standing rigidly to attention. He put this down to their IRA training rather than any threats from their guards.

Sergeant Dennis Holt remembers that Walker jumped to attention every time he was spoken to. Mr Holt was in charge of the cells at Queen's Road on both the nights the men spent there. He says he did not witness any violence and says that no one could have entered the cell area without his knowing. On one occasion he remembers hearing a thumping sound from the other side of the cell block wall. He went outside and found the officer on guard kicking the wall. 'I said, "What the hell are you doing?" He replied, "If I've got to be awake all night, I don't see why they shouldn't, too."'

Sergeant Holt also recalls that normal procedures weren't always followed. Usually every prisoner has a 'Persons in Custody Sheet' on which details of every movement made by a prisoner within the police station are supposed to be recorded. Details of meals, visitors and even every cup of tea delivered are also supposed to be noted. In serious cases, the investigating officers are also supposed to maintain a log recording their movements. In this case, according to Sergeant Holt, the custody sheet was almost non-existent. 'I spoke to Harry Robinson about this. He said, "That's all right. Me and Mr Buck will take care of that."'

That did not satisfy Holt. 'I said to him, "I'm in charge of the station. Your men are only guests." But Harry Robinson made it quite clear to me that they would do it their way.'

Ronald Rawsthorne, the chief inspector in charge of the Lock-up at Steelhouse Lane, has now retired to the Isle of Wight. The story he tells today is the same as the one he told the court. He saw the men stripped and could see no sign of injury, but they appeared to be terrified out of their wits. The light, he says was dim and he was not looking for injuries. Mr Rawsthorne offers one significant addition to his earlier account. 'I did hear afterwards about the incident with the noose.' At the trial, Gerry Hunter testified that, at Steelhouse Lane, one of the armed guards, PC Coffey, had made a noose from a piece of string and hung it over the hatch on his cell door. Billy Power also said someone had held a noose in his face. The two armed guards, PC Coffey and DC Jennings, both testified that this did not happen. Chief Inspector Rawsthorne now says that it did.

We come to the prison officers. As we have seen, early in 1976, they were persuaded to provide their lawyers with frank statements of what took place at Winson Green. Chapters Twenty and Twenty-One are based on these statements, the contents of which have never before been made public. The statements are of interest, however, not only for what they say about the conduct of the prison officers but also for what they say about the behaviour of the police who delivered the men to the prison (see pages 127–8). At both the Lancaster trial and at the trial of the prison officers, a succession of policemen of all ranks up to Chief Inspector John Moore testified that they had seen and offered no abuse or violence on arrival at the prison. Some even testified that the prisoners walked unaided up the steps into the reception. Apart from the prisoners, there was no one to challenge this version of events. None of the prison officers on duty at reception were called as witnesses at Lancaster. And, at their own trial, they all declined to testify. If the prison officers are right, then many of the policemen committed perjury.

In their statements several prison officers also say they saw signs of injuries which appeared to have been inflicted before the men arrived at the prison. Patrick Murtagh, the officer in charge of handing out the prison clothes, saw Johnny Walker stripped immediately after his arrival. Mr Murtagh says, 'As he stripped, I noticed there were a number of marks on his body. I believe it was Walker who had a long and discoloured bruise from the waist up and across the front of his ribs ... It was yellow and green.'

Brian Sharp was with Murtagh when Walker stripped off. He says, 'I saw bruises on many parts of his body and his torso was more or less covered. They were all colours, black, blue, yellow, purple and most of them looked oldish.'

Gordon Willingham, one of the officers who two hours later supervised the bathing, saw all the men naked. 'From the marks I saw on them, I would say that their facial markings were recent, but their bodily marks were ... at least one or more days old. These were consistent with a systematic beating below the neck while in police custody.'

So, the unfortunate Dr Harwood may not have been far wrong, after all. His mistake was to try to cover up for his colleagues in the prison service by maintaining that all the injuries could have been inflicted before the men reached Winson Green. It will be argued that the prison officers, too, have an axe to grind. Of course they do, but what lends their statements credibility is the fact that the prison officers also implicate themselves.

Then there is Dr David Paul. He is now the Coroner for the City of

233

London. If he were ever allowed to testify, he would repeat the opinion he gave at the trial of the prison officers in 1976. Namely, that the photographs taken at Queen's Road do show signs of beatings. Dr Paul, of course, was available all along. There is no reason why he could not have been called at the original trial. He says, 'Their solicitors could have contacted the Royal Academy of Forensic Science or the Forensic Science Society for help. So far as I know, we had no inquiry.'

At the end of the day the issue can only be conclusively resolved if a policeman who had been at either Morecambe or Queen's Road were to come forward and say he saw or heard the men being beaten. More than ten years have now passed and there is no sign of any policeman breaking ranks. This may be because no beatings took place. Or it may be because, whatever happened, everyone involved sincerely believes that they got the right men. When asked about the basis for their certainty, the answer is always the same:

'How do you explain those forensic tests?'

37

Controversy has always surrounded Dr Frank Skuse's confident assertion that the positive Greiss tests against Power and Hill made him ninety-nine per cent certain that the men had been in contact with explosives. There have always been forensic scientists who shared Dr Black's view that other, innocent, substances could also yield a positive Greiss test. Until recently, however, no one had ever proved that this was so.

The first serious doubts arose in February 1976 when Howard Yallop, the former Principal Scientific Officer in charge of explosives at Woolwich Arsenal, gave evidence for the defence at the trial of the Maguire family. Mrs Annie Maguire, her husband, three sons, her lodger, a neighbour and a relative from Belfast were accused of making bombs in the kitchen of their council house in Acton. It was dubbed 'Aunt Annie's Bomb Factory' by the popular press. No trace of explosives was found in the house or garden. Nor was there any independent evidence to suggest that the Maguires had been involved in bomb-making. The only evidence against them were positive Greiss and TLC tests.

Mr Yallop ought to have been a formidable defence witness for it was he who, in the 1960s, had developed the TLC test as a method of detecting explosives. At the trial of the Maguire family, he testified that there were other substances that could produce a positive Greiss test. Mr Yallop said he had carried out laboratory tests in which a range of common substances had produced a positive Greiss test. These included 1001 carpet shampoo, Goddard's silver polish, Electrolux carpet shampoo and even cigarette smoke. Some of these, said Yallop, also produced positive TLC tests. His evidence failed to impress the jury, however. The Maguires and their co-defendants were found guilty and received sentences of up to fourteen years. To this day they, too, have vociferously protested their innocence.

Attempts to persuade Mr Yallop to repeat his experiments failed. In 1978 he was contacted by Kieran Morgan, a young solicitor in Armagh, and asked if he would be prepared to go to help in the case of the Birmingham men. To begin with Mr Yallop agreed. Later, however, he backed out. 'At first Dr Yallop was very helpful, but then he changed completely,' Mr Morgan recalls. 'He would have nothing more to do with the case. I pressed him either to proceed or to explain why he could not, but he would do neither.'

No one else has ever claimed that cigarette smoke could produce a positive Greiss test. Nor, until 1985, does anyone seem to have tested the competing claims made by Dr Skuse and Dr Black. It does seem, however, that Home Office laboratories no longer, if they ever did, give the Greiss test the weight that Dr Skuse suggested it was given.

According to a letter from Home Office minister, Giles Shaw, to Joan Maynard MP, in April, 1985, Greiss is no longer much used. Mr Shaw wrote, 'New and more sensitive techniques for the detection of nitroglycerine have been developed and these have largely replaced the Greiss test.' He added, however, that Greiss might still be used for screening purposes, 'in conjunction with other techniques.'

Mr Shaw goes on, 'The weight attached to the Greiss test is now somewhat less than ten years ago, but this should not be interpreted as a loss of confidence.' He said that no research on the Greiss test had been commissioned since 1974, but earlier research had been conducted by the Royal Armament Research and Development Establishment. The hands of 936 people from a variety of backgrounds had been swabbed. 'In none of these cases was there an indication of material which could be mistaken for nitroglycerine.'

In May 1985 the Granada Television programme *World in Action* commissioned two distinguished forensic scientists, Dr Brian Caddy and Mr David Baldock, to carry out a series of Greiss tests on a range of common substances, including nitrocellulose.

Mr Baldock was a senior scientific officer at the Home Office laboratories at Nottingham until 1982 when he set up in business as a consultant. During his time with the Home Office he gave evidence for the Crown on many occasions, including at trials involving bombs and explosives. Before conducting the tests, Mr Baldock obtained from the Home Office Forensic Science Laboratory at Chorley, where Dr Skuse was based, precise details of the chemical re-agents used by Skuse in his tests at Morecambe. Mr Baldock then prepared and used exactly the same solution. The director of the Chorley laboratory also sent Baldock a Home Office briefing paper which described Greiss as a 'presumptive' and not a definitive test for nitroglycerine, which makes Dr Skuse's ninety-nine per cent certainty hard to justify. Thirty-five samples were tested. These included various types of meat pies similar to the one Paddy Hill might have eaten at Crewe station. They also included Embassy tipped and Park Drive cigarettes, the brands smoked by the men on their train journey to Heysham, several packs of playing cards, nitrocellulose lacquer, nitrocellulose chips and nitrocellulose aerosol spray.

Tests on the three nitrocellulose products proved positive. All the rest were negatives. Dr Black had been right and Dr Skuse had been wrong.

Further tests showed that the Greiss reaction to nitrocellulose was dependent on room temperature. At normal room temperature the three samples all gave positive reactions, while in rooms without heating the tests were negative. (Dr Skuse had testified that nitrocellulose would have to be heated to sixty degrees centigrade before it would give a positive reading.) Mr Baldock was later asked to comment on the result of his tests. 'I wasn't surprised,' he said. 'The chemical formula of nitrocellulose and nitroglycerine isn't very different... There is obviously a range of substances that will give a positive reaction to the Greiss test.'

Was he surprised that Dr Skuse had been so certain of his own results? 'Frankly, I was amazed.'

Mr Baldock was also asked to comment on the one laboratory test that had proved positive against Paddy Hill, a GCMS test on a sample from Hill's left hand. Dr Black had disputed this. Black said that Skuse should have taken three readings from the oscilloscope, whereas Skuse had taken only one. Mr Baldock agreed with Dr Black. Normally, said Baldock, a positive GCMS test for nitroglycerine should produce three readings. In this case, Skuse found only one. What should Skuse have told the court? 'He should have said ... that it did not confirm the presence of nitroglycerine.'

Support for this view also comes from Mr R. A. Hall, director of the Northern Ireland Forensic Laboratory, which has more experience than any other in Britain of detecting explosives. Mr Hall says, 'The appearance of a fragment of mass 46 (the result that Skuse obtained from the GCMS test on the sample from Hill's left hand) is not in itself an identification of the presence of nitroglycerine.'

David Baldock also threw another spanner in the works. In the early seventies, he said, Home Office forensic scientists were in the habit of cleaning their GCMS equipment by saturating it with a solution of nitroglycerine. It was a practice they had tried to keep from defence scientists. There was a danger, he said, that the equipment could be contaminated.

Why, he was asked, was this practice never challenged in court? 'Possibly because nobody knows it was done.'

Dr Brian Caddy's tests were of still greater interest. Dr Caddy is head of the Forensic Science Unit at Strathclyde University where many of the country's forensic scientists are trained. He, too, tested a wide range of domestic materials and discovered that those containing nitrocellulose gave a positive Greiss test. Among the items which gave positive readings were Spectra Clear Lacquer, a wooden surface coated with ten year old varnish containing nitrocellulose, as well as a cigarette packet and a picture postcard both of which had nitrocellulose coatings. Most interesting of all, however, Dr Caddy obtained a positive reading from two packs of old playing cards. As we have seen, the five men were playing cards on the trains from Birmingham to Heysham.

Dr Caddy then went one step further. He asked *World in Action* producer, Ian McBride, to shuffle the cards for five minutes and then tested McBride's hands. He repeated this test twice. On both occasions the result was positive. Or, as Dr Skuse might put it, there was a ninety-nine per cent chance that McBride had recently handled explosives.

That effectively destroys the evidence of Dr Skuse. The forensic evidence was described by Mr Justice Bridge as one of two 'absolutely critical' chapters in the evidence against the six men. It follows, therefore, that the destruction of the forensic evidence demolishes one of the main planks of the prosecution case. The other main plank is the confessions and they, as we have seen, are deeply flawed.

On being shown the results of Dr Caddy's tests, Roy Jenkins, who was Home Secretary at the time of the bombings, told Granada Television: 'The new evidence I have seen would be sufficient to create in my mind what's sometimes called a lurking doubt as to whether the convictions in these cases were safe.'

Mr Jenkins went on, 'What I would do, if I were Home Secretary and I received a document like the one you have produced, then I would summon a Home Office meeting and say, "On the face of it this seems to me to amount to a case for referring the matter to the Court of Criminal Appeal..."'

No one, however, should underestimate the capacity of the judiciary for moving the goal-posts. Lord Widgery prepared the ground in his appeal judgement as long ago as 1976. 'This is not, as we see it, a point of great importance,' he said, referring to the positive tests on Hill and Power.

Lord Denning made a similar point in his remarkable judgement dismissing the men's attempt to sue the West Midlands police. 'The forensic evidence was quite insufficient to warrant a conviction unless the men's statements were admitted in evidence. The judge so told the jury. He said that, apart from their statements, he would not have left this case for their consideration.' This appears to be based on a misreading of Mr Justice Bridge's summing up. Bridge made those remarks in relation to the circumstantial evidence, including that of Walker's workmates. About the forensic evidence he was quite clear. It was one of two 'absolutely critical' chapters. No one, not even Lord Denning, should be allowed to rewrite the script.

The key point is that the forensic tests, as Lord Widgery accepted, convinced the police that they had the right men. '*You're covered in gelignite from head to toe. You've got more on you than Judith Ward,*' Sergeant Bennett is alleged to have shouted at Hill during their first encounter at Morecambe police station. When Hill called him a liar, Bennett is said to have retorted, '*It's not us who says it, it's the scientist.*'

Three days after the World in Action programme was shown Dr Skuse retired from the Home Office Forensic Laboratory at Chorley. At the time of retirement he was aged fifty. Asked to give the reason for Skuse's early retirement the Home Secretary, Douglas Hurd, replied, 'Dr Skuse retired voluntarily, and it is not the practice to divulge reasons for such retirements. Dr Skuse retired on the terms which are payable to mobile civil servants who retire in the public interest.' Asked to say whether there was any connection between his early retirement and the experiments carried out by *World in Action*, Dr Skuse replied 'I can't tell you. It's in the hands of the Home Office.'

38

There is no special secret about the identity of those who organised the Birmingham pub bombings. Many people know, or at least have a pretty good idea. The identity of those who carried out the bombings is, however, a deeper secret.

Before August, 1974, when the first major arrests were made, the Birmingham IRA was a fairly leaky organisation. In the pubs and clubs where Irish people gather there were many people who were not involved in the bombings, but had a pretty good idea who was. As they now admit, Johnny Walker, Richard McIlkenny, Billy Power and Gerry Hunter were certainly amongst those in a position to make an educated guess. It was dangerous knowledge and nobody asked questions. Many saw the bombings as a way of bringing home to British people what was going on in Northern Ireland. They condoned it as long as no one was getting hurt. And with the exception of an army bomb-disposal officer who was killed in September, 1973, no innocent person was hurt in any of the Birmingham IRA's fifty or so bombings that preceded the explosions at the Mulberry Bush and the Tavern in the Town.

Until the bombings started, Irish Republicans in Birmingham operated quite openly. Sinn Fein in Birmingham was divided into five lodges or *cumman*, as they were known, each named after a different Republican hero. A *cumman* had about fifteen to twenty members and activities consisted mainly of selling newspapers and organising demonstrations to mark the anniversaries of internment and Bloody Sunday. In January, 1973, for example, over 1,000 people marched from Small Heath to Digbeth Civic Hall to mark the first anniversary of Bloody Sunday. A band came from Belfast for the occasion and there was a colour party bearing IRA flags, clad in black berets and dark glasses.

'Are you ready to go?' a superintendent in charge of policing the demonstration asked Sinn Fein organiser George Lynch, as the marchers assembled in Small Heath Park.

'Not yet,' said Lynch, 'We're waiting for the colour party.'

'Oh,' said the superintendent, 'It's nice to see the coloured people getting involved.'

In the following two weeks, there were another five bombs in Birmingham, all targeted against commercial premises. There was also an outbreak of incendiaries in Manchester.

One of the Birmingham bombs was found by a group of children and fortunately did not explode. At the scene of one explosion, a motor accessory firm at Sutton Coldfield, a youth was injured jumping out of a window. On September 17, 1973, the bombers claimed their first fatality. Captain Ronald Wilkinson was killed trying to defuse a bomb at Edgbaston.

At first the West Midlands police had little to go on. An examination of bombs that had failed to explode showed that they all seemed to be the work of the same team. Several had been placed in plastic shopping bags. There was only one arrest, a thirty-seven year old Irishman called Patrick Dowling who was said to have been found with bomb-making pamphlets. He was later sentenced to four years in prison.

The West Midlands bombings came in waves. There was nothing in the last three months of 1973 and then, on January 2, 1974 two bombs exploded in shops near the city centre. In March a lone incendiary device ignited, and then in April there came a new wave of bombings in Birmingham, Wolverhampton, Walsall and Manchester. Targets included Lloyds Bank in the Rotunda at New Street.

The bombings were usually preceded by a warning, but it was not always precise. The one on April 6, for example, said simply that three bombs had been planted in the city centre. It was a Saturday night. The police had no choice but to seal off the entire city centre.

In February, 1974, there was the most horrific explosion so far. A bomb exploded on a coach carrying soldiers and their families from Manchester to the army base at Catterick. The coach was on the M62 when the bomb exploded. Twelve people died, including a family of four. Judith Ward, a young woman from Stockport, would later be convicted of planting the bomb and sentenced to a minimum of thirty years in prison.

Meanwhile letter bombs had started arriving at the homes of prominent people: judges, generals and the former Home Secretary, Reginald Maudling.

By the end of April there had been more than twenty explosions in the West Midlands. A Bomb Squad had been set up under the command of Detective Chief Superintendent Harry Robinson. Hundreds of police were engaged in the search for the bombers, but they were getting nowhere. For every genuine bomb warning, there were a dozen hoaxes. Every one had to be taken seriously. It was a frustrating time for the police.

The first break came not in Birmingham, but in Manchester. At four o'clock on the afternoon on Friday, April 26, there was an explosion in the bedroom of a council house in the southern part of the City. Neighbours watched in astonishment as two girls and two young men, one of them with his clothes smouldering, clambered out of an upstairs window and sped off in an old grey van. One of the men later turned up in the Salford Royal Infirmary with serious burns. He was Eddie Byrne, a painter by trade and he came from 11 Woodpecker Walk, Chelmsley Wood, Birmingham. The girls were Ann and Eileen Gillespie. They were arrested the next day boarding the ferry to Ireland. The other young man was Patrick Guilfoyle, known to his friends as Tip, after his family's home county, Tipperary. It would be another three months before the police caught up with him.

By now the police were keeping a close watch on Sinn Fein members in Birmingham. In the middle of June, two or three coach-loads of Sinn Fein supporters from Birmingham went to Dublin for the annual Wolfe Tone commemoration. As we have seen, a dozen or more regulars from the Crossways were on that trip, including Johnny Walker, Gerry Hunter and Paddy Hill. Hill, as ever, had trouble raising the money for the fare and eventually solved the problem by buying three watches from Walker and raffling them. None of them were members of Sinn Fein or the IRA, but there were many on the trip who were. Gerry Hunter remembers overhearing a conversation about tarring and feathering a pub landlord who was refusing to allow the sale of *Republican News*. Martin Coughlan, who police believed to be the leader of the IRA in Birmingham, was on the coach. So were Mick Murray, Micky Sheehan and Hunter's cousin, Seamus McLoughlin. Hunter says he had suspected McLoughlin's IRA connections since McLoughlin had tried to recruit him earlier that year. After which, he says, he gave McLoughlin a wide berth.

The police followed the Birmingham contingent every inch of the way to Bodenstown and back. They eaves-dropped on conversations in pubs and they took photographs (one of Johnny Walker at Bodenstown surfaced eventually in the *Guardian* on the day after the trial). Still, they found no hard evidence.

July saw a new wave of bombings in Birmingham, the most extensive there had been. There were two bombs and about twenty incendiary devices. As before, the targets were all commercial premises. There were no casualties, but considerable disruption. The biggest explosion was in a Central Electricity Generating Board cable tunnel which caused a black-out in the Nechells area. Other targets included the Rotunda (again), Maples the furniture store in Corporation Street, the ABC cinema in Bristol Road, and four cinemas including the Odeon in New Street.

It was at the end of July that the police had their first big break.

It was not detective work that led to the first arrests, but a tip-off. One of the IRA men, Patrick Christie, became involved in a row over a girl and was summoned to account by his colleagues. The girl, Valerie Hardy, panicked and told the police he had been taken to a house in Sparkbrook, number 232 Clifton Road. After keeping watch on the house, the police identified a second house at 38 Baker Street, also in Sparkbrook. On the night of Friday, August 2, they swooped. At 232 Clifton Road they arres-ted Gerry Small.

At 38 Baker Street they found Mick Mooney (alias Joseph Duffy) and Tip Gulfoyle, the survivor of the fiasco in Manchester. Bomb-making equipment was recovered from both houses. It included a Smith's alarm clock with the outer lens removed and the minute hand and alarm indi-cator snipped off, Ever Ready batteries, weedkiller (used in incendiaries) and a partly finished incendiary.

A fourth man, Stephen Blake, was arrested at a nearby flat, having been followed home from the house in Clifton Road.

The police then kept a watch on Blake's flat and the next day they were rewarded when Martin Coughlan and Gerry Young turned up. Coughlan and Young were later alleged to be, and IRA sources confirm that they were, the first and second in command of the Birmingham IRA. On the same day, after a brief chase, they arrested Joseph Ashe who had turned up at 232 Clifton Road unaware that it had been raided.

An eighth young man, Tony Madigan, who had been photographed leaving the house in Clifton Road, was picked up at home a week later.

When they appeared in court on first remand, Jimmy Ashe took off his shirt and tried to show the magistrate cigarette burns on his back which, he said, had been inflicted by the police. He got precious little sympathy.

'Take that ape-man down,' said the magistrate. Later Ashe admitted that he had inflicted the burns himself.

The August arrests were a serious blow to the IRA in Birmingham. Within two weeks of the arrests two more incendiaries were planted. They were poor efforts, one failed to ignite and the other caused only minor damage.

It was another six weeks before the Birmingham IRA were heard from again and this time they struck without warning. On October 24, a bomb was found under a car belonging to a woman magistrate. It failed to explode. Four days later, another was found attached to the car of another magistrate, a retired army colonel. It, too, failed to ignite. On the same day, a bomb was found under a car belonging to the wife of Labour MP, Denis Howell. It exploded but she escaped unhurt.

Meanwhile, the IRA had re-opened their bombing campaign in the South of England with a vengeance. Bombs exploded without warning at two pubs in Guildford known to be used by off-duty soldiers and their friends. Five people died and about sixty were injured. At the beginning of November, the King's Arms in Woolwich – also used by soldiers – was bombed. Two people died and more than thirty others were injured.

November also saw the final round of the IRA's West Midlands campaign which was to culminate in the carnage of November 21. In the two weeks leading up to the pub bombings, seven bombs and incendiary devices exploded without warning in the West Midlands. Targets included the Conservative Party offices in Edmund Street, Birmingham, Inland Revenue offices in Birch Street, Wolverhampton and, of course, the telephone exchange at Coventry, where James McDade met his end. McDade's death, together with the eight arrested in August, accounts for nine Birmingham IRA members. The arrest of Raymond McLaughlin, who was caught running away from the scene, makes ten.

Mick Murray, arrested three days after the pub bombings, makes eleven. He admitted he was an IRA member, though that was all he owned up to. Mick Sheehan, who was shopped by Kelly, makes twelve.

But that was not all. After the pub explosions, the bombings stopped, but the arrests didn't. The following year saw the arrest of another five men who were charged with complicity in the bombings up to August 1974. They were all in their twenties. Four had homes in Birmingham and one came from Wolverhampton. All except one were of Irish origin. The exception was David Owen, a Welshman who was said to have left the Welsh nationalists because they were too tame. The others were Michael Reilly, Brian McLaughlin, Peter Toal and Patrick Christie. It was Christie whose girlfriend was said to have informed on the men arrested in August the previous year. He was not charged that time round, but later he was of no further use to the police and he went down with the others. That made a total of seventeen Birmingham IRA members in custody by the end of 1975. Another man, John Callaghan, was named in court as having got away. It was, said the judge who sentenced the last five, the final round up. But he was wrong.

39

One day in July 1985, seven months after I first let it be known that I wished to meet one or more of those responsible for the pub bombings, I received word that a meeting had been arranged. I was told to report to an address in Dublin on the morning of Saturday, 27 July 1985. Waiting in a car outside was the man who had arranged the meeting. A minute later we were joined by the man I had come to meet. He climbed into the back seat and directed us to a block of flats a few streets away. He got out and went to make arrangements for us to use one of the flats. There was a delay of about fifteen minutes before he returned. Apparently the occupant was still in bed. By the time we went inside, however, there was no sign of anyone else.

We sat in the living room and talked for three hours. The basis of the interview was that I would disclose his identity to no one and that, when we came to a question he did not wish to answer, he would say so, but that he would not mislead me. We had two further meetings, in November 1985 and April 1986. At our second meeting he made clear that he was not at all keen to speak to me. He said: 'I think you are only doing this for yourself. You're a member of the British Labour Party, so you're part of the Establishment as far as I am concerned.' He had only agreed to see me at the request of someone high up in the Republican movement. Despite his reluctance my source – whom I shall refer to as X – provided a detailed account of what happened on the night of the bombing. At our first meeting he had refused to discuss his own role, but at our second and third meetings he was frank. He was one of two men who had made the bombs, and it was he who had phoned through the warning.

The account that follows is not dependent upon X's version of events. In the nine months following my first meeting with him, I traced and interviewed another twelve of those who took part in the IRA's West Midlands bombing campaign, including one of the two people who placed the bombs in the pubs. I have carefully cross-checked their accounts and, with the exception of one who told me a pack of lies (and whose evidence I have discounted) their stories tally.

It is not conceivable that all these people can have been part of a conspiracy to mislead. Most have not met for many years. Some have never met. Some were captured and some escaped. Some are in Northern Ireland, some are in the Republic, and some are in England. Some still have links with the IRA and some do not. Most are unaware to this day which of their erstwhile colleagues I have interviewed. Most I have traced independently of contacts in the Republican movement and most had no advance warning of my appearance on their doorstep.

About one thing they are all agreed: none of the six men serving sentences for the pub bombings was at any time a member of the Birmingham IRA.

The Birmingham IRA began to be assembled in the summer of 1973. The leaders were mainly men in their thirties who were long-time residents of the city. From Birmingham's large Irish community they recruited younger men, some still in their teens. An IRA unit was also set up in Manchester, under the control of the Birmingham leadership. Many of the young recruits had cut their teeth at Sinn Fein demonstrations against internment and on the anniversary of Bloody Sunday. Some admit to being attracted by the cloak and dagger aspects of IRA operations. Others say they were anxious to bring home to people in England the realities of the war in Ireland.

Martin Coughlan, the first commander of the Birmingham IRA, ran his units according to strict principles. The bombing campaign was to be targeted solely against property. Civilian casualties were to be avoided at all costs. If anyone going out on a bombing mission allowed a drop of alcohol to pass his lips, he would be sent home at once and, if necessary, the mission would be aborted. During Coughlan's year as commander of the Birmingham IRA, which saw a total of thirty-eight bombings, the only serious casualty was the bomb disposal officer killed in September 1973.

Coughlan's recruits were organised into four or five Active Service Units, each consisting of three or four volunteers. Each unit had its own Officer Commanding or O/C. A man came from London and taught them how to make bombs. One of the early recruits recalls spending a day learning the trade at a house near the top of Icknield Port Road, in Winson Green.

Coughlan had two deputies. One was Gerry Young, the intelligence officer, responsible for assessing potential targets. The other – the man known as Belfast Jimmy – was the quartermaster, responsible for weapons and finance. Explosives came from Ireland by car.

No bombing could take place without the approval of the commander, although members of an ASU could suggest their own targets. As the bombing campaign progressed there were regular meetings of O/Cs to discuss tactics. Because of Birmingham's central location the O/Cs of all the units in the country would congregate in Birmingham, usually at a house in Chelmsley Wood. National leaders of the IRA would also attend.

At one such meeting early in 1974 the O/Cs were warned that something big was about to happen and that they should make sure their homes were clean. A few days later the M62 coach bomb exploded.

The O/C meetings were run along democratic lines. An O/C would make a proposal, not necessarily his own (it might have been put up by a member of his unit), which would be discussed and voted upon. At an O/C meeting about six weeks after the coach bombing, there was talk of shooting policemen. This was rejected on the grounds that the police force in Britain was legitimate and that the IRA had no quarrel with it. One of those present recalls, 'Someone even said he wouldn't object to standing up for "God Save the Queen" in an English cinema, but he would not do so in Ireland. It drew a laugh, but everyone knew what he meant.' Someone also suggested ambushing army convoys from motorway bridges. This, too, was rejected.

At a third O/C meeting in July there was a suggestion that the IRA should shoot prison officers involved in the force-feeding of the Price sisters, who were then on hunger strike. This was referred to Dublin. Before Dublin had a chance to answer, however, the Birmingham IRA suffered its first wave of arrests.

Until August 1974 there were between twenty-five and thirty people active in the Birmingham IRA, but with varying degrees of activity. Some had safehouses, some took initiatives, some acted only when ordered. Some people just enjoyed attending secret meetings. The arrests scared a lot of people away. It was known that Christie's girl friend had named more people than just those picked up, and several left town for good. Others just kept their heads down. Eventually word came from Dublin to reorganise.

The new head of the Birmingham IRA was the man known as Belfast Jimmy. The man I have referred to as X was one of his deputies. Three new units were set up composed mainly of people who had been active before August. There were also several new recruits. By October plans were being laid for hitting new targets. One of those involved recalls attending a meeting at a house in Bordesley Green when there was talk of assassinating magistrates, prison officers and MPs. It was shortly after this that bombs were found under the cars of two Birmingham magistrates and the Labour MP, Denis Howell. The Conservative MP, Jill Knight, was also mentioned as a possible target, but nothing came of this. There was also talk of blowing up the Winson Green prison officers' social club and the police station at Bradford Street in retalliation for the rough treatment those arrested in August are alleged to have received. The men in prison were consulted and apparently vetoed the idea.

There was considerable disagreement over the choice of targets and one O/C was reduced to the ranks for refusing to take part in the attacks on politicians and magistrates. The position of the IRA commander, Belfast Jimmy, on this issue is unclear. There is some evidence to suggest that he favoured a hard line. One of those who knew him describes him as 'ruthless'. Another of those most closely involved says, 'If certain people had had their way there would have been a lot of dead prison officers.'

The attacks against magistrates were unsuccessful and by the beginning of November the Birmingham IRA had reverted to attacks on property, except that by now it was the practice not to give warnings.

The timing of a bombing campaign was determined by the availability of explosives. The policy was not to hold on to explosives, so once a consignment arrived it was used as quickly as possible. Other equipment, such as batteries and cheap watches, was purchased locally at stores like Woolworth's.

There were usually two main dumps for arms and detonators. The dumps were usually in the houses of trusted IRA members or supporters and would be rotated regularly to minimise the risk of detection. A person whose home was to be used as a dump would first be carefully tested, as Jimmy Kelly had been. A pistol would be left for a few days. It would then be taken away again and returned several times over a period of weeks. If there were no leaks, then the custodian of the pistol would be asked to take care of more important consignments. X was adamant that Johnny Walker's home was never used as a dump. 'Walker was too well known for his raffles and totes,' he said. X was equally adamant that Kelly's house was a main dump and that he had been tried and tested over a period of months. An ASU setting off on a mission would withdraw a pistol and anything else needed from a dump immediately before an operation and return it immediately afterwards. The Birmingham IRA was not, however, as highly organised as X would have us believe. One of those involved in the final round of bombings recalls an occasion when his wife found a bag of incendiary materials under their bed and he had to fob her off with a story that he was a petty thief. The same man also relates that he had several sticks of gelignite hidden behind his fridge. He adds, 'And I once had to collect gelly from a guy who had it stored in the back of an old TV set.'

The bombs were made either in rented houses or lock-up garages. There were other safe houses besides those discovered by the police in Clifton Road and Baker Street. There were always two people making a bomb: one to assemble the circuit and the other to check it. Two detonators were frequently used because often one did not work. The circuits were only dangerous when put together with explosives and this was usually done at the last moment. The bomb that killed McDade was, for example, connected up in the back of a van near the scene of the explosion.

James McDade collected the bomb that killed him from a house in Bordesley Green. It was from this same house that the bombs which destroyed the two pubs were collected one week later.

'McDade had a choice of two bombs that night,' says X. 'He could have done the Conservative Club in Solihull. Instead he chose the bigger bomb and went to Coventry. He knew the risks.'

At the time of his death, McDade was in charge of the ASU which consisted of himself, Ray McLaughlin (who was captured running away from the scene) and a third man who escaped. The third man was the driver. He still lives in Birmingham. He was badly shaken by what happened and drove back to Birmingham and reported to Belfast Jimmy who told him to take a few days off.

Belfast Jimmy was also apparently shaken by McDade's death. They had been close friends. According to one of those who spoke to Belfast Jimmy in the few days between McDade's death and the explosions in the pubs, he said, 'They will pay for Jamsie.' It was at about this time the pub bombings were conceived.

40

Those who organised and carried out the pub bombings insist that there was never any intention to kill civilians. X flatly denies that the bombings had anything to do with McDade's death or that the explosions were timed to coincide with the day of his funeral. He says, 'There was nothing special about the targets. They were picked the weekend before by the ASUs. The explosives came in on the Monday or Tuesday. Then we had to contact the ASUs.'

According to X, the pubs were chosen for their location and not for their clientele. The Mulberry Bush is in the Rotunda, which had been hit twice before. The Rotunda is a landmark in Birmingham and one of the aims of the bombers was to close it down. The Tavern in the Town was underneath the New Street tax office. Security was tight in the area around New Street and the Rotunda. 'We, therefore, decided to plant the bombs in the pubs and give a warning. At that time it was not our policy to give warnings, but in this case we decided on thirty minutes.'

According to X, the bombs for both Hagley Road and the pubs were made by two men, himself and one other. He says that he personally delivered the bombs to the O/Cs of the two units who were to plant them: 'I delivered all the bombs to two separate places about an hour before they set out.' X declines to say where he handed over the bombs, other than that the handover took place at pre-arranged times and at venues which were not private houses. 'I travelled to one by public transport. From there I walked to the other.'

The original intention had been to plant the bombs soon after opening time, but on the day before this was changed to around eight o'clock because one of the volunteers could not get home from work on time. The bombs were made in a rented lock-up garage. X would not comment on the location.

According to X, each of the bombs consisted of about ten pounds of explosive, and not the twenty-five to thirty pounds described in court by forensic scientists. X is adamant on this point. Pressed to account for the discrepancy, he points to the difficulty of estimating the size of bombs after they had exploded. By way of example, he cites the bomb planted in July at the Central Electricity Board cable tunnel in Nechells. That had contained around forty pounds of explosives and yet at the time the police had given a much smaller estimate.

X's explanation for the size of the pub bombs does not, however, apply to the Hagley Road bomb. That was recovered intact and was later the subject of a controlled explosion. According to the forensic scientist, Percy Lidstone, the Hagley Road bomb contained about thirteen and a half pounds of explosive made up of six ounce cartridges. X says it was his policy at the time only to use around ten pounds per bomb.

As to what the bombs were contained in, X says that they were in plastic bags when he handed them over, but they should not have been in plastic bags when planted. 'Volunteers were forbidden to carry bombs in plastic bags because by this time the police were on the look out for plastic bags.' Asked why the Hagley Road bomb was recovered in a plastic bag he said only that it must have been carried to the scene in some other container. As we shall see, it was not, but there is no reason for X to have known this.

The Hagley Road bomb was planted by three men. I have identified and traced all three. Two escaped to Ireland and the third was later arrested and sentenced for other offences. He has since been released and still lives in England. One of those involved describes his role on the day of the bombing: 'Someone called for me at work and told me to pick up the gear from a lock-up in a block of council maisonettes at Saltley.' He went there either in his lunch hour or after work (he cannot recall which) and picked up a ready-made timing device and a detonator. 'There was other stuff there, but I was told not to touch anything else.'

He was then instructed to rendezvous that evening at the underpass at Fiveways with the O/C of his unit, who would bring the bomb. He and the other man in his unit waited at Fiveways at the appointed hour and in due course the O/C arrived with the bomb in a plastic bag (having presumably been given it by X). 'I connected the detonator with the explosives in a nearby toilet. We then walked up Hagley Road to the bank. The O/C carried the bomb, still in its plastic bag. It was not that big. I remember he carried it tucked under his arm.'

They walked up the side of the road opposite the bank. Before crossing over there was a final piece of wire that needed taping to the bomb. 'There was a building site nearby, separated from the road by a low wall. The O/C went behind the wall to make the final connection, but his nerve failed and I had to do it. He was also supposed to plant the bomb, but in the end I and the other lad did it. The O/C said he would wait for us at a bus stop, but I never saw him again in Birmingham. I did see him once about three years later on a street in Dublin.'

The other two crossed the road with the bomb and put it down behind the bank. 'I opened the bag and threw the switch, but there was something wrong. The light flickered on and off, which it shouldn't do. We stood there in the dark fiddling with it for about five minutes.'

Eventually, they gave up and went home, agreeing to meet later in the White Swan pub in Ladywood. They were in the White Swan playing pool with a crowd of friends when the wife of one of them arrived with news that bombs had gone off in the city centre and that many people had been killed. He went white. The Hagley Road bomb was still ticking away. 'I said to the other fellow, "We'd better get on the phone and give a warning." But we couldn't get out of the pub without drawing attention to ourselves so we just sat tight and prayed.'

Having handed over the pub bombs, the man to whom I have referred as X had to place himself in a position from which he could telephone the warning. This meant a further rendezvous with one of the planters. Obviously it had to be as close as possible to the targets since, once the bombs were in place, time was of the essence. At the same time, it had to be sufficiently far away to avoid his being caught up in any dragnet the police might throw round the scene as soon as the warning was received. X declines to say from where he phoned the warning other than that it was about ten minutes' walk from the pubs, and that there was more than one telephone box on the same site.

X says he made the phone call as soon as the planter appeared. There was no contact between them. The phone boxes had been checked out that afternoon and found to be working. By now, however, two of them were out of order. 'I, therefore, pushed off and found another. It didn't take long.' The warning was preceded by a code which had been communicated well in advance to the police and was designed to indicate that the call was genuine and not one of the many hoaxes. 'The codeword I used was "Double X". I repeated it once at the beginning of the warning and once at the end.' On the instructions of the judge, the code was not made public at the trial. Until today it would have been known only to the police, to Ian Cropper the telephonist at the *Birmingham Post and Mail* who received the warning, to the man who phoned through the warning and perhaps to one or two other senior IRA men in Birmingham.

By now every second was vital. According to X, he had allowed an hour's delay on each of the bombs with the intention of leaving the authorities half an hour to clear the pubs. Given that the planting will have taken anywhere up to twenty minutes and that another ten minutes or so will have elapsed by the time the planter made it to his rendezvous with X, the schedule would have been tight, even supposing it had gone according to plan.

There are a number of discrepancies between X's version of the warning and that given to the court. According to the telephonist, Ian Cropper, it was phoned through at 8.11. According to the police the first bomb exploded at 8.17 and the second a few minutes later. X disputes this. 'The first went off at 8.28. That's our time.' X says he heard the explosion clearly and noted the time. A colleague, with whom he had synchronised watches, also heard the explosion. When they met two days later to compare notes they both noted the time as 8.28.

This may be an attempt to justify the inadequacy of the warning. Even if the IRA times were correct, this would not help to explain why the warning was so misleading – '*There is a bomb planted in the Rotunda and there is a bomb in New Street . . . At the tax office.*' Here again X disputes the wording: 'I said there was a bomb in the Rotunda *building* and a bomb in the tax office *building*.' Pressed on the matter he concedes, 'We can be criticised for bungling the warning, but any sane person would have cleared the buildings. Instead of clearing out the people, the police went looking for the bombs.'

I asked how he felt when he heard what had happened. He declined to answer. It was like talking to a bomber pilot whose bombs had been intended for an enemy factory, but had inadvertently been discharged onto a nearby housing estate. In war these things happen.

It soon became clear that, if I were to prove decisively that the six convicted men did not plant the pub bombs, it was not enough to have talked to the man who made the bombs and phoned through the warning since the police never claimed to have caught either. I would, therefore, have to speak to one of the men who planted the bombs.

When I started on this inquiry I believed that the identity of the planters was reasonably well-known in certain circles. I now know differently. The identity of the men who planted the bombs in the Mulberry Bush and the Tavern in the Town is a very deep secret.

X was naturally not keen to discuss the identity of his colleagues. He would say no more than that one other person helped him make the bombs and that the same two people planted both bombs in both pubs. Inadvertently, however, he did confirm the identity of one other man, though he would not tell me his role. Let us call this other man Y.

Y is in his forties. He has been a member of the IRA since his youth. In the late 1950s he served three years in the British Army, based mainly at Aldershot. He was by this time already an IRA member.

In the 1960s he married an English woman. They lived at Bordesley Green in Birmingham and had a large family. He worked as a pipelayer and travelled the country advising other IRA units on such matters as the geography of British Army bases.

During the course of a three-hour interview, Y was prepared to own up to involvement from the beginning in the IRA's West Midlands campaign. When it came to the pub bombings, however, he flatly denied that he was involved. Instead he stuck doggedly to the remarkable view that the bombings may have been the work of British agents bent on discrediting the IRA – something which the IRA itself has never alleged. His reasons for this became clear as the interview progressed.

There had, said Y, been an IRA inquiry into the pub bombings. When they got back to Ireland the survivors of the Birmingham IRA, including Y, were interviewed. Y then makes a remarkable revelation: 'We told the inquiry that we were not responsible.'

If Y is to be believed, it seems that the Birmingham IRA men were so shocked by what they had done that they decided to pretend that it was nothing to do with them. Had this been the explanation offered for public consumption, it might have been understandable, if not in the least plausible. That they should attempt to sell this line to the Army Council of the IRA is incredible. It might, however, explain why David O'Connell's promise that the results of the inquiry would be published, 'no matter how unpalatable', was never honoured.

I later interviewed a veteran IRA man who had sat on the inquiry into the Birmingham bombings. He said, 'A lot of lies were told. The people who had come out of England were interviewed. They all said, "It wasn't us". I firmly believed them at the time.' He goes on, 'Eighteen months later I was sitting in the house of one of the people who had been active in Birmingham. People had had a few drinks and they started talking. It became clear that we had done it. A second inquiry was held. It concluded that we had been lied to and that the people who had done it were walking around free.'

I had asked the contacts who had set up my meeting with X, if they could put me in touch with one of the planters. Several months passed and it became clear that they were either unable or unwilling to do so. I, therefore, decided to try and solve the mystery under my own steam.

One by one I traced and questioned the likely candidates, eliminating each as I established their whereabouts on the night in question. Gradually one name began to emerge. At about the same time an inquiry I had made through someone in the British prison system bore fruit. Again, it was the same name.

Through an intermediary I established that the individual concerned would be willing to see me. I then put his name to the contact who had arranged my meeting with X. He said, 'Yes, that's it. I wasn't going to tell you unless you found out for yourself.'

One rainy day in the spring of 1986 I made my sixth and last trip to Ireland in connection with this case. The man who I went to see lives in a bleak public housing estate. He is aged around thirty and was, therefore, still in his teens at the time of the pub bombings. He joined the Birmingham IRA in the summer of 1973 and remained a member throughout the entire West Midlands campaign. He was involved in seven or eight bombings, including one of the cinemas, an Army and Navy Stores and one of the bombs in Stephenson Street and one of the two Conservative clubs bombed in early November. To say any more about him would be to risk disclosing his identity, and that I have pledged not to do.

He began by giving me a sanitised version of his career. As we drew nearer to the night of 21 November 1974 his voice began to tremble and at times almost faded. At first he did not tell the truth, saying that he had been warned to stay at home because something big was going to happen and had spent the evening at home watching television. Once we had passed 21 November his voice grew stronger.

Eventually I said to him, 'I think you were in the pubs.'

There was a long silence. We were sitting on the floor. He stared straight ahead, smoking. Then it all came out. This is his story:

On the evening of the bombing a person came to see me and said,

'You're needed for an operation.' I went with him to a house. We went by car. The bombs were in the parlour. Behind the sofa. One was in a duffle bag and the other was a small brown luggage case.

I was given the duffle bag and a pistol. I was wearing some kind of duffle coat. I put the gun in my coat pocket. The other man carried the case.

We walked into town. It was a good mile. The other guy told me the targets about ten minutes before we arrived. He said, 'The one in the Tavern is for the tax office and the one in the Mulberry Bush is for the Rotunda.' He said, 'There'll be plenty of warning.' Believe it or not I accepted it. I didn't want a stigma [of cowardice] attached to me. He kept saying, 'Don't worry. Those people will be well out of there.' I kept on about it and he repeated that there would be a substantial warning.

We approached down Digbeth. Just before we arrived we stopped in the entrance to a row of shops. The other guy opened the case and fiddled with something. Then he reached inside my duffle bag. That's when the bombs were primed. We crossed the road without using the underpass because the police were sometimes down there. There was hardly any traffic about.

We did the Tavern first. Up New Street, past the Mulberry Bush. The other fellow went to the bar and ordered two drinks. I took both bags and found a seat. I was shitting myself. The other person came back with the drinks. We took a sip and then got up, leaving the duffle bag under a seat.

I drew a crude diagram of the Tavern in my notebook and asked him to mark the spot where the bomb had been left. Without hesitation he drew a seat which, he said, ran along the wall abutting New Street to the right of the stairs, as you enter. In front of that he drew the table at which he had sat. The bomb, he said, was left under the seat near the table.

Only two categories of people could have indicated the site of the bomb with such accuracy. Either someone with access to the trial transcript containing the evidence of the Home Office forensic scientist, Donald Lidstone, or someone who was present when the bomb was planted.

At the Mulberry Bush the procedure was the same. The other man was carrying the case: 'We entered through the doors at the front. This time I ordered the drinks. The other person found a table at the back. The bomb was left by a telephone.'

Again I drew a rough sketch of the pub and asked him to mark the site of the bomb. Again without hesitation he marked a spot at the rear. For good measure he also drew in the rear exit which I had omitted. On my diagram I had inadvertently drawn in a staircase and he remarked that he could not recall any stairs in that place. When I returned home and examined the plan of the pub, I saw that he was right. It is hard to see how someone who cannot possibly have had access to the forensic evidence at the trial could accurately mark the spot where the bomb was placed. Unless, of course, he was present when the bomb was planted.

We went outside. The other fellow took the gun off me. He told me to go home and keep my head down. Nobody would be hurt. No need to worry. I last saw the other guy walking off down Digbeth. I've never heard of him again. I don't know whether it was his intention to kill people. If they'd have said, 'We're going to kill people', there is no way I would have gone. They just needed a carrier and I was available. I'm not blaming anyone or making excuses. What's done is done.

I walked home. Took about an hour. Didn't hear the bang. Then all those people got killed. Jesus, I can't make excuses . . .

We talked for nearly four hours. I pressed him repeatedly for the name of the other man. He refused saying he had been told never to divulge what he knew. He did, however, reveal from where the bombs had been collected. It was Y's house in Bordesley Green. The same address from which McDade collected the bomb that killed him.

I also asked X about the identity of the second man. He would say nothing except that the man is free and in Ireland.

There are only two possible candidates for the second man. One is Y himself, although he is more likely to be the man who helped X make the bombs.

The favourite, therefore, is a man, let us call him Z, who – along with Y – left Birmingham in January 1975. He remained active in the IRA and is now in his mid-thirties. When last heard of Z was living in Dublin and said to be engaged to a woman from Birmingham. Needless to say she will have to come to Ireland, if she wants to live with him.

As for the man who admits to planting the bomb, he remained in Birmingham for at least a year after the bombings, working as a lump labourer on building sites. Although he now lives in Ireland, he visited Birmingham as recently as 1982. He has lived alone with his secret for eleven years. 'There was no one I could talk to. The guy who was with me had disappeared. The others didn't have a clue what had happened. I didn't tell my wife. None of my relatives know. There was no one I could talk to until now.'

As we parted he said, 'No offence, but I don't ever want to see you again.'

At the moment of the explosions, Belfast Jimmy, the commander of the Birmingham IRA who perhaps conceived and undoubtedly authorised the pub bombings, was at Birmingham Airport waiting to accompany the remains of James McDade back to Ireland. The airport was surrounded by eight hundred policemen. It is hard to imagine a better alibi.

He now lives in the centre of Dublin where for a while he worked in a Republican social club. I realise now that my first interview with X took place in Belfast Jimmy's flat. I have never set eyes on him but someone who saw him recently says he is virtually an alcoholic. 'He is incoherent and he has the shakes. Nowadays he says, "I fucked it up." At the time I heard he was saying, "Three or four more of those and the Brits will pull out."'

It was eleven years before the IRA could bring itself to admit that its men were responsible for the Birmingham pub bombings. The first public admission came from Joe Cahill, a senior figure in the IRA and a former commander of the IRA's Belfast Brigade. He was speaking on Granada TV's *World in Action* on 28 October 1985. Cahill went on to say, 'The volunteers who did carry out those operations are freely walking about today.'

The interviewer asked, 'You're saying they've escaped justice?'

'If that's the term you want to use, yes.'

Postscript

Belief in the innocence of the six convicted men is not confined to Republican sympathisers or to their families. In the prisons where they have been held for any length of time they are widely regarded as innocent both by other prisoners and by some of the prison authorities. At Long Lartin Prison in Worcestershire, where Johnny Walker and Gerry Hunter were held for many years (Walker is still there at time of writing), the authorities long ago abandoned the pretence that these are IRA men. For three years they have been receiving unsupervised visits in the main visiting hall alongside ordinary criminal prisoners. These are supposed to be two of the IRA men responsible for killing twenty-one people. At their trial it was alleged that Walker was an IRA Brigadier. By contrast, IRA men in the same jail for much lesser offences still receive closed visits with a prison officer present.

On one occasion, while visiting a prison where Billy Power and Richard McIlkenny were held, I met an assistant governor. 'Between you and me,' I said, 'these men are innocent, aren't they.'

He replied: 'I know, it's awful isn't it? A lot of people in here believe that.'

At the time of writing, the six Irishmen have served nearly twelve years for a crime they did not commit. Had the death penalty been in force at the time of their conviction, they would all have hanged. Unless the Home Office and the judges can summon up the courage to admit publicly what many people are saying in private, these men are destined to remain in prison for the rest of their natural lives.

Notes on sources

The allegations of violence while the men were in police custody were all made during the trial. Most were made twice. Once during the 'trial within a trial' in the absence of the jury and later before a jury. They are to be found in the seventeen-volume trial transcript from which most of the quotations are taken. Occasionally quotes have been taken from statements the men made to their solicitors, but only to describe allegations that were made in open court. As we have seen, all the allegations were denied by the police and the police evidence was accepted by the jury.

The following notes provide a reference for each allegation against a named police officer. The first number indicates the volume of the trial transcript and the second indicates the page.

Chapter 8

1 – 5, 43
2 – 2, 124
3 – 5, 156
4 – 6, 48
5 – 6, 21
6 – 5, 44
7 – 5, 157
8 – 5, 158 Hunter also testified that he had overheard the remark about Judith Ward: 6, 21
9 – 5, 159
10 – 10, 98

Chapter 9

1 – 5, 40
2 – 5, 41
3 – 5, 43
4 – 5, 47
5 – 5, 48
6 – 5, 49
7 – 5, 47
8 – 5, 51–3
9 – 5, 56–63
10 – 5, 62

Chapter 10

1 – 5, 157–161
2 – 6, 68
3 – 6, 68
4 – 6, 70–1
5 – 6, 71–2
6 – 6, 72
7 – 6, 23
8 – 13, 92
9 – 13, 92–3

Chapter 11

1 – 6, 74
2 – 13, 17
3 – 6, 74–5
4 – 6, 74–5
5 – 5, 162–3
6 – 5, 163–4
7 – 11, 12
8 – 11, 13
9 – 6, 26–7
10 – 6, 27–8
11 – 13, 94
12 – 14, 46
13 – Interviewed by author and Charles Tremayne, 19.3.85

Chapter 13

1 – 5, 118
2 – 13, 25
3 – 13, 21
4 – 13, 23
5 – 13, 22
6 – 13, 22
7 – 6, 31
8 – 6, 32

Chapter 14

1 – 6, 76
2 – 6, 77
3 – 6, 78
4 – 6, 78
5 – 6, 79
6 – 6, 79
7 – 6, 80

Chapter 15

1 – 6, 48
2 – 6, 49
3 – 13, 132
4 – 6, 51–3
5 – 6, 55–6

Chapter 16

1 – 12, 16
2 – 12, 16–17
3 – 12, 17
4 – 12, 17
5 – 5, 168–9
6 – 5, 169
7 – 12, 19

Chapter 17

1 – Words from proof of evidence describing allegations made at 5, 120
    and 5, 135
2 – 11, 92
3 – Words from proof of evidence describing alegations made at 5, 128;
    5, 134 and 5, 142.

Chapter 18

1 – 11, 97
2 – 12, 20

Chapter 19

1 – Interviewed by author and Charles Tremayne 22.4.85
2 – 5, 43
3 – 13, 35–6

Index

269